Also by Edward Seidensticker

Japan (1961)
Kafū the Scribbler (1965)
Genji Days (1977)
This Country: Japan (1979)

TRANSLATIONS

Yasunari Kawabata
Snow Country (1956)
Thousand Cranes (1959)
House of the Sleeping Beauties (1969)
The Sound of the Mountain (1970)
The Master of Go (1972)

The Mother of Fujiwara Michitsuna
The Gossamer Years (1955, revised 1964)

Yukio Mishima
The Decay of the Angel (1974)

Murasaki Shikibu
The Tale of Genji (1976)

Junichirō Tanizaki
Some Prefer Nettles (1955)
The Makioka Sisters (1957)

LOW CITY,
HIGH CITY

LOW CITY, HIGH CITY

TOKYO FROM EDO TO THE EARTHQUAKE

Edward Seidensticker

ALFRED A. KNOPF · NEW YORK · 1983

THIS IS A BORZOI BOOK
PUBLISHED BY ALFRED A. KNOPF, INC.

Copyright © 1983 by Edward Seidensticker
All rights reserved under International and Pan-American Copyright Con-
ventions. Published in the United States by Alfred A. Knopf, Inc., New
York, and simultaneously in Canada by Random House of Canada Limited,
Toronto. Distributed by Random House, Inc., New York.

Library of Congress Cataloging in Publication Data
Seidensticker, Edward.
Low city, high city: Tokyo from Edo to the earthquake.
Includes index.
1. Tokyo (Japan)—History. 2. Tokyo (Japan)—
Popular culture. I. Title.
DS896.64.S44   1983   952'.135   82-48867
ISBN 0-394-50730-4

Manufactured in the United States of America
First Edition

CONTENTS

Preface   *vii*

1 The End and the Beginning   3

2 Civilization and Enlightenment   25

3 The Double Life   90

4 The Decay of the Decadent   144

5 Low City, High City   185

6 The Taishō Look   252

  Notes   287

  Index   293

Color illustrations follow pages 48 and 208

PREFACE

When young, I did not dedicate books. Dedications seemed overblown and showy. It is too late to begin; but if this book carried a dedication, it would be to the memory of Nagai Kafū.

Though he was not such a good novelist, he has come to seem better and better at what he was good at. He was his best in brief lyrical passages and not in sustained narrative and dramatic ones. He is the novelist whose views of the world's most consistently interesting city accord most closely with my own. He has been my guide and companion as I have explored and dreamed and meditated upon the city.

I do not share his yearning for Edo, the city when it was still the seat of the Tokugawa shoguns and before it became the Eastern Capital. The Tokugawa Period is somehow dark and menacing. Too many gifted people were squelched, and, whether gifted or not, I always have the feeling about Edo that, had I been there, I would have been among the squelched ones.

I share Kafū's affection for the part of the city which had its best day then. The twilight of that day lasted through the succeeding Meiji reign and down to the great earthquake. It is the Shitamachi, the plebeian flatlands, which I here call the Low City. Meiji was when the changes that made Japan modern and economically miraculous were beginning. Yet the Low City had not lost its claim to the cultural hegemony which it had clearly possessed under the Tokugawa.

Many exciting things have occurred in the six decades since the earthquake, which is slightly farther from the present than from the beginning of Meiji. Another book asks to be written, about those decades and especially the ones since the surrender. Perhaps it will be written, but it would have to be mostly about the other half (these days considerably more than half), the hilly High City, the Yamanote. That is where the artist and the intellectual, and to an increasing extent the manager and the magnate, have been. If there is less in this book about the High City than the Low City, it is because one is not drawn equally to everything in a huge and complex city, and a book whose beginnings lie in personal experience does have a way of turning to what interests and pleases.

Kafū was an elegist, mourning the death of Edo and lamenting the emergence of modern Tokyo. With such a guide and companion, an elegiac tone is bound to emerge from time to time. The departure of the old and the emergence of the new are inextricably entwined, of course. Yet, because the story of what happened to Edo is so much the story of the Low City, matters in which it was not interested do not figure much. It was not an intellectual sort of place, nor was it strongly political. Another consideration has urged the elimination of political and intellectual matters: the fact that Tokyo became the capital of Japan in 1868. A distinction may be made between what occurred in the city because it was the capital, and what occurred because it was a city.

So this book contains little political and intellectual history, and not much more literary and economic history. The major exception in literary matters is the drama, the great love of the Edo townsman. The story of what happened to Kabuki is central to the story of the city, and not that of the capital. The endeavor to describe a changing city as if it were an organism is perhaps not realistic, since cities change in all ways and directions, as organisms and specific institutions do not. The subject here is the changing city all the same, the legacy of Edo and what happened to it. To a much smaller degree is it the story of currents that have flowed in upon the city because it was the capital.

Japanese practice has been followed in the rendition of personal names. The family name comes before the given name. When a single element is used, it is the family name if there is no elegant pen-name (distinguished in principle from a prosy one like Mishima Yukio), and the pen-name when there is one. Hence Kafū and Shigure, both of them pen-names; but Tanizaki, Kubota, and Shibusawa, all of them family names.

The staff of the Tokyo Metropolitan Archives was very kind in helping assemble illustrations. The prints, woodcut and lithograph, are from Professor Donald Keene's collection and my own, except as noted in the captions. I am also in debt to the Tokyo Central Library and the Tōyō Keizai Shimpō. Mr. Fukuda Hiroshi was very helpful in photographing photographs that could not be taken across the Pacific for reproduction.

The notes are minimal, limited for the most part to the sources of direct quotations. A very important source, acknowledged only once in the notes, is the huge work called A *History of the Tokyo Century* (although it begins with the beginnings of Edo), published by the municipal government in the early 1970s, with a supplemental chronology published in 1980. Huge it certainly is, six volumes (without the chronology), each of them some fifteen hundred pages long. Uneven it is as well, and indispensable.

Guidebooks, four of them acknowledged in the notes, were very useful, the two-volume guide published by the city in 1907 especially so. Then there were ward histories, none of them acknowledged, because I have made no direct quotation from them. The Japanese are energetic and accomplished local historians, as much so as the British. Their volumes pour forth in bewildering numbers, those Japanese equivalents of the "admirable history of southeast Berks" one is always seeing reviewed in the *Times Literary Supplement*. Every ward has at least one history. Some are better than others, not because some are especially unreliable, but because some are better organized and less given to axe-grinding. I do not pretend to have been through them all, but none that I have looked at has been valueless.

The most important source is Nagai Kafū. To him belongs the final acknowledgment, as would belong the dedication if there were one.

E.S.

April, 1982

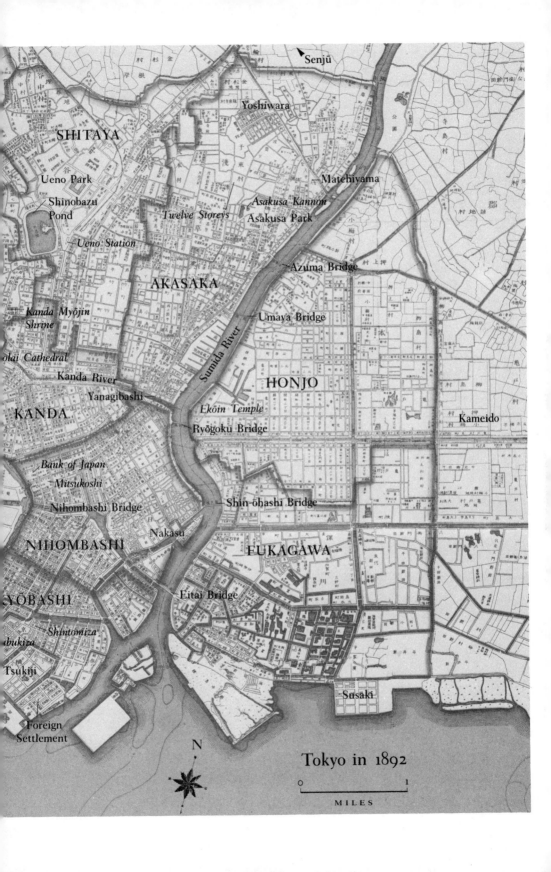

Tokyo in 1892

SHITAYA

Ueno Park

Shinobazu
Pond

Ueno Station

Kanda Myōjin
Shrine

olai Cathedral

Kanda River

Yanagibashi

KANDA

Bank of Japan

Mitsukoshi

Nihombashi Bridge

NIHOMBASHI

YOBASHI

Shintomiza

Tsukiji

bukiza

Foreign
Settlement

Senjū

Yoshiwara

Matchiyama

Asakusa Kannon

Asakusa Park

Twelve Storeys

AKASAKA

Azuma Bridge

Umaya Bridge

Sumida River

HONJO

Ekōin Temple

Ryōgoku Bridge

Kameido

Shin-ōhashi Bridge

Nakasu

FUKAGAWA

Eitai Bridge

Susaki

N

0   1

MILES

Tokyo in 1914

LOW CITY, HIGH CITY

1

THE END
AND THE BEGINNING

There was foreboding in Japan on September 1, 1923. September 2 would be the Two-Hundred-Tenth Day, counting from the day in early February when spring is held to begin. Awaited each year with apprehension, it comes during the typhoon season and the harvest. The conjunction of the two, harvest and typhoon, can mean disaster. The disaster of that year came instead on September 1.

The morning was warm, heavy, as most days of late summer are, with the shrilling of locusts. The mugginess was somewhat relieved by brisk winds, which shifted from east to south at about nine. A low-pressure zone covered the southern part of the Kantō Plain, on the fringes of which the city lies. The winds became stronger as the morning drew on. Rain fell, stopping at eleven. The skies cleared.

The city was awaiting the *don*, the "bang" of the cannon which since 1871 had been fired at noon every day in the palace plaza.

At one minute and fifteen and four-tenths seconds before noon, the great earthquake struck. The initial shocks were so violent that the seismographs at the Central Weather Bureau went out of commission. The surviving seismograph at Tokyo Imperial University made the only detailed record of the long series of quakes, more than seventeen hundred over the next three days. The epicenter was in Sagami Bay, southeast of the city. There was sinkage along a deep trough and a rising along the sides. The eastern limits of the modern city follow one earthquake zone, which runs along the Edo River and out into Tokyo Bay, and lie very near another, which crosses the wide mouth of Sagami Bay from the tip of the Chiba Peninsula to the tip of the Izu Peninsula. There had been a disastrous quake in 1855, centered on the Edo River zone, and a major though less disastrous one in the summer of 1894, also centered on the nearer of the two zones. It was assumed at that time that there would presently be another, and it is so assumed today, in 1982. Talk in 1923 of moving the capital to safer regions had been quieted by a proclamation from the emperor himself.

Between noon of September 1 and the evening of September 2, most of the Tokyo flatlands—the eastern sections of the city, the Shitamachi or "Low City"—went up in flames. The Low City produced most of what was original in the culture of Edo (as Tokyo had been known until the Meiji emperor moved there from Kyoto in 1867). Much of the Low City survived on the morning of September 1, and then, in forty hours or so, most of it disappeared.

Though we do not know how many died in the earthquake and the fires that followed, initial reports in the Western press almost certainly exaggerated. The *Los Angeles Times* informed a large and alarmed Japanese readership that half a million had died. The highest estimates today put the figure for Tokyo at something over a hundred thousand. Far more were killed in the fires than in the earthquake itself, and there seem to have been more deaths from drowning than from collapsed buildings.

Almost half the deaths, or perhaps more than half, if lower estimates are accepted for the total, occurred in an instant at a single place in the Low City, a park, formerly an army clothing depot, near the east or left bank of the Sumida River. Fires had started in several parts of the city soon after the initial shocks. There were whirlwinds of fire up and down the Sumida from midafternoon; the largest of them, according to witnesses, covered about the area of the Sumō wrestling gymnasium, much the largest building east of the river, and was several hundred feet high. A flaming whirlwind came down upon the park at about four in the afternoon, and incinerated upwards of thirty thousand people who had fled there from the fires sweeping the Low City.

Akutagawa Ryūnosuke, the great writer of short stories and a man of strong suicidal impulses, liked to tell people that had he then been in his native Honjo, east of the river, he would probably have taken refuge where everyone else did, and been spared the trouble of suicide.

"In a family of nine, relatives of my wife, only a son, about twenty, survived. He was standing with a shutter over his head to ward off sparks when he was picked up by a whirlwind and deposited in the Yasuda garden. There he regained consciousness."

The traditional wooden house has great powers of resistance to wind, flood, and earthquake. It resisted well this time too, and then came the fires, leaving only scattered pockets of buildings across the Low City. The damage would have been heavy if the quakes alone had caused it, but most of the old city would have survived. Even then, seventy years after the arrival of Commodore Perry and fifty-five years after the resignation of the last Edo shogun, it was built mostly of wood. Buildings of more substantial materials came through the quakes well, though many were gutted by the fires. There has been much praise for the aplomb with which Frank Lloyd Wright's Imperial Hotel came through, built as it was of volcanic stone on an "earthquake-proof" foundation. It did survive, and deserves the praise; yet so did a great many other modern buildings (though not all). The Mitsukoshi Department Store suffered only broken windows from the quake, but burned as brightly as the sun, people who saw it said, when the fires took over. That the Imperial Hotel did not burn brightly was due entirely to chance.

It is difficult to judge earthquake damage when fires sweep a city shortly afterwards. Memories shaken and distorted by the horror of it all must be counted on to establish what was there in the brief interval between quake and fire. The best information suggests that after it was over almost three-quarters of the buildings in the city had been destroyed or seriously damaged, and almost two-thirds of them were destroyed or gutted by fire. The earthquake itself can be held clearly responsible only for the difference between the two figures.

Fifteen wards made up the city; a single one remained untouched by fire. It lay in the High City, the hilly regions to the west. In five wards the loss was above 90 percent and in a sixth only slightly less. The five all lay in the Low City, along the Sumida and the bay. The sixth lay mostly in the Low City, but extended also into the hills. In Shitaya Ward, half Low City and half High City, the flat portions were almost completely destroyed, with the line of the fires stopping cleanly at the hills. Had Ueno Park in Shitaya been hit as the erstwhile clothing depot was, the casualty lists might well have doubled.

Determining the number and cause of the fires has been as diffi-

Ruins in Asakusa, including the Twelve Storeys, after the earthquake

cult as distinguishing between earthquake damage and fire damage. The best estimate puts the total number at upwards of a hundred thirty, of which well over half could not be controlled. Most of the damage occurred during the first afternoon and night. It was early on the morning of September 2 that the Mitsukoshi was seen burning so brightly. Nineteen fires, the largest number for any of the fifteen wards, began in Asakusa, east of Shitaya. By the morning of September 3 the last of them had burned themselves out or been extinguished.

It is commonly said that the chief reason for the inferno was the hour at which the first shocks came. Lunch was being prepared all over the city, upon gas burners and charcoal braziers. From these open flames and embers, common wisdom has it, the fires began.

But in fact many fires seem to have had other origins. Chemicals have been identified as the largest single cause, followed by electric wires and burners. This suggests that the same disaster might very well have occurred at any hour of the day. The earthquake of 1855 occurred in the middle of the night. Much of the Low City was destroyed then too. Most of the damage was caused by fire—yet in the mid-nineteenth century there were no electric lines and probably few

6

chemicals to help the fire on. Fires will start, it seems, whenever buildings collapse in large numbers. No fire department can cope with them when they start simultaneously at many points on a windy day. Tokyo is now a sea of chemicals and a tangle of utility wires. It is not as emphatically wooden as it once was, to be sure, but the Low City, much of it a jumble of small buildings on filled land, will doubtless be the worst hit when the next great earthquake comes.

Among the rumors that went flying about the city was the imaginative one that an unnamed country of the West had developed an earthquake machine and was experimenting upon Japan. There were, nevertheless, no outbreaks of violence against "foreigners," which in Japan usually means Westerners. Instead, the xenophobia of the island nation turned on Koreans.

The government urged restraint, not to make things easier for Koreans, but because the Western world might disapprove: it would not do for such things to be reported in the Western press. Rumors spread that Koreans were poisoning wells. The police were later accused of encouraging hostility by urging particular attention to wells, but probably not much encouragement was needed. A willingness, and indeed a wish, to believe the worst about Koreans has been a consistent theme in modern Japanese culture. The slaughter was considerable, in any event. Reluctant official announcements put casualties in the relatively low three figures. The researches of the liberal scholar Yoshino Sakuzō were later to multiply them by ten, bringing the total to upwards of two thousand.

Not all the things of Edo were destroyed. The most popular temple in the city, the great Asakusa Kannon, survived. An explanation for its close escape was that a statue of the Meiji Kabuki actor Danjūrō, costumed as the hero of *Shibaraku* (meaning "One Moment, Please"), held back flames advancing from the north. But fire did destroy the Yoshiwara, most venerable of the licensed quarters that had been centers of Edo culture.

Several fine symbols of Meiji Tokyo were also destroyed. The old Shimbashi Station, northern terminus of the earliest railroad in the land, was among the modern buildings that did not survive. The Ryōunkaku (literally "Cloud Scraper"), a twelve-storey brick tower in Asakusa, had survived the earthquake of 1894, when many a brick chimney collapsed and brick architecture in general was brought into

7

disrepute. It had been thought earthquake-proof, but in 1923 it broke off at the eighth storey. The top storeys fell into a lake nearby, and the rest were destroyed the following year by army engineers.

The great loss was the Low City, home of the merchant and the artisan, heart of Edo culture. From the beginnings of its existence as the shogun's capital, Edo was divided into two broad regions, the hilly Yamanote or High City, describing a semicircle generally to the west of the shogun's castle, now the emperor's palace, and the flat Low City, the Shitamachi, completing the circle on the east. Plebeian enclaves could be found in the High City, but mostly it was a place of temples and shrines and aristocratic dwellings. The Low City had its aristocratic dwellings, and there were a great many temples, but it was very much the plebeian half of the city. And though the aristocracy was very cultivated indeed, its tastes—or the tastes thought proper to the establishment—were antiquarian and academic. The vigor of Edo was in its Low City.

The Low City has always been a vaguely defined region, its precise boundaries difficult to draw. It sometimes seems as much an idea as a geographic entity. When in the seventeenth century the Tokugawa regime set about building a seat for itself, it granted most of the solid hilly regions to the military aristocracy, and filled in the marshy mouths of the Sumida and Tone rivers, to the east of the castle. The flatlands that resulted became the abode of the merchants and craftsmen who purveyed to the voracious aristocracy and provided its labor.

These lands, between the castle on the west and the Sumida and the bay on the east, were the original Low City. Of the fifteen Meiji wards, it covered only Nihombashi and Kyōbashi and the flatlands of Kanda and Shiba. Asakusa, most boisterous of the Meiji pleasure centers, was scarcely a part of the old city at all. It lay beyond one of the points guarding approaches to the city proper, and was built initially to serve pilgrims to its own great Kannon temple. Later it was linked to the theater district, and was a part of the complex that catered to the Yoshiwara licensed quarter, yet farther to the north.

Today everything east of the Sumida is regarded as part of the Low City, but until Meiji only a thin strip along the east bank of the Sumida was so considered, and not even that by everyone.

The heart of the Low City was Nihombashi, broadest of the lands first reclaimed by the shogunate. Nihombashi set the tone and made the definitions. Nihombashi proper, the "Japan Bridge" from which the district took its name, was the spot where all roads began. Distances from the city were measured from Nihombashi. A proper resident of Nihombashi did not have to go far east, perhaps only as far as the Sumida, perhaps a few paces beyond, to feel that he had entered the land of the bumpkin. The Low City was small, tight, and cozy.

It changed a great deal between the resignation of the last shogun and the earthquake. As time runs on, new dates for the demise of Edo are always being assigned by connoisseurs of the subject. In 1895, we are told, or in 1912, Edo finally departed, and only Tokyo remained. Yet even today the Low City is different from the High City, and so it may be said that even today something of Edo survives. The earthquake was all the same a disaster from which the heart of the Low City did not recover. Already before 1923 the wealthy were moving away from Nihombashi, and vitality was departing as well. The earthquake accelerated the movement to the south and west, first apparent in the rise of Ginza. Today the most prosperous centers for drinking and shopping lie beyond the western limits of the Meiji city.

Nihombashi and the Low City in general were conservative. There

Tokiwa Bridge, Nihombashi, in early Meiji. Later site of the Bank of Japan

was, of course, resentment at the rigid Tokugawa class structure, which put the merchant below everyone else. By way of fighting back, a satirical vein in the literature and drama of the Low City poked fun at the High City aristocrat, but never strongly enough to make the urban masses a threat to the old order. The Edokko, the "child of Edo," as the native of the Low City called himself, was pleased to be there "at the knee" of Lord Tokugawa, and the shogunate was wise enough to take condescending notice of the populace on certain festival days. When the threat to the regime eventually came, it was from the far provinces, and the Edokko was more resentful of the provincial soldiers who became the new establishment than he had ever been of the old.

He may be taxed with complacency. The professional child of Edo has descendants today, and they are proud of themselves to the point of incivility. They tend to divide the world between the Low City and other places, to the great disadvantage of the latter. The novelist Tanizaki Junichirō, a genuine Edokko, born in 1886 of a Nihombashi merchant family, did not like his fellow Edokko, whom he described as weak, complaining, and generally ineffectual. Yet the Low City of Edo had high standards and highly refined tastes, and if exclusiveness was necessary to maintain them, as the years since have suggested, that seems a small price to pay.

Kyōbashi, to the south of Nihombashi, included Ginza, which came aggressively forward to greet the new day. An artisan quarter under the old regime, Ginza stood at the terminus of the new railway and eagerly brought new things in from Yokohama and beyond. Tanizaki and others have described the diaspora of the Edokko, with Nihombashi its chief victim, as the new people came in. It can be exaggerated, and one suspects that Tanizaki exaggerated for literary effect. He made much also of the helplessness of the Edokko before the entrepreneur from the West Country. Yet many an Edo family did very well. Among those who did best were the Mitsui, established in Nihombashi since the seventeenth century. Not many children of Edo had been there longer. The demographic and cultural movement to the south and west was inexorable all the same, and more rapid after the earthquake.

The High City was much less severely damaged than the Low City. The growing suburbs, many of them later incorporated within the city limits, were hurt even less. Through the years before and after the earthquake, industrial production remained fairly steady for Tokyo Prefecture, which included large suburbs as well as the city proper. Within the fifteen wards of the city, it fell sharply in the same period. The suburban share was growing.

With the Low City pleasure quarters lost in the fires, those of the High City throve. They did not have the same sort of tradition, and the change meant the end of something important in the life of the city. The novelist Nagai Kafū—not, like Tanizaki, a real son of Edo, both because he was not from the merchant class and because his family had not been in the city the three generations held necessary to produce one—was even so an earnest student of Edo and Tokyo. All through his career (he was born in 1879 and died in 1959) he went on lamenting the fact that the latter had killed the former; and all through his career, with lovable inconsistency, he went on remembering how Edo yet survived at this and that date later than ones already assigned to the slaying. Though he is commonly considered an amorous and erotic novelist, his writings are essentially nostalgic and elegiac. The pleasure quarters were central to Edo culture, and it was in those conservative regions if anywhere that something of Edo survived. So it was natural that they should be his favorite subject. He had many harsh things to say about the emergent pleasure centers of the High City, and their failure to keep sex in its place—pleasurable, no doubt, but not the only thing at which the great ladies of the older quarters thought it necessary to excel. The old quarters were genuine centers of the higher arts.

The seventy-seventh of the Chinese sexagenary cycles came to a close in 1923. When Cycle Seventy-seven began, in 1864, the Tokugawa shogunate was in its final convulsions. The short administration of the last shogun was soon over, and the "Restoration," as it is called in English, occurred. Edo became Tokyo, with the Meiji emperor in residence. "Restoration" is actually a bad translation of the Japanese *ishin*, which means something more like "renovation" or "revitalization."

Edo could not have known, at the beginning of the Cycle Seventy-seven, that Lord Tokugawa would so soon be in exile. Yet there were ample causes for apprehension, not the least of which was the presence of the foreigner. He obviously did not mean to go away. At first, upon the opening of the ports, foreigners seem to have been greeted with friendliness and eager curiosity. Presently this changed. A Dutch observer dated the change as 1862, subsequent to which there were many instances of violence, including the stoning of an American consul. The Dutchman put the blame upon the foreigners themselves, an unruly lot whom the port cities attracted. The Edo townsman seems to have had little to do with the violence; his feelings were not that strong. Yet he seems to have agreed with the rustic soldiers responsible for most of the violence that the barbarian should be put back in his place, on the other side of the water.

Early in 1863, the new British legation was destroyed by arsonists of the military class—among them Itō Hirobumi, later to become the most prominent of Meiji statesmen. The legation had been built in the part of the city closest to the relative security of Yokohama. It was not yet occupied, and nothing came of plans for other legations on the same site. The Edo townsman seems to have received news of the fire with satisfaction.

Edo was not, like the great capitals of Europe, a commercial center in its own right, with interests independent of and sometimes in conflict with those of the sovereign. More like Washington than London or Paris, it was an early instance, earlier than Washington, of a fabricated capital. Technically it was not the capital at all, since the emperor remained in Kyoto through the Tokugawa centuries. It was, however, the seat of power. The first shogun established himself there for military reasons, and the commercial and artisan classes gathered, as in Washington, to be of service to the bureaucracy. It was an enormous bureaucracy, because the Tokugawa system required that provincial potentates maintain establishments in the city. The Edo townsman was happy, on the whole, to serve and to make money. He saw enough of the bureaucracy to know that its lesser members, at least, looked upon his own life with some envy.

Land-use maps, though they disagree in matters of detail, are consistent in showing a very large part of the city given over to the aristocracy and to temples and shrines, and a very small part to the plebeian classes, mercantile and artisan. If the expression "aristocracy" is defined broadly to include everyone attached in some fashion to the central bureaucracy and the establishments of the provincial lords, then the Edo townsman occupied perhaps as little as a fifth of the city. Not even the flatlands commonly held to be his abode belonged entirely to him. The banks of the Sumida were largely aristocratic all the way to Asakusa. The aristocracy possessed most of the land east of the river, and very large expanses as well in eastern Nihombashi and to the east of Ginza. There were extensive temple lands along the northern and southern fringes of the flatlands. A half million townsmen were crowded into what was indeed a small part of the city, scarcely enough to make up two of the present inner wards, or four of the smaller Meiji wards.

In the late eighteenth and early nineteenth centuries, Edo was probably the largest city in the world. The population was well over a million, perhaps at times as much as a million and two or three hundred thousand, in a day when the largest European city, London, had not yet reached a million. The merchant and artisan population was stable at a half million. The huge military aristocracy and bureaucracy made up most of the rest. There were also large numbers of priests, Buddhist and Shinto, numbering, with their families, as many as a hundred thousand persons; and there were pariahs, beneath even the merchants, the lowest of the four classes established by Tokugawa orthodoxy. There were indigents and transients. And finally there were entertainers, accommodated more and more uncomfortably by the Tokugawa regime as it moved into its last years.

Pictures of Edo—woodcuts and screens—make it seem the loveliest of places to live. Elegant little shops are elegantly disposed among temples and shrines, each of which offers a range of amusing sights and performers, jugglers and acrobats and musicians and swordsmen, and perhaps a tiger or an elephant brought from abroad in response to the exotic yearnings of a sequestered populace.

Prominent in such representations are the main streets of Nihombashi. They suggest a pleasant buzz of life, which indeed there must have been, but they do not reveal the equally probable crowding of the back streets. The main or "front" streets were for the better shops and the wealthier merchants. Lesser people occupied the alleys behind, living in rows of shingled huts along open gutters, using common wells and latrines.

The old city did not fill the fifteen wards of the Meiji city, much less the twenty-three wards of the present city. "It is Edo as far as the

Kaneyasu," said the Edo maxim, with reference to a famous shop in the Hongō district, not far from the present Hongō campus of Tokyo University. There the provinces were said to begin, even though the jurisdiction of the city magistrates extended somewhat farther; and today the Kaneyasu is practically downtown. The city extended no more than a mile or two in most directions from the castle, and a considerably shorter distance before it reached the bay on the east. In a fifth or so of this limited area lived the steady and permanent populace of a half million townsmen, a twentieth, roughly, of the present population, on much less than a twentieth of the present land. In the back alleys the standard dwelling for the artisan or the poorer tradesman was the "nine-by-twelve," two rooms, one of them earth-floored, with nine feet of frontage on the alley and extending twelve feet back from it. The wealthier merchants lived, some of them, as expansively and extravagantly as the aristocrats of the High City, but lesser inhabitants of the Low City lived with mud, dust, darkness, foul odors, insects, and epidemics. Most of the huts in the back alleys had roofs of the flimsiest and most combustible sort. They burned merrily when there was a fire. The city was proud of its fires, which were called *Edo no hana,* "the flowers of Edo," and occurred so frequently and burned so freely that no house in the Low City could expect to last more than two decades. Some did, of course, and some have survived even into our day, but actuarial figures announced doom at intervals of no more than a quarter of a century.

It is easy to become sentimental about Edo and the beautiful way of life depicted on the screens. Nostalgia is the chief ware offered by the professional Edokko. But Meiji was an exuberant period, and even for the most conservative inhabitant there must have been a sense of release at its advent.

Tanizaki had a famous vision after the earthquake of what the rebuilt city would be like. He was in the Hakone mountains, some forty miles southwest of Tokyo, when the earthquake struck. He rejoiced in the destruction of the old city, and looked forward to something less constricting. Since he doubtless had the Nihombashi of his boyhood in mind, and the mood of Edo was still strong in that place and in those days, we may feel in his musings something of what the son of Edo must have felt upon leaving Edo and the repressive old regime behind.

Lafcadio Hearn once said that a person never forgets the things seen and heard in the depths of sorrow; but it seems to me that, whatever the time of sorrow, a person also thinks of the happy, the bright, the comical, things quite the opposite of sorrowful. When the earthquake struck I knew that I had survived, and I feared for my wife and daughter, left behind in Yokohama. Almost simultaneously I felt a surge of happiness which I could not keep down. "Tokyo will be better for this!" I said to myself. . . .

I have heard that it did not take ten years for San Francisco to be a finer city than before the earthquake. Tokyo too would be rebuilt in ten years, into a solid expanse of splendid buildings like the Marunouchi Building and the Marine Insurance Building. I imagined the grandeur of the new metropolis, and all the changes that would come in customs and manners as well. An orderly pattern of streets, their bright new pavements gleaming. A flood of automobiles. The geometric beauty of block towering upon block, and elevated lines and subways and trolleys weaving among them, and the stir of a nightless city, and pleasure facilities to rival those of Paris and New York. . . . Fragments of the new Tokyo passed before my eyes, numberless, like flashes in a movie. Soirees, evening dresses and swallowtails and dinner jackets moving in and out, and champagne glasses floating up like the moon upon the ocean. The confusion of late night outside a theater, headlights crossing one another on darkly shining streets. The flood of gauze and satin and legs and illumination that is vaudeville. The seductive laughter of streetwalkers beneath the lights of Ginza and Asakusa and Marunouchi and Hibiya Park. The secret pleasures of Turkish baths, massage parlors, beauty parlors. Weird crimes. I have long had a way of giving myself up to daydreams in which I imagine all manner of curious things, but it was very strange indeed that these phantasms should be so stubbornly entwined among sad visions of my wife and daughter.

In the years after the Second World War, one was frequently surprised to hear from the presumably fortunate resident of an unbombed

Kotsukappara execution grounds

pocket that he would have been happier if it too had been bombed. A lighter and airier dwelling, more consonant with modern conveniences, might then have taken its place. The Edo townsman must have shared this view when the gates to the back alleys were dismantled and, after disappearing in fires, the alleys themselves were replaced by something more in keeping with Civilization and Enlightenment, as the rallying call of the new day had it.

Meiji brought industrial soot and other forms of advanced ugliness, and Nagai Kafū's laments for a lost harmony were not misplaced. But it also brought liberation from old fears and afflictions. In the spring of 1888 services were held on the site of the old Kotsukappara execution

16

grounds, in the northern suburbs, for the repose of the souls of those who had been beheaded or otherwise put to death there. The number was then estimated at a hundred thousand. The temple that now stands on the site claims to comfort and solace two hundred thousand departed spirits. If the latter figure is accepted, then about two persons a day lost their lives at Kotsukappara through the three hundred years of its use—and Kotsukappara was not the only execution grounds at the disposal of the Edo magistracy. The Meiji townsman need fear no such judicial harshness, and he was gradually rescued from epidemics and fires as well.

There was also spiritual liberation. The playwright Hasegawa Shigure, a native of Nihombashi, thus described the feelings of her father upon the promulgation, on February 11, 1889, of the Meiji constitution: "His joy and that of his fellows had to do with the end of the old humiliation, the expunging of the stigma they had carried for so many years as Edo townsmen."

One should guard against sentimentality, then; but there is the other extreme to be guarded against as well. The newly enlightened elite of Meiji was strongly disposed to dismiss Edo culture as vulgar and decadent, and the latter adjective is one commonly applied even now to the arts and literature of the early nineteenth century.

Perhaps it was "decadent," in a certain narrow sense, that so much of Edo culture should have centered upon the pleasure quarters, and it is certainly true that not much late-Edo literature seems truly superior. The rigid conservatism of the shogunate, and the fact that the pleasure quarters were the only places where a small degree of democracy prevailed (class did not matter, only money and taste), may be held responsible for the decadence, if decadence there was. As for the inadequacy of late-Edo literature, good taste itself may have been more important than the products of good taste.

Because of its exquisite products we think of the Heian Period, when the Shining Genji of the tale that bears his name did everything so beautifully, as a time when everyone had good taste. But it is by its nature something that not everyone possesses. Courtly Heian and mercantile Edo must have been rather similar in that good taste was held to be important and the devices for cultivating it were abundant.

Edo culture was better than anything it left to posterity. Its genius was theatrical. The *chanoyu*, the tea ceremony, that most excellent

product of an earlier age, was also essentially theatrical. In the hands
of the affluent and cultivated, it brought together the best in handi-
crafts, in painting, and in architecture, and the "ceremony" itself was
a sort of dance punctuated by ritualized conversation. The objects that
surrounded it and became a part of it survived, of course, but, whatever may have been the effect on the minds and spirits of the participants, the occasion itself was an amalgam of beautiful elements put
together for a few moments, and dispersed.

So it was too with the highest accomplishments of Edo—and the
likening of an evening at the Yoshiwara to an afternoon of tea is not to
be taken as jest. In both cases, the performance was the important
thing. The notion of leaving something behind for all generations was
not relevant. Much that is good in the Occidental theater is also satis-
fying as literature, but writings for the Tokugawa theater, whether of
Edo or of Osaka, tend not to be.

The best of Edo was in the Kabuki theater and in the pleasure
quarters, whose elegant evenings also wore a theatrical aspect. It was a
very good best, a complex of elements combining, as with *chanoyu*, into
a moment of something like perfection. The theater reached in many
directions, to dominate, for instance, the high demimonde. The theaters and the pleasure quarters were in a symbiotic relationship. The
main business of the Yoshiwara and the other quarters was, of course,
prostitution, but the preliminaries were theatrical. Great refinement
in song and dance was as important to the Yoshiwara as to the theater.
There were many grades of courtesan, the lowest of them an un-
adorned prostitute with her crib and her brisk way of doing business,
but letters and paintings by the great Yoshiwara ladies turn up from
time to time in exhibitions and sales, to show how accomplished they
were.

The pleasure quarters were culture centers, among the few places
where the townsman of affluence could feel that he had things his
way, without censorious magistrates telling him to stay down there at
the bottom of an unchanging social order. The Yoshiwara was central
to the culture of Edo from its emergence in the seventeenth century as
something more than a provincial outpost.

The elegance of the Yoshiwara was beyond the means of the poorer
shopkeeper or artisan, but he shared the Edo passion for things theatrical. The city was dotted with Yose, variety or vaudeville halls, where

he could go and watch and pass the time of day for a very small admission fee. There he found serious and comic monologues, imitations of great actors, juggling and balancing acts, and mere oddities. At no expense whatever there were shows on festival days in the precincts of shrines and temples. A horror play on a summer night was held to have a pleasantly chilling effect; and indeed summer, most oppressive season for the salaried middle class of the new day, was for the Edo townsman the best of seasons. He could wander around half naked of a warm evening, taking in the sights.

He did it mostly on foot. A scarcity of wheels characterized Edo, and the shift from feet to wheels was among the major revolutions of Meiji. The affluent of Edo had boats and palanquins, but almost no one but draymen used wheels. More than one modern Japanese city has been described as "the Venice of Japan," and the appellation might have been used for Edo—it was not as maritime in its habits as Venice, and the proportion of waterways to streets was certainly lower, but

Pleasure boats moored in the northern suburbs in winter, early Meiji

there was a resemblance all the same. Edo had a network of water-ways, natural and artificial, and the pleasantest way to go to the Yoshiwara was by boat. Left behind by movements and concentrations of modern power, Venice remained Venice. Not Edo. No Japanese city escaped the flood of wheeled vehicles, and there really is no Venice of modern Japan. Something more of the Edo canal and river system might have survived, however, if the city had not become the political center of the modern country, leading the way into Civilization and Enlightenment.

In late Edo the resident of Nihombashi had to go what was for him a long distance if he wished a day at the theater or a night in the Yoshiwara. The theaters and the Yoshiwara were there side by side, leagued geographically as well as aesthetically in the northern suburbs. The Yoshiwara had been there through most of the Tokugawa Period. It was popularly known as "the paddies." The Kabuki theaters were moved north only in very late Edo, when the shogunate had a last seizure of puritanical zeal, and sought to ease its economic difficulties by making the townsman live frugally.

Asakusa was already a thriving center because of its Kannon tem-ple, and it had long been the final station for wayfarers to the Yoshiwara. Now it had the Kabuki theaters to perform a similar service for. In the last decades of Edo, the theaters and the greatest of the pleasure quarters both lay just beyond the northeastern fringe of the city, and Asakusa was that fringe. The efforts of the shogunate to discourage indulgence and prodigality among the lower classes thus had the effect of making Asakusa, despite its unfortunate situation in watery suburban lands, the great entertainment district of the city. This it was to become most decisively in Meiji.

The Kannon drew bigger crowds of pilgrims, many of them more intent upon pleasure than upon devotion, than any other temple in the city, and a big crowd was among the things the city loved best. Crowds were their own justification, and the prospect of a big crowd was usu-ally enough to make it even bigger. When the Yoshiwara was first moved north in the seventeenth century, the Kannon sat among tidal marshes, a considerable distance north of Nihombashi, and beyond one of the points guarding access to the city proper. That is why the Yoshiwara was moved there. The shogunate did not go to the extreme of outlawing pleasure, but pleasure was asked, like funerals and ceme-teries, to keep its distance.

The same happened, much later, to the theaters. The Tempō sumptuary edicts, issued between 1841 and 1843, were complex and meticulous, regulating small details of the townsman's life. The number of variety halls in the city was reduced from upwards of five hundred to fifteen, and the fifteen were required to be serious and edifying. Ladies in several trades—musicians, hairdressers, and the proprietresses of archery stalls in such places as the Asakusa Kannon—were held to be a wanton influence, and forbidden to practice.

In 1842 the Kabuki theater was picked up and moved to the northern limits of the city, a five-minute walk nearer Asakusa than the Yoshiwara. Kabuki was enormously popular in the early decades of the nineteenth century. The more successful actors were cultural heroes and leaders of fashion and taste, not unlike television personalities today. When two major theaters burned down, permission to rebuild was denied, and the possibility was considered of outlawing Kabuki completely. There was disagreement among the city magistrates, and a compromise was reached, permitting them to rebuild, but far from their old grounds. The suburban villa of a daimyo was taken over for the purpose. There the theaters remained even after the reforming zeal had passed, and there they were when Edo became Tokyo, and the Meiji Period began.

So Asakusa was well placed to provide the city of the new era with its pleasures. It has declined sadly in recent decades, and its preeminence in late Edo and early Meiji may have been partly responsible. People had traveled there on foot and by boat. Now they were to travel on wheels. The future belonged to rapid transit and to places where commuters boarded suburban trains. Overly confident, Asakusa chose not to become one of these.

It is of course a story of gradual change. The city has always been prone to sudden change as well, uniformly disastrous. It cannot be said, perhaps, that disasters increased in frequency as the end of Edo approached. Yet they were numerous after the visit of Commodore Perry in 1853, an event which many would doubtless have listed first among them. A foreboding hung over the government and the city.

The traditional system of chronology proceeds not by a single sequence, as with B.C. and A.D., but by a series of era names, which can be changed at the will of the authorities. In premodern Japan, they were often changed in hopes of better fortune; when one name did not seem to be working well, another was tried. The era name was changed a year after the Perry visit, and four times in less than a decade before the Meiji Restoration finally brought an end to the agonies of the Tokugawa.

Half the Low City was destroyed in the earthquake of 1855. There were two great fires in 1858 and numbers of lesser but still major fires through the remaining Tokugawa years, one of which destroyed the Yoshiwara. The main redoubt of the castle was twice destroyed by fire during the 1860s. Rebuilding was beyond the resources of the shogunate. A lesser redoubt, hastily and roughly rebuilt after yet another fire, became the Meiji palace, and served in that capacity until it was destroyed again, early in the new era. A fire which destroyed yet another of the lesser redoubts was blamed on arson. The Meiji emperor spent most of his first Tokyo decades in a Tokugawa mansion to the southwest of the main palace compound. It later became the Akasaka Detached Palace and the residence of the crown prince, and is now the site of the guest house where visiting monarchs and prelates are put up.

There were, as there had always been, epidemics. It was possible to see ominous portents in them too. A nationwide cholera epidemic in 1858 was laid to the presence of an American warship in Nagasaki.

The opening of the ports meant the arrival of the foreign merchant and missionary, and the undisguised adventurer. The Tokugawa regime never got around to lifting the anti-Christian edicts of the seventeenth century, but Christianity was tolerated so long as the congregations were foreign. Inflation followed the opening of the ports. The merchant was blamed. On a single night in 1864, ten Japanese merchants were killed or injured, in attacks that must have been concerted.

"Rice riots" occurred in the autumn of 1866 while the funeral of the fourteenth shogun was in progress. The coincidence was ominous. Indeed, everything about the death of the shogun was ominous, as if the gods had withdrawn their mandate. He had been a very young man, barely past adolescence, and his election had quieted factional disputes which now broke out afresh. He died of beriberi in Osaka, the first in the Tokugawa line to die away from Edo.

The riots began in Fukagawa, east of the Sumida River, as peaceful assemblies of poor people troubled by the high cost of food. In a few days, crowds were gathering in the flatlands west of the river, so large and dense as to block streets. There were lesser gatherings in the hilly districts as well, and four days before the climax of the funeral ceremonies violence broke out. Godowns (as warehouses were called in the East) filled with rice were looted, as were the shops of *karamonoya*, "dealers in Chinese wares," by which was meant foreign wares in general and specifically the products beginning to enter the country through Yokohama. It was in the course of the disturbances that the American consul was stoned, at Ueno, where he was observing the excitement.

What had begun as protests over economic grievances were colored by fright and anger at the changes that had come and were coming. The regime was not seriously endangered by the disturbances, which were disorganized and without revolutionary goals, but the antiforeign

*Doughnut cloud forms above the Central Weather Bureau in Kōjimachi
as fires sweep the Low City after the earthquake*

strain is significant. Though the past may have been dark and dirty, the city did not, on the whole, want to give it up.

Yet the Tokugawa regime had brought trouble upon itself, and upon the city. The population had begun to shrink even before the Restoration. In 1862 relaxation was permitted of an institution central to the Tokugawa system, the requirement that provincial lords keep their families and spend part of their own time in Edo. Families were permitted to go to their provincial homes. There was a happy egress. The Mōri of Nagato, most aggressive of the anti-Tokugawa clans, actually dismantled their main Edo mansion and took it home with them. It had stood just south of the castle, where a vacant expanse now seemed to mark the end of an era.

Widespread unemployment ensued among the lower ranks of the military, and a great loss of economic vitality throughout the city. An attempt in 1864 to revive the old system, under which the families of the daimyo were in effect held hostage in Edo, was unsuccessful. It may be that these changes did not significantly hasten the Tokugawa collapse, but they affected the city immediately and harshly. They plainly announced, as did the presence of foreigners, that things would not be the same again.

In 1863 the fourteenth shogun, Iemochi, he whose funeral coincided with the rice riots, felt constrained to go to Kyoto, the emperor's capital, to discuss the foreign threat. The dissident factions were clamoring for immediate and final expulsion. Iemochi was the first shogun to visit Kyoto since the early seventeenth century. Though he returned to Edo for a time, the last years of his tenure were spent largely in and near Kyoto. His successor Keiki (Yoshinobu), the fifteenth and last shogun, did not live in Edo at all during his brief tenure.

The Tokugawa system of city magistrates continued to the end, but the shogun's seat was for the most part without a shogun after 1863. The city could not know what sort of end it would be. The shogun was gone, and his prestige and the city's had been virtually identical. Would someone of similar qualities take his place, or would Edo become merely another provincial city—a remote outpost, even, as it had been before 1600? The half-million townsmen who remained after the shogun and his retainers had departed could but wait and see.

2

CIVILIZATION
AND ENLIGHTENMENT

The fifteenth and last shogun, no longer shogun, returned to Edo early in 1868.

Efforts to "punish" the rebellious southwestern clans had ended most ingloriously. The Tokugawa regime did not have the resources for further punitive expeditions. The southwestern clans already had the beginnings of a modern conscript army, while the Tokugawa forces were badly supplied and perhaps not very militant, having had too much peace and fun in Edo over the centuries. Seeing the hopelessness of his cause, the shogun resigned early in 1868 (by the solar calendar; it was late 1867 by the old lunar calendar). He himself remained high in the esteem of the city. Late in Meiji, when his long exile in Shizuoka was at an end, he would be invited to write "Nihombashi" for that most symbolic of bridges. Subsequently carved in stone, the inscription survived both earthquake and war. The widow of his predecessor was to become the object of a romantic cult. A royal princess married for political reasons, she refused to leave Edo during the final upheaval.

Politically inspired violence persuaded retainers of the shogunate to flee Edo. The provincial aristocracy had already fled. Its mansions were burned, dismantled, and left to decay. Common criminals took advantage of the political violence to commit violence of their own. The city locked itself in after dark, and large sections of the High City and the regions near the castle were unsafe even in the daytime.

The lower classes stayed on, having nowhere to go, and—as their economy had been based on serving the now-dispersed bureaucracy— little to do either. The population fell to perhaps half a million immediately after the Restoration. The townsmen could scarcely know the attitude of the new authorities toward the foreign barbarians and intercourse with barbarian lands. Yokohama was the most convenient port for trading with America, the country that had started it all, but if the new regime did not propose to be cosmopolitan, then placing the capital in some place remote from Yokohama would be an act of symbolic importance. Some did indeed advocate making Osaka the capital, or having Osaka and Edo as joint capitals.

Even when, in 1868, Edo became Tokyo, "the Eastern Capital," the issue was not finally resolved. By a manipulation of words for which a large Chinese vocabulary makes the modern Japanese language well suited, a capital was "established" in Edo, or Tokyo. The capital was not, however, "moved" from Kyoto. So Kyoto, which means "capital," could go on performing a role it was long accustomed to, that of vestigial or ceremonial capital. The Meiji emperor seems to have gone on thinking of Kyoto as his city; his grave lies within the Kyoto city limits.

Some scholars have argued that the name of the city was not changed to Tokyo at all. The argument seems extreme, but the complexities of the language make it possible. The crucial rescript, issued in 1868, says, insofar as precise translation is possible: "Edo is the great bastion of the east country. Upon it converge the crowds, and from it one can personally oversee affairs of state. Accordingly the place known as Edo will henceforth be Tokyo."

This could mean that Edo is still Edo, but that it is now also "the eastern capital," or, perhaps, "the eastern metropolitan center." Another linguistic curiosity made it possible to pronounce the new designation, whether precisely the same thing as a new name or not, in two ways: "Tokei" or "Tokyo." Both pronunciations were current in early Meiji. W. S. Griffis's guide to the city, published in 1874, informs us that only foreigners still called the city Edo.

The townsmen who stayed on could not know that the emperor would come to live among them in Tokyo, or Tokei. The economic life of the city was at a standstill, and its pleasures virtually so. The theaters closed early in 1868. Few came asking for the services of the

Yoshiwara. Forces of the Restoration were advancing upon the city. Restoration was in fact revolution, and it remained to be seen what revolution would do to the seat of the old regime. The city had helped very little in making this new world, and the advancing imperial forces knew that the city had no high opinion of their tastes and manners. Gloom and apprehension prevailed.

The city waited, and the Meiji armies approached from the west. One of the songs to which they advanced would be made by Gilbert and Sullivan into the song of the Mikado's troops. It was written during the march on Edo, the melody by Omura Masujirō, organizer of the Meiji armies. The march was halted short of the Hakone mountains for conferences in Shizuoka and in Edo. It was agreed that the castle would not be defended. The last shogun left the city late in the spring of 1868, and the transfer of city and castle was accomplished, bloodlessly, in the next few days. Advance parties of the revolutionary forces were already at Shinagawa and Itabashi, the first stages from Nihombashi on the coastal and inland roads to Kyoto.

Resistance continued in the city and in the northern provinces. Though most of the Tokugawa forces scattered through the city surrendered, one band took up positions at Ueno, whence it sent forth patrols as if it were still in charge of the city. The heights above Shitaya, now Ueno Park, were occupied by the great Kan-eiji, one of the Tokugawa mortuary temples, behind which lay the tombs of six shoguns. The holdouts controlled the person of the Kan-eiji abbot, a royal prince, and it may have been for this reason that the victors hesitated to attack.

In mid-May by the lunar calendar, on the Fourth of July by the solar, they finally did attack. From early morning, artillery fire fell upon Ueno from the Hongō rise, across a valley to the west. It was only late in the afternoon that the south defenses were breached, at the "Black Gate," near the main entrance to the modern Ueno Park, after a fierce battle. Perhaps three hundred people had been killed, twice as many among the defenders as among the attackers. Much of the shelling seems to have fallen short, setting fires. Most of the Kan-eiji was destroyed, and upwards of a thousand houses burned in the regions between Ueno and the artillery emplacements. The abbot fled in disguise, and presently left the city by boat.

.   .   .

If we may leave aside linguistic niceties and say that Edo was now Tokyo and the capital of Japan, it was different from the earlier capitals, Nara and Kyoto. It was already a large city with a proud history. Edo as the shogun's seat may have been an early instance of a fabricated capital or seat of power, but it had both Chinese and Japanese forebears. Nara and Kyoto had been built upon rural land to become capitals; there had been no urban class on hand to wish that the government had not come. So it had been with Edo when it first became the shogun's seat, but when it became the emperor's capital there were the centuries of Edo to look back upon. The proper son of Edo had acquired status by virtue of his nearness to Lord Tokugawa, and when he had the resources with which to pursue good taste, he could congratulate himself that he did it impeccably. Now came these swarms of bumpkins, not at all delicate in their understanding of Edo manners.

> Destroyed, my city, by the rustic warrior.
> No shadow left of Edo as it was.

This is Tanizaki Junichirō, speaking, much later, for the son of Edo. It is an exaggeration, of course, but many an Edo townsman would have echoed him.

The emperor departed Kyoto in the autumn of 1868. He reached the Shinagawa post station, just south of the city, after a journey of some three weeks, and entered the castle on the morning of November 26. Townsmen turned out in huge numbers, but the reception was reverent rather than boisterous; utter silence prevailed. By way of precaution against the city's most familiar disaster, businesses requiring fires were ordered to take a holiday. Then the city started coming back to life. Despite its affection for Lord Tokugawa, it was happy to drink a royal cup. Holidays were decreed in December (the merchant class of Edo had allowed itself scarcely any holidays); two thousand five hundred sixty-three casks of royal sake were distributed through the city, and emptied.

The emperor returned to Kyoto early in 1869, after the pacification of the northern provinces. He was back in Tokyo in the spring, at which time his permanent residence may be said to have begun. He did not announce that he was leaving Kyoto permanently, and the old capital went on expecting him back. It was not until 1871 that the last

court offices were removed from Kyoto, and most of the court aristocracy settled in Tokyo. Edo castle became what it is today, the royal
palace, and Tokyo the political center of the country. Until 1923 there
was scarcely a suggestion that matters should be otherwise.

The outer gates to the palace were dismantled by 1872, it having
early been decided that the castle ramparts were exaggerated, and that
the emperor did not need such ostentatious defenses. Several inner
gates, though not the innermost, were released from palace jurisdiction, but not immediately dismantled. The stones from two of the
castle guard points were used to build bridges, which the new regime
favored, as the old had not.

Initial policy towards the city was cautious, not to say confused. In
effect the Edo government was perpetuated, with a different terminol-
ogy. The north and south magistrates, both with offices in the flatlands east of the castle, were renamed "courts," and, as under the
Tokugawa, charged with governing the city in alternation.

A "red line" drawn in 1869 defined the city proper. It followed
generally the line that had marked the jurisdiction of the Tokugawa
magistrates. A few months later the area within the red line was divided into six wards. The expression "Tokyo Prefecture," meaning the
city and larger surrounding jurisdiction, had first been used in 1868.
In 1871 the prefecture was divided into eleven wards, the six wards of
the inner city remaining as before. In 1878 the six were divided into
fifteen, covering an area somewhat smaller than the six inner wards of
the city today and the two wards immediately east of the Sumida.
There were minor revisions of the city limits from time to time, and in
1920 there was a fairly major one, when a part of the Shinjuku district
on the west (not including the station or the most prosperous part of
Shinjuku today) was brought into Yotsuya Ward. The fifteen wards
remained unchanged, except in these matters of detail, until after the
Second World War, and it was only in 1932 that the city limits were
expanded to include thirty-five wards, covering generally the eleven
wards, or the Tokyo Prefecture, of 1872. The red line of early Meiji
takes some curious turns, jogging northwards above Asakusa, for instance, to include the Yoshiwara, and showing in graphic fashion how
near the Yoshiwara was, and Asakusa as well, to open paddy land.

The Tokyo Prefecture of early Meiji was not as large as the prefecture of today, and the prefecture has never been as large as the old

Musashi Province in which Edo was situated. The Tama district, generally the upper valley of the Tama River, which in its lower reaches was and is the boundary between Tokyo and Kanagawa prefectures, was transferred to Kanagawa Prefecture in 1871. Because it was the chief source of the Tokyo water supply and an important source of building materials as well, there was earnest campaigning by successive governors to have it back. In 1893 it was returned, and so the area of the prefecture was tripled. The Izu Islands had been transferred from Shizuoka Prefecture in 1878 and the Ogasawara or Bonin Islands from the Ministry of the Interior in 1880. The Iwo Islands were added to the Ogasawaras in 1891, and so, with the return of the Tama district two years later, the boundaries of the prefecture were set as they remain today. Remote though they are, the Bonin and Iwo Islands, except when under American jurisdiction, have continued to be a part of Tokyo. It is therefore not completely accurate to say that Okinawa was the only prefecture invaded during the Second World War.

A still remoter region, the Nemuro district of Hokkaido, was for a time in early Meiji a part of Tokyo Prefecture. The economy of the city was still in a precarious state, because it had not yet been favored with the equivalent of the huge Tokugawa bureaucracy, and the hope was that these jurisdictional arrangements would help in relocating the poor.

Tokyo Prefecture was one of three *fu,* which might be rendered "metropolitan prefecture." The other two were Osaka and Kyoto. Local autonomy was more closely circumscribed in the three than in other prefectures. They had their first mayors in 1898, almost a decade later than other cities. Osaka and Kyoto have continued to be *fu,* and to have mayors as well as governors. Tokyo became a *to,* or "capital district," during the Second World War, the only one in the land. Today it is the only city, town, or village in the land that does not have a mayor.

On September 30, 1898, the law giving special treatment to the three large cities was repealed, and so October 1 is observed in Tokyo as Citizens' Day, the anniversary of the day on which it too was permitted a mayor. He was chosen through a city council voted into office by a very small electorate. The council named three candidates, of whom one was appointed mayor by imperial rescript, upon the recommendation of the Ministry of the Interior. It became accepted practice for the candidate with the largest support in the council to be named mayor. The first mayor was a councilman from Kanda Ward, in the Low City. Tokyo has had at least two very famous mayors, Ozaki Yukio, who lived almost a century and was a stalwart defender of parliamentary democracy in difficult times, and Gotō Shimpei, known as "the mayor with the big kerchief," an expression suggesting grand and all-encompassing plans. Though it cannot be said that Gotō's big kerchief came to much of anything, he is credited by students of the subject with having done more than any other mayor to give the city a sense of its right to autonomy. He resigned a few weeks before the great earthquake to take charge of difficult negotiations with revolutionary Russia, but his effectiveness had already been reduced considerably by the assassination in 1921 of Hara Takeshi, the prime minister, to whom he was close. Before he became mayor he had already achieved eminence in the administration of Taiwan (then a Japanese possession) and in the national government.

The first city council was elected in 1889, the year other cities were permitted to elect mayors. There were three classes of electors, divided according to income, each of which elected its own councilmen. Some very eminent men were returned to the council in that first election, and indeed lists of councilmen through successive elections are worthy of a body with more considerable functions. The Ministry of the Interior had a veto power over acts of the city government and from time to time exercised the power, which had an inhibiting effect on the mayor and the council. Fukuzawa Yukichi, perhaps the most successful popularizer of Civilization and Enlightenment, the rallying call of the new day, was among those elected to the first council. Yasuda Zenjirō, founder of the Yasuda (now the Fuji) financial empire, was returned by the poorest class of electors.

The high standards of the council did not pervade all levels of government. There were scandals. The most sensational was the one known as the gravel scandal. On the day in 1920 that the Meiji Shrine was dedicated (to the memory of the Meiji emperor), part of a bridge just below the shrine collapsed. Investigation revealed that crumbly cement had been used, and this in turn led to revelations of corruption in the city government. The gravel scandal coincided with a utilities scandal, and the mayor, among the most popular the city has had, resigned, to be succeeded by the famous Gotō Shimpei. Tokyo deserves the name it has made for itself as a well-run city, but City Hall does have its venalities from time to time.

The Meiji system, local and national, could hardly be called democratic, but it was more democratic than the Tokugawa system had been. It admitted the possibility of radical departures. Rather large numbers of people, without reference to pedigree, had something to say about how they would be governed. Meiji was a vital period, and gestures toward recognizing plebeian talents and energies may help to account for the vitality. The city suffered from "happy insomnia," said Hasegawa Shigure, on the night the Meiji constitution went into effect. Her father made a speech. The audience was befuddled, shouting, "No, no!" when prearranged signals called for "Hear, hear!" and vice versa; but it was happy, so much so that one man literally drank himself to death. It is an aspect of Meiji overlooked by those who view it as a time of dark repression containing the seeds of 1945.

The population of the city increased from about the fifth year of Meiji. It did not reach the highest Edo levels until the mid-1880s. The sparsely populated High City was growing at a greater rate than the Low City, though in absolute terms the accretion was larger in the Low City. The new population came overwhelmingly from the poor rural areas of northeastern Japan. Despite its more stable population, the Low City had a higher divorce rate than the High City, and a higher rate than the average for the nation. But then the Low City had always been somewhat casual toward sex and domesticity. It had a preponderantly male population, and Tokyo continues to be one of the few places in the land where men outnumber women. The High City changed more than the Low City in the years between the Restoration and the earthquake, but when sons of Edo lament the death of their city, they refer to the dispersal of the townsman and his culture, the culture of the Low City. The rich moved away and so their patronage of the arts was withdrawn, and certain parts of the Low City, notably those immediately east of the palace, changed radically.

Change, as it always is, was uneven. Having heard the laments of the sons of Edo and turned to scrutinize the evidence, one may be more surprised at the continuity. The street pattern, for instance, changed little between Restoration and earthquake. In his 1874 guide to the city, W. E. Griffis remarked upon "the vast extent of open space as well as the lowness and perishable material of which the houses are

The Meiji emperor, photographed in 1872

built." Pictures taken from the roof of the City Hall in the last years of Meiji still show astonishing expanses of open land, where once the mansions of the military aristocracy had stood. Photographs from the Nikolai Cathedral in Kanda, taken upwards of a decade earlier, show almost unbroken expanses of low wooden buildings all the way to the horizon, dissolving into what were more probably photographic imperfections than industrial mists.

One would have had to scan the expanses carefully to find precise and explicit survivals among the back alleys of Edo. Fires were too frequent, and the wish to escape the confines of an alley and live on a street, however narrow, was too strong. Yet one looks at those pictures taken from heights and wonders what all those hundreds of thousands of people were doing and thinking, and the very want of striking objects seems to offer an answer. The hundreds of thousands must have been far closer to their forebears of a hundred years before than to the leaders, foreign and domestic, of Civilization and Enlightenment. Even today the Low City is different from the High City— tighter, more conservative, less given to voguish things. The difference is something that has survived, not something that has been wrought by the modern century.

It was considered very original of Charles Beard, not long before the earthquake, to characterize Tokyo as a collection of villages, but the concept was already familiar enough. John Russell Young, in attendance upon General and Mrs. Grant when they came visiting in 1879, thus described a passage up the river to dine at an aristocratic mansion:

> The Prince had intended to entertain us in his principal town-house, the one nearest the Enriokwan, but the cholera broke out in the vicinity, and the Prince invited us to another of his houses in the suburbs of Tokio. We turned into the river, passing the commodious grounds of the American Legation, its flag weather-worn and shorn; passing the European settlement, which looked a little like a well-to-do Connecticut town, noting the little missionary churches surmounted by the cross; and on for an hour or so past tea houses and ships and under bridges, and watching the shadows descend over the city. It is hard to realize that Tokio is a city—one of the greatest cities of the world. It looks like a series of villages, with bits of green and open spaces and inclosed grounds breaking up the continuity of the town. There is no special character to Tokio, no one trait to seize upon and remember, except that the aspect is that of repose. The banks of the river are low and sedgy, at some points a marsh. When we came to the house of the Prince we found that he had built a causeway of bamboo through the marsh out into the river.

The city grew almost without interruption from early Meiji to the earthquake. There was a very slight population drop just before the First World War, to be accounted for by economic disquiet, but by the end of Meiji there were not far from two million people. Early figures, based on family registers, proved to be considerably exaggerated when, in 1908, the national government made a careful survey. It showed a population of about a million and two-thirds. This had risen to over two million by 1920, when the first national census was taken. The 1920 census showed that almost half the residents of the city had been born elsewhere, the largest number in Chiba Prefecture, just across the bay; and so it may be that the complaints of the children of Edo about the new men from the southwest were exaggerated. In the decade preceding the census (the figures are based upon family registers) the three central wards seem to have gained population at a much lower rate than the city as a whole. The most rapid rate of increase was in Yotsuya Ward, to the west of the palace. The High City was becoming more clearly the abode of the elite, now identified more in terms of money than of family or military prowess. Wealthy merchants no longer had to live in the crowded lowlands, and by the end of Meiji most of them had chosen to leave. Asakusa Ward stood first both in population and in population density.

Tokyo had been somewhat tentatively renamed and reorganized, but it passed through the worst of the Restoration uncertainty by the fourth or fifth year of Meiji, and was ready for Civilization and Enlightenment: *Bummei Kaika*. The four Chinese characters, two words, very old, provided the magical formula for the new day. *Bummei* is generally rendered as "civilization," though it is closely related to *bunka*, usually rendered as "culture." *Kaika* means something like "opening" or "liberalization," though "enlightenment" is perhaps the commonest rendering. Both words are ancient borrowings from Chinese. As early as 1867 they were put together and offered as an alternative to the dark shadows of the past.

"Examining history, we see that life has been dark and closed, and that it advances in the direction of civilization and enlightenment." Already in 1867 we have the expression from the brush of Fukuzawa Yukichi, who was to coin many another new word and expression for the new day. Though in 1867 Fukuzawa was still a young man, not far into his thirties, the forerunner of what was to become his very own

35

Keiō University had been in session for almost a decade. No other university seems so much the creation of a single man. His was a powerful and on the whole benign personality. In education and journalism and all manner of other endeavors he was the most energetic and successful of propagandizers for the liberal and utilitarian principles that, in his view, were to beat the West at its own game.

For the Meiji regime, *Bummei Kaika* meant Western modes and methods. Though not always of such liberal inclinations as Fukuzawa, the regime agreed that the new formula would be useful in combatting Western encroachment. Tokyo and Osaka, the great cities of the old day, led the advance, together with the port cities of the new.

The encroachment was already apparent, and it was to be more so with the arrival of large-nosed, pinkish foreigners in considerable numbers. The formal opening of Edo was scheduled to occur in 1862. Unsettled conditions brought a five-year delay. The shogunate continued building a foreign settlement all the same. Tsukiji, on the bay east of the castle and the Ginza district, was selected for reasons having to do with protecting both foreigner from native and native from foreigner. Isolated from the rest of the city by canals and gates and a considerable amount of open space known as Navy Meadow, the settlement was ready for occupation in 1867. The foreign legations, of which there were then eleven, received word some weeks after the Restoration that the opening of the city must wait until more equable conditions prevailed. The government finally announced it towards the end of the year. Several legations, the American legation among them, moved to Tsukiji.

The gates to the settlement were early abandoned, and access became free. Foreigners employed by the government received residences elsewhere in the city, in such places as "the Kaga estate" (*Kaga yashiki*), the present Hongō campus of Tokyo University. Others had to live in the Tsukiji quarter if they were to live in Tokyo at all. Not many of them did. Tsukiji was never popular with Europeans and Americans, except the missionaries among them. The foreign population wavered around a hundred, and increasingly it was Chinese. Though small, it must have been interesting. A list of foreign residents for 1872 includes a Frenchman described as an "equestrian acrobat."

Among them were, of course, bad ones, opium dealers and the like, and the gentle treatment accorded them by the consulates aroused great resentment, which had the contradictory effect of increasing enthusiasm for Civilization and Enlightenment—faithful application of the formula, it was felt, might persuade foreign powers to do without extraterritoriality.

The two chief wonders of Tsukiji did not lie within the foreign settlement. The Tsukiji Hoterukan was across a canal to the south. The New Shimabara licensed quarter, established to satisfy the presumed needs of foreign gentlemen, was to the north and west, towards Kyōbashi.

The Hoterukan could only be early Meiji. Both the name and the building tell of the first meetings between Meiji Japan and the West. *Hoteru* is "hotel," and *kan* is a Sino-Japanese term of roughly the same meaning. The building was the delight of early photographers and late print-makers. One must lament its short history, for it was an original, a Western building unlike any building in the West. The structure, like its name, had a mongrel air, foreign details applied to a traditional base or frame. The builder was Shimizu Kisuke, founder of the Shimizu-gumi, one of the largest modern construction companies. Shimizu was a master carpenter, or perhaps a sort of building contractor, who came from a province on the Japan Sea to study foreign architecture in Yokohama.

Although the Hoterukan was completed in early Meiji, it had been planned from the last days of Tokugawa as an adjunct to the foreign settlement. It took the shape of an elongated U. Records of its dimensions are inconsistent, but it was perhaps two hundred feet long, with more than two hundred rooms on three floors, and a staff numbering more than a hundred. Tokugawa instincts required that it face away from the sea and towards the nondescript Ginza and Navy Meadow; the original design, taking advantage of the grandest prospect, was reversed by xenophobic bureaucrats, who wished the place to look more like a point of egress than a point of ingress. There was a pretty Japanese garden on the bay side, with a tea cottage and a pergola, but the most striking features of the exterior were the tower, reminiscent of a sixteenth-century Japanese castle, and walls of the traditional sort called *namako,* or "trepang," dark tiles laid diagonally with white interstices. From the outside, little about it except the height and the window sashes seems foreign at all, though perhaps an Anglo-Indian influence is apparent in the wide verandas. Wind bells hung along chains from a weathervane to the corners of the tower. The interior was plastered and painted in the foreign manner.

Through the brief span of its existence, the Hoterukan was among the wonders of the city. Like the quarter itself, however, it does not seem to have been the sort of place people wished to live in. It was sold in 1870 to a consortium of Yokohama businessmen, and in 1872 it disappeared in the great Ginza fire. (It may be of interest to note that this calamity, like the military rising of 1936, was a Two-Two-Six Incident, an event of the twenty-sixth day of the Second Month. Of course the later event was dated by the solar calendar and the earlier one by the old lunar calendar; yet the Two-Two-Six is obviously one of those days of which to be apprehensive.) The 1872 fire began at three in the afternoon, in a government building within the old castle compound. Fanned by strong winds, it burned eastward through more than two hundred acres before reaching the bay. Government buildings, temples, and mansions of the old and new aristocracy were taken, and fifty thousand people of the lesser classes were left homeless. It was not the largest fire of the Meiji Period, but it was perhaps the most significant. From it emerged the new Ginza, a commercial center for Civilization and Enlightenment and a symbol of the era.

Then there was that other marvel, the New Shimabara. For the accommodation of the foreigner a pleasure quarter was decreed. It was finished in 1869, among the first accomplishments of the new government. The name was borrowed from the famous Shimabara quarter of Kyoto. Ladies arrived from all over the Kantō district, but most of them came from the Yoshiwara. In 1870, at the height of its short career, it had a very large component indeed, considering the small size of the foreign settlement and its domination by missionaries. It followed the elaborate Yoshiwara system, with teahouses serving as appointment stations for admission to the grander brothels. Upwards of seventeen hundred courtesans and some two hundred geisha, twenty-one of them male, served in more than two hundred establishments, a hundred thirty brothels and eighty-four teahouses.

The New Shimabara did not prosper. Its career, indeed, was even shorter than that of the Hoterukan, for it closed even before the great fire. A report informed the city government that foreigners came in considerable numbers to look, but few lingered to play. The old military class also stayed away. Other pleasure quarters had depended in large measure upon a clientele from the military class, but the New Shimabara got only townsmen. In 1870 fire destroyed a pleasure quarter in Fukagawa, across the river (where, it was said, the last of the real Edo geisha held out). The reassigning of space that followed led to the closing of the New Shimabara. Its ladies were moved to Asakusa. There were no further experiments in publicly sponsored (as opposed to merely licensed) prostitution.

The most interesting thing about the quarter is what it tells us of changing official standards. In very early Meiji it was assumed that the foreigner, not so very different from the Japanese, would of course desire bawdy houses. Prudishness quickly set in, or what might perhaps better be described as deference to foreign standards. When the railway was put through to Yokohama, a land trade resulted in a pleasure quarter right beside the tracks and not far from the Yokohama terminus. Before long, the authorities had it moved away: foreign visitors would think it out of keeping with Civilization and Enlightenment.

The foreign settlement seems to have been chiefly a place of bright missionary and educational undertakings. Such eminent institutions as Rikkyō University, whose English name is St. Paul's, had their beginnings there, and St. Luke's Hospital still occupies its original Tsukiji site.

The reaction of the impressionable townsman to the quarter is as interesting as the quarter itself. The word "Christian" had taken on sinister connotations during the centuries of isolation. In appearance so very Christian, the settlement was assumed to contain more than met the eye.

At about the turn of the century Tanizaki Junichirō was sent there for English lessons. Late in his life he described the experience:

There was in those days an English school run by ladies of the purest English stock, or so it was said—not a Japanese among them. . . . Exotic Western houses stood in unbroken rows, and among them an English family named Summer had opened a school. At the gate with its painted louver boards was a wooden plaque bearing, in Chinese, the legend "Bullseye

School of European Letters." No one called it by the correct name. It was known rather as "The Summer." I have spoken of "an English family," but we cannot be sure that they were really English. They may have been a collection of miscellaneous persons from Hong Kong and Shanghai and the like. They were, in any event, an assembly of "she foreigners," most alluring, from eighteen or nineteen to perhaps thirty. The outward appearance was as of sisters, and there was an old woman described as their mother; and there was not a man in the house. I remember that the youngest called herself Alice and said she was nineteen. Then there were Lily, Agnes, and Susa [sic]. . . . If indeed they were sisters, it was curious that they resembled each other so little. . . .

Even for us who came in groups, the monthly tuition was a yen, and it must have been considerably more for those who had private lessons. A yen was no small sum of money in those days. The English lived far better, of course, than we who were among the unenlightened. They were civilized. So we could not complain about the tuition. . . .

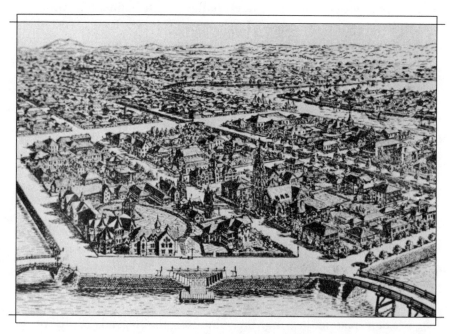

Bird's-eye view of Tsukiji foreign settlement

Wakita spoke in a whisper when he told me—he had apparently heard it from his older brother—that the she foreigners secretly received gentlemen of the Japanese upper classes, and that they were for sale also to certain Kabuki actors (or perhaps in this instance they were the buyers). The Baikō preceding the present holder of that name, he said, was among them. He also said that the matter of private lessons was a strange one, for they took place upstairs during the evening hours. Evidence that Wakita's statement was not a fabrication is at hand, in the "Conference Room" column of the *Tokyo Shimbun* for January 27, 1954. The article, by the recently deceased actor Kawarazaki Gonjūrō, is headed: "On the Pathological Psychology of the Sixth Kikugorō." I will quote the relevant passage:

"There was in those days an English school in Tsukiji called the Summer. I was sent to it. The old Uzaemon and Baikō, and Fukusuke, who later became Utaemon, had all been there before me, and it would seem that their object had to do less with the English language than with the Sanctuary of the Instincts. Among the Summer girls was a very pretty one named Susa. She was the lure that drew us."

Later Sasanuma, to keep me company, also enrolled in the Summer. The two of us thought one day to see what the upstairs might be like. We were apprehended along the way, but we succeeded in catching a glimpse of florid decorations.

Here is a description of Tsukiji from another lover of the exotic, the poet Kitahara Hakushū, writing after the settlement had disappeared in the earthquake, not to return:

> A ferry—off to Boshū, off to Izu?
> A whistle sounds, a whistle.
> Beyond the river the fishermen's isle,
> And on the near shore the lights of the Metropole.

This little ditty written in his youth by my friend Kinoshita Mokutarō, and Eau-de-vie de Dantzick, and the print in three colors of a Japanese maiden playing a samisen in an iris garden in the foreign settlement, and the stained glass and the ivy of the church, and the veranda fragrant with lavender paulownia blossoms, and a Chinese amah pushing a baby carriage, and the evening stir, "It's silver it's green it's red," from across the river, and, yes, the late cherries of St. Luke's and its bells, and the weird secret rooms of the Metropole, and opium, and the king of trumps, and all the exotic things of the proscribed creed—they are the faint glow left behind from an interrupted dream.

The foreign settlement was rebuilt after the Ginza fire, but not the Hoterukan. As the reminiscences of Hakushū tell us, there were other hotels. The Metropole was built in 1890 on the site of the American legation when the latter moved to the present site of the embassy. The Seiyōken is recommended in Griffis's guide of 1874. It was already in Tsujiki before the first railway was put through, and food fit for foreigners was brought from Yokohama by runner. The Seiyōken enterprise survives as a huge and famous restaurant in Ueno.

The Tsukiji foreign settlement lost its special significance when, at the end of the nineteenth century, revision of "the unequal treaties" brought an end to extraterritoriality. By way of bringing Japan into conformity with international practice in other respects as well, foreigners were allowed to live where they chose. The quarter vanished in the earthquake and fire of 1923, leaving behind only such mementoes as St. Luke's.

Very soon after the Restoration the city set about changing from water and pedestrian transport to wheels. A significant fact about the first stage in the process is that it did not imitate the West. It was innovative. The rickshaw or jinrickshaw is conventionally reviled as a symbol of human degradation. Certainly there is that aspect. It might be praised for the ingenuity of the concept and the design, however, and if the city and the nation were determined to spin about on wheels, it was a cheap, simple, and clean way of getting started. Though the origins of the rickshaw are not entirely clear, they seem to be Japanese, and of Tokyo specifically. The most widely accepted theory offers the names of three inventors, and gives 1869 as the date of the invention. The very first rickshaw is thought to have operated in Nihombashi. Within the next few years there were as many as fifty thousand in the city. The iron wheels made a fine clatter on rough streets and bridges, and the runners had their distinctive cries among all the other street cries. The populace does not seem to have paid as close attention as it might have. Edward S. Morse, an American professor of zoology who arrived in the tenth year of Meiji to teach at the university, remarked upon the absentminded way in which pedestrians received the warning cries. They held their ground, as if the threat would go away.

Some of the rickshaws were artistically decorated, and some, it would seem, salaciously, with paintings on their rear elevations. In 1872 the more exuberant styles of decoration were banned. Tokyo (though not yet the provinces) was discovering decorum. Runners were required to wear more than the conventional loincloth. Morse describes how a runner stopped at the city limits to cover himself properly.

For a time in early Meiji four-wheeled rickshaws carrying several passengers and pushed and pulled by at least two men operated between Tokyo and Yokohama. There are records of runners who took loaded rickshaws from Tokyo to Kyoto in a week, and of women runners.

From late Meiji the number of rickshaws declined radically, and runners were in great economic distress. On the eve of the earthquake there were fewer than twenty thousand in the city proper. The rickshaw was being forced out to the suburbs, where more advanced means of transportation were slower in coming.

It was an excellent mode of transport, particularly suited to a crowded city of narrow streets. It was dusty and noisy, to be sure, but no dustier and in other respects cleaner than the horse that was its first genuine competitor. An honest and good-natured runner, not difficult to find, was far less dangerous than a horse. Most people seem to have liked the noise—leastways Meiji reminiscences are full of it. Rubber tires arrived, and the clatter went away, though the shouting lingered on. The best thing about the rickshaw, perhaps, was the sense it gave of being part of the city.

Even this first and simplest vehicle changed the city. The canals and rivers became less important, and places dependent on them, such as old and famous restaurants near the Yoshiwara, went out of business. Swifter means of transportation come, and people take to them. Yet it seems a pity that the old ones disappeared so completely. The rickshaw is gone today, save for a few score that move geisha from engagement to engagement.

In its time the rickshaw itself was the occasion for the demise of another traditional way of getting about. The palanquin, which had been the chief mode of transport for those who did not walk, almost disappeared with the sudden popularity of the rickshaw. It is said that after 1876, with the departure for Kagoshima of the rigidly conservative Shimazu Saburō of the Satsuma clan, palanquins were to be seen only at funerals and an occasional wedding. The bride who could not afford a carriage and thought a rickshaw beneath her used a palanquin. With the advent of motor hearses and cheap taxis the palanquin was deprived of even these specialized functions.

The emperor had his first carriage ride in 1871, on a visit to the Hama Detached Palace, where General and Mrs. Grant were to stay some years later. Horse-drawn public transportation followed very quickly after the first appearance of the rickshaw. There were omnibuses in Yokohama by 1869, and not many years later—the exact date is in doubt—they were to be seen in Ginza. A brief span in the 1870s saw two-level omnibuses, the drivers grand in velvet livery and cocked hats. The first regular route led through Ginza from Shimbashi on the south and on past Nihombashi to Asakusa. Service also ran to Yokohama, and westwards from Shinagawa, at the southern edge of the city. The horse-drawn bus was popularly known as the Entarō, from the name of a vaudeville story-teller who imitated the bugle call of the conductor, to great acclaim. Taxis, when their day came, were long known as *entaku,* an acronym from Entarō and "taxi," with the first syllable signifying also "one yen."

The horse trolley arrived in 1883. The first route followed the old omnibus route north from Shimbashi to Nihombashi, and eventually to Asakusa. In the relentless advance of new devices, horse-drawn transportation had a far shorter time of prosperity than in Europe and America. There was already experimentation with the electric trolley before the horse trolley had been in use for a decade. An industrial exposition featured an electric car in 1890. In 1903 a private company laid the first tracks for general use, from Shinagawa to Shimbashi, and later to Ueno and Asakusa. The electric system was very soon able to carry almost a hundred thousand passengers a day, for lower fares than those asked by rickshaw runners, and so the rickshaw withdrew to the suburbs. Initially in private hands, the trolley system was no strong argument for private enterprise. There were three companies, and the confusion was great. In 1911, the last full year of Meiji, the city bought the system.

Horse-drawn buses in Ginza Bricktown, from a print by Hiroshige III
(Courtesy Tokyo Central Library)

The confusion is the subject of, or the occasion for, one of Nagai Kafū's most beautiful prose lyrics, "A Song in Fukagawa" (*Fukagawa no Uta*), written in 1908. The narrator boards a trolley at Yotsuya and sets forth eastwards across the city. As it passes Tsukiji, an unplanned but not unusual event occurs, which sends him farther than he has thought to go.

> The car crossed Sakura Bridge. The canal was wider. The lighters moving up and down gave an impression of great activity, but the New Year decorations before the narrow little shops and houses seemed punier, somehow, than in Tsukiji. The crowds on the sidewalks seemed less neat and orderly. We came to Sakamoto Park, and waited and waited for a sign that we would be proceeding onwards. None came. Cars were stopped in front of us and behind us. The conductor and motorman disappeared.
>
> "Again, damn it. The damned power's gone off again."
>
> A merchant in Japanese dress, leather-soled pattens and a cloak of rough, thick weave, turned to his companion, a red-faced old man in a fur muffler.

A boy jumped up, a delivery boy, probably. He had a bundle on his back, tied around his neck with a green kerchief.

"A solid line of them, so far up ahead you can't see the end of it."

The conductor came running back, change bag under his arm, cap far back on his head. He mopped at his brow.

"It might be a good idea to take transfers if you can use them."

Most of us got up, and not all of us were good-humored about it.

"Can't you tell us what's wrong? How long will it be?"

"Sorry. You see how it is. They're stopped all the way to Kayabachō.". . .

Caught in the general rush for the doors, I got up without thinking. I had not asked for one, but the conductor gave me a transfer to Fukagawa.

So Kafū finds himself east of the river, and meditates upon the contrast between that backward part of the city and the advanced part from which he has come. He yearns for the former, and must go back and live in the latter; and we are to suppose that he would not have had his twilight reverie if the trolley system had functioned better.

The rickshaw changed patterns of commerce by speeding people past boat landings. The trolley had a more pronounced effect, the Daimaru dry-goods store being a case in point. It was one of several such establishments that were to develop into department stores. Established in Nihombashi in the eighteenth century, it was in mid-Meiji the most popular of them all, even more so than Mitsukoshi, foundation of the Mitsui fortunes. "The Daimaru," said Hasegawa Shigure, "was the center of Nihombashi culture and prosperity, as the Mitsukoshi is today." In her girlhood it was a place of wonder and excitement. It had barred windows, less to keep burglars out than to keep shop boys (there were no shop girls in those days) in. Sometimes a foreign lady with foxlike visage would come in to shop, and the idle of Nihombashi would gather to stare. But the Daimaru did not lie, as its rivals did, on a main north-south trolley line. By the end of the Meiji it had closed its Tokyo business and withdrawn to the Kansai, whence only in recent years it has returned to Tokyo, this time not letting the transportation system pass it by. It commands an entrance to Tokyo Central Station.

For some, Nagai Kafū among them, the trolley was a symbol of disorder and ugliness. For others it was the introduction to a new world, at once intimidating and inviting. The novelist Natsume Sōseki's *Sanshirō*, a university student from the country, took the advice of a friend and dashed madly and randomly about, seeking the rhythms of this new world.

Construction of a railway, financed in London, began in 1870. The chief engineer was English, and a hundred foreign technicians and workers were engaged to run it. Not until 1879 were trains entrusted to Japanese crews, and then only for daylight runs. The first line was from Shimbashi, south of Ginza, to Sakuragichō in Yokohama, a stop that still serves enormous numbers of passengers, though it is no longer the main Yokohama station. The Tokyo terminus was moved some four decades later to the present Tokyo Central Station, and the old Shimbashi Station became a freight office, disappearing in 1923.

Daimaru Department Store, Nihombashi. Woodcut by Kiyochika

The very earliest service, in the summer of 1872, was from Shinagawa, just beyond the southern limits of the city, to Yokohama. The Tokyo terminus was opened in the autumn, amid jubilation. The emperor himself took the first train. He wore foreign dress, but most of the high courtiers were in traditional court dress; Western dress was still expensive and very difficult to come by. Among the notables present was the king of Okinawa.

The fare was higher than for a boat or horse-drawn bus. Everyone wanted a ride, but only the affluent could afford a ride daily. Eighty percent of the passengers are said to have been merchants and speculators with business in Yokohama. The first tickets carried English, German, and French translations. From 1876 on, there was only English. It was in 1877 that an early passenger, E. S. Morse, made his famous discovery of the shell middens of Omori, usually considered the birthplace of Japanese archeology. The train took almost an hour to traverse its twenty-five kilometers, and Omori was then a country village offering no obstructions, and so, without leaving his car, Morse was able to contemplate the mounds at some leisure and recognize them for what they were.

The Tokyo–Yokohama line was the first segment of the Tōkaidō line, put through from Tokyo to Kobe in 1889. Unlike the Tōkaidō, the main line to the north was built privately, from Ueno. It was completed to Aomori, at the northern tip of the main island, in 1891. By the turn of the century private endeavor had made a beginning at the network of suburban lines that was to work such enormous changes on the city; in 1903 Shibuya Station, outside the city limits to the southwest, served an average of fifteen thousand passengers a day. When it had been first opened, less than two decades before, it served only fifteen.

Shimbashi Station possessed curious ties with the Edo tradition. The Edo mansion of the lords of Tatsuno had stood on the site. Tatsuno was a fief neighboring that of the Forty-seven Loyal Retainers of the most famous Edo vendetta. The Forty-seven are said to have refreshed themselves there as they made their way across the city, their vendetta accomplished, to commit suicide.

If the railroad caused jubilation, it also brought opposition. The opposition seems to have been strongest in the bureaucracy. Carrying Yokohama and its foreigners closer to the royal seat was not thought a good idea. If a railroad must be built, might it not better run to the

General Grant admiring Kegon Falls during his 1879 visit. Woodcut by Kunimasa.

Above: Advertising throwaway from the Mitsui dry-goods store (later Mitsukoshi Department Store) showing the traditional first floor, with many clerks, and the new-fangled second floor (top), with glass display cases.

Left: An ingenious inside-and-outside view of the Shintomiza by Kamiyama Seishichi, 1881. The artist has removed the roof to improve the effect.

Right: Yoshiwara ladies in the eighties—two varieties of *haute couture*.

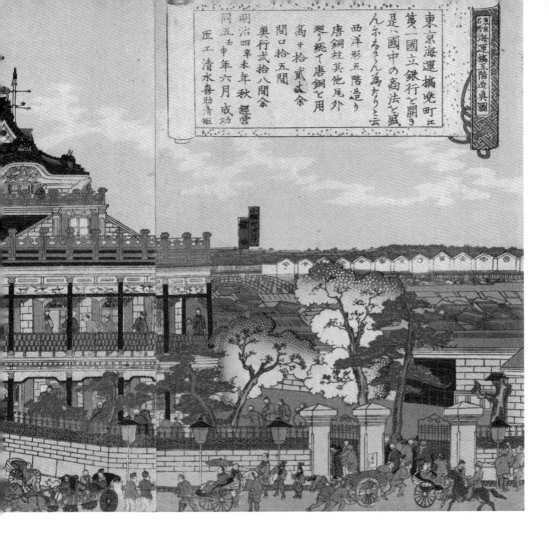

Above: The First National Bank, designed by Shimizu Kisuke, with the Kaiun Bridge in the foreground, early 1870s.

Far left: The first Bank of Japan building, designed by Conder. Woodcut by Inoue Yasuji, after Kiyochika.

Left: A vision of the Rokumeikan at night, by Yasuji after Kiyochika.

Traffic jams at Shinagawa. While locomotives approach each other on an apparent collision course, more traditional bustle fills the street above. Woodcut by Yoshitora.

Spencer the Balloon Man, shown performing his various aerial tricks at Ueno, in a woodcut dated 1890. All the airborne figures seem to be Spencer.

north, where it could be used against the most immediately apparent threat, the Russians? Along a part of its course, just south of the city, it was in the event required to run inland, because for strategic reasons the army opposed the more convenient coastal route.

Among the populace the railway does not seem to have aroused as much opposition as the telegraph, about which the wildest rumors spread, associating it with the black magic of the Christians and human sacrifice. People seem to have been rather friendly towards the locomotive. Thinking that it must be hot, poor thing, they would douse it with water from embankments.

By the eve of the earthquake there were ten thousand automobiles in the city, but they did not displace the railroad as railroad and trolley had displaced the rickshaw. In one important respect they were no competition at all. When the railroad came, the Ukiyoe print of Edo was still alive. The art, or business, had considerable vigor, though many would say that it was decadent. Enormous numbers of prints were made, millions of them annually in Tokyo alone, almost exclusively in the Low City. Few sold for as much as a penny. They were throwaways, little valued either as art or as investment. Nor were technical standards high. Artists did not mind and did not expect their customers to mind that the parts of a triptych failed to join precisely. Bold chemical pigments were used with great abandon. Yet Meiji prints often have a contagious exuberance. They may not be reliable in all their details, but they provide excellent documents, better than photographs, of the Meiji spirit. Losses over the years have been enormous. Today such of them as survive are much in vogue, bringing dollar prices that sometimes run into four figures, or yen prices in six figures.

The printmakers of early Meiji loved trains and railroads. Many of the prints are highly fanciful, like representations of elephants and giraffes by people who have never seen one. A train may seem to have no axles, and to roll on its wheels as a house might roll on logs. Windows are frivolously draped, and two trains will be depicted running on the same track in collision course, as if that should be no problem for something so wondrous. The more fanciful images can seem prophetic, showing urban problems to come, smog, traffic jams, a bureaucracy indifferent to approaching disaster.

Sometimes the treatment was realistic. The manner of Kobayashi Kiyochika, generally recognized as the great master of the Meiji print, is both realistic and effective, as beautiful a treatment of such unlikely subjects as railroads, surely, as is to be found anywhere.

Kiyochika was born in Honjo, east of the Sumida, in 1847, near the present Ryōgoku Station and not far from the birthplace of the great Hokusai. The shogunate had lumber and bamboo yards in the district. His father was a labor foreman in government employ. Though the youngest of many sons, Kiyochika was named the family heir, and followed the last shogun to Shizuoka. The shogun in exile was himself far from impoverished, but many of his retainers were. Kiyochika put together a precarious living at odd jobs, one of them on the vaudeville stage. Deciding finally to return to Tokyo, he stopped on the way, or so it is said—the details of his life are not well established—to study art under Charles Wirgman, the British naval officer who became Yokohama correspondent for the *Illustrated London News*. Missing nothing, Kiyochika is said also to have studied photography under Shimooka

Train on Takenawa embankment. Woodcut by Kiyochika

Renjō, the most famous of Meiji photographers, and painting in the Japanese style as well.

His main career as a printmaker lasted a scant five years, from 1876 to 1881, although he did make an occasional print in later life. In that brief period he produced more than a hundred prints of Tokyo. The last from the prolific early period are of the great Kanda fire of 1881, in which his own house was destroyed. (That fire was, incidentally, the largest in Meiji Tokyo.)

All the printmakers of early Meiji used Western subjects and materials, but Kiyochika and his pupils (who seem to have been two in number) achieved a Western look in style as well. It may be that, given his Westernized treatment of light and perspective, he does not belong in the Ukiyoe tradition at all.

The usual Meiji railway print is bright to the point of gaudiness, and could be set at any hour of the day. The weather is usually sunny, and the cherries are usually in bloom. Kiyochika is best in his nocturnes. He is precise with hour and season, avoiding the perpetual springtide of his elders. His train moves south along the Takanawa fill and there are still traces of color upon the evening landscape; so one knows that the moon behind the clouds must be near full.

The prints of Kiyochika's late years, when he worked mostly as an illustrator, are wanting in the eagerness and the melancholy of prints from the rich early period. The mixture of the two, eagerness and melancholy, seems almost prophetic—or perhaps we think it so because we know what was to happen to his great subject, the Low City. His preference for nocturnes was deeply appropriate, for there must have been in the life of the Low City this same delight in the evening, and with it a certain apprehension of the dawn.

The lights flooding through the windows of Kiyochika's Rokumeikan, where the elite of Meiji gathered for Westernized banquets and balls, seem about to go out. Lights are also ablaze in the great and venerable restaurant outside the Yoshiwara, but they seem subdued and dejected, for the rickshaws on their way to the quarter do not stop as the boats once did. In twilight fields outside the Yoshiwara stands a little shrine, much favored by the courtesans. Soon (we know, and Kiyochika seems to know too) the city will be flooding in all around it. Other little shrines and temples found protectors and a place in the new world, but this one did not. No trace of it remains.

Shrine near the Yoshiwara. Woodcut by Inoue Yasuji, after Kiyochika

Kiyochika had a knack one misses in so many travel writers of the time for catching moods and tones that would soon disappear. Other woodcut artists of the day, putting everything in the sunlight of high spring, missed the better half of the picture. Kiyochika was a gifted artist, and that period when Edo was giving way to Tokyo provided fit subjects for the light of evening and night. He outlived the Meiji emperor by three years.

The importance of the waterways declined as the city acquired wheels and streets were improved. The system of rivers, canals, and moats had been extensive, drawing from the mountains to the west of the city and the Tone River to the north. Under the shogunate most of the produce brought into the city had come by water. At the end of Taishō, or three years after the earthquake, most of it came by land. This apparent shift is something of a distortion, since it ignores Yokohama, the international port for Tokyo. The decline of water transport is striking all the same. There was persistent dredging at the mouth of the Sumida, but Tokyo had no deep harbor. It could accommodate ships of not more than five hundred tons. All through the Meiji Period the debate continued as to whether or not the city should seek to become an international port. Among the arguments against the proposal was the old xenophobic one: a harbor would bring in all manner of foreign rogues and diseases. What is remarkable is that such an argument could still be offered seriously a half-century after the question of whether or not to have commerce with foreign rogues had presumably been settled.

The outer moats of the palace were filled in through the Meiji Period, and the Tameike reservoir, to the southwest of the palace, which had been among the recommended places in guides to the pleasures of Edo for gathering new herbs in the spring and, in high summer, viewing lotus blossoms and hearing them pop softly open, was allowed to gather sediment. Its military importance having passed, it became a swamp in late Meiji, and in Taishō quite disappeared.

The system of canals was still intact at the end of Meiji, and there were swarms of boats upon them and fish within them. Life on the canals and rivers seems to have been conservative even for the conservative Low City. An interesting convention in the woodcuts of Meiji is doubtless based upon fact. When bridges are shown, as they frequently are, the roadway above is generally an exuberant mixture of the new and the traditional, the imported and the domestic; on the waters below there is seldom a trace of the new and imported.

Pleasure-boating of the old sort almost disappeared. Advanced young people went rowing on the Sumida, and the university boathouse was one of the sights on the left bank. A 1920 guide to Japan, however, lists but a single *funayado* in the city. The *funayado,* literally "boat lodge" or "boating inn," provided elegant boating for entertainment on the waters or for an excursion to the Yoshiwara. The boats were of the roofed, high-prowed sort, often with lanterns strung out along the eaves, that so often figure in Edo and Meiji woodcuts. Since the customer expected to be entertained as well as rowed, the *funayado* provided witty and accomplished entertainers, and so performed services similar to those of the Yoshiwara teahouses. As the network of canals disappeared, some of them made the transition into the new day and became the sort of restaurant to which geisha are summoned, but a great many merely went out of business. Ginza and Kyōbashi were the southern terminus for passage to the Yoshiwara. The *funayado* of that region were therefore among the ingredients from which the Shimbashi geisha district, still one of the finest in the city, was made.

Connoisseurs like Nagai Kafū said that Edo died of flood and fire, but it may be that the loss of boats and waterways had an even more destructive effect on the moods of Edo. Kafū himself implies as much when, in an elegiac evocation of late Edo, he has a famous writer set forth from a *funayado* and take stock of events. He is a victim of the puritanical edicts of the 1840s, and a quiet time on the Sumida is best for surveying the past and the future. The wheels of Meiji disrupted old patterns and rhythms. There was no longer the time or the inclination to put together a perfect outing, and so the arts of plebeian Edo were not in demand as they once had been.

This is not to say that the moods of the Sumida, so important to Edo, were quite swept away. They were still there, if somewhat polluted and coarsened. A "penny steamer" continued to make its way up and down the river, and on to points along the bay, even though it had by the time of the earthquake come to cost more than a penny. Ferries across the river were not completely replaced by bridges until after the Second World War. The most conservative of the geisha quarters, Yanagibashi, stood beside the river, and mendicant musicians still had themselves paddled up and down before it. One could still go boating of a summer night with geisha and music and drink. The great celebration called the "river opening" was the climactic event of the Low City summer.

In 1911 and 1912 the playwright Osanai Kaoru published an autobiographical novel called *Okawabata* (*The Bank of the Big River,* with reference to the Sumida). Osanai was a pioneer in the Westernized theater. Some years after the earthquake he was to found the Little Theater of Tsukiji, most famous establishment in an energetic and venturesome experimental-theater movement. Like Nagai Kafū, whose junior he was by two years, he was a sort of Edokko manqué. His forebears were bureaucratic and not mercantile, and he had the added disability that he spent his early childhood in Hiroshima. Such people often outdid genuine Edokko, among whom Tanizaki Junichirō could number himself, in affection for the city and especially vestiges of Edo, abstract and concrete. *The Bank of the Big River* has the usual defects of Japanese autobiographical fiction—weak characterization, a

The Yaomatsu restaurant on the Sumida, looking towards Asakusa

rambling plot, a tendency towards self-gratification; but it is beautiful in its evocation of the moods of the Sumida. The time is 1905 or so, with the Russo-Japanese War at or near a conclusion. The setting is Nakasu, an artificial island in the Sumida, off Nihombashi.

> Sometimes a lighter would go up or down between Ohashi Bridge and Nakasu, an awning spread against the sun, banners aloft, a sad chant sounding over the water to the accompaniment of bell and mallet, for the repose of the souls of those who had died by drowning.
> Almost every summer evening a boat would come to the stone embankment and give us a shadow play. Not properly roofed, it had a makeshift awning of some nondescript cloth, beneath which were paper doors, to suggest a roofed boat of the old sort. Always against the paper doors, yellowish in the light from inside, there would be two shadows. . . . When it came up the river to the sound of drum and gong and samisen, Masao would look happily at Kimitarō, and from the boat there would be voices imitating Kabuki actors. . . .

Every day at exactly the same time a candy boat would pass, to the beating of a drum. Candy man and candy would be like distant figures in a picture, but the drum would sound out over the river in simple rhythm, so near that he might almost, he thought, have reached out to touch it. At the sound he would feel a nameless stirring and think of home, forgotten so much of the time, far away in the High City. The thought was only a thought. He felt no urge to leave Kimitarō.

The moon would come up, a great, round, red moon, between the godowns that lined the far bank. The black lacquer of the river would become gold, and then, as the moon was smaller and whiter, the river would become silver. Beneath the dark form of Ohashi Bridge, across which no trolleys passed, it would shimmer like a school of whitefish.

The old wooden bridges, so pretty as they arched their way over river and canal, were not suited to heavy vehicular traffic. Wood was the chief material for wider and flatter bridges, but steel and stone were used for an increasing number of important new ones. Of 481 bridges in the city at the end of the Russo-Japanese War, 26 were steel and 166 were stone. The rest were wood. A new stone Nihombashi was dedicated in 1911. It is the Nihombashi that yet stands, and the one for which the last shogun wrote the inscription. He led the ceremonial parade, and with him was a lady born in Nihombashi a hundred years before, when there were yet four shoguns to go. The famous Azuma Bridge at Asakusa, often called "the big bridge," was swept away by a flood in 1885. A steel Azuma Bridge with a decorative superstructure was finished in 1882, occasioning a great celebration at the dedication, geisha and lanterns and politicians and all. It quickly became one of the sights of the city. The floor was still wooden at the time of the earthquake. It caught fire, as did all the other bridges across the river; hence, in part, the large number of deaths by drowning.

Nagai Kafū accused the Sumida, which he loved, of flooding twice annually. "Just as when summer gives way to autumn, so it is when spring gives way to summer: there are likely to be heavy rains. No one was surprised, for it happened every year, that the district from Senzoku toward the Yoshiwara should be under water."

So begins the last chapter of his novella *The River Sumida*. It is an exaggeration, and in other respects not entirely accurate. Late summer and autumn was the season for floods. The rains of June are more easily contained than the violent ones of the typhoon season. The passage of the seasons so important to Kafū's story required a flood in early summer. Records through the more than three centuries of Edo and Meiji suggest that the Sumida flooded on an average of once every three years. It may be that, for obscure reasons, floods were becoming more frequent. In the last half of Meiji the rate was only a little less than one every two years, and of eight floods described as "major," two were in late Meiji, in 1907 and 1910.

The flood of 1910, commonly called the Great Meiji Flood, submerged the whole northern part of the Low City, eastwards from the valleys of Koishikawa. Rising waters breached the levees of the Sumida and certain lesser streams. Asakusa, including the Yoshiwara and the setting of the Kafū story, suffered the worst damage, but only one of the fifteen wards was untouched, and the flood was a huge disaster.

Azumabashi, Asakusa. From a lithograph dated 1891

The damage has been calculated at between 4 and 5 percent of the national product for that year. Kafū liked to say that Edo disappeared in the Great Flood and the Yoshiwara fire of the following year. The flood was the occasion for the Arakawa Drainage Channel, to put an end to Sumida floods forever (see page 263).

Of all Meiji fires, the Ginza fire of 1872 had the most lasting effect upon the city. From it emerged the new Ginza.

Ginza had not been one of the busier and more prosperous sections of mercantile Edo. Compared to Nihombashi, farther north, it was cramped and narrow, caught between the outer moats of the great Tokugawa citadel and a bay shore occupied in large measure by the aristocracy. The great merchant houses were in more northerly regions. Ginza was a place of artisans and small shops.

W. E. Griffis gave a good account of what he saw there in 1870, before the fire. It contained no specific reference to Ginza, but a long walk, on his first visit to the city, took him from Tsukiji and the New Shimabara (which he wrongly calls the Yoshiwara) to Kanda. It must have been the Ginza district through which he first strolled.

> I pass through one street devoted to bureaus and cabinets, through another full of folding screens, through another of dyers' shops, with their odors and vats. In one small but neat shop sits an old man, with horn-rimmed spectacles, with the mordant liquid beside him, preparing a roll of material for its next bath. In another street there is nothing on sale but bamboo poles, but enough of these to make a forest. A man is sawing one, and I notice he pulls the saw with his two hands toward him. Its teeth are set contrary to ours. Another man is planing. He pulls the plane toward him. I notice a blacksmith at work: he pulls the bellows with his foot, while he is holding and hammering with both hands. He has several irons in the fire, and keeps his dinner boiling with the waste flame. . . . The cooper holds his tub with his toes. All of them sit while they work. How strange! Perhaps that is an important difference between a European and an Asian. One sits down to his work, and the other stands up to it. . . .

I emerge from the bamboo street to the Tori, the main street, the Broadway of the Japanese capital. I recognize it. The shops are gayer and richer; the street is wider; it is crowded with people.

Turning up Suruga Chō, with Fuji's glorious form before me, I pass the great silk shop and fire-proof warehouses of Mitsui the millionaire.

Ginza had once been something of a theater center, until the Tempō edicts of the 1840s removed the Kabuki theaters to the northern suburbs. Theater quickly returned to the Ginza region when it was allowed to, after the Restoration, but the beginning of Ginza as a thriving center of commerce and pleasure came after the fire.

The governor decided that the city must be made fireproof, and the newly charred Ginza offered a place to begin. An English architect, Thomas Waters, was retained to build an entire district of red brick. The government subsidized a special company "for building and for the management of rentals." The rebuilding took three years, when it could have been accomplished in the old way almost overnight. Rather proud of its fires, the old city had also been proud of the speed with which it recovered.

There seem to have been at least two brick buildings in the Ginza district even before the great fire, one of them a warehouse, the other a shop, "a poorer thing than the public latrines of later years," says an eminent authority on the subject. When the rebuilding was finished there were almost a thousand brick buildings in Kyōbashi Ward, which included Ginza, and fewer than twenty in the rest of the city. An 1879 list shows a scattering of Western or Westernized buildings through most of the other wards, and one ward, Yotsuya in the High City, with none at all.

The hope was that the city would make itself over on the Ginza model, and become fireproof. Practice tended in the other direction. Only along the main street was a solid face of red brick presented to the world. Very soon there was cheating, in the form of reversion to something more traditional. Pictures from late Meiji inform us that Bricktown, as it was called, lasted longest in what is now the northern part of Ginza. Nothing at all survives of it today.

The new Ginza was not on the whole in good repute among for-

Ginza Bricktown, with trees

eigners. Already in the 1870s there were complaints about the Americanization of the city. Isabella Bird came visiting in 1878 and in 1880 described Tokyo as less like an Oriental city than like the outskirts of Chicago or Melbourne. She did not say what part of the city she had reference to, but almost certainly it was Ginza. Pierre Loti thought that Bricktown had about it *une laideur americaine*. Philip Terry, the English writer of tour guides, likened it, as Griffis had likened Nihombashi, to Broadway, though not with Griffis's intent to praise. "Size without majesty, individuality divorced from all dignity and simplicity, and convenience rather than fitness or sobriety are the salient characteristics of this structural hodge-podge." Not much of Bricktown survived when Terry wrote, in 1920. What did survive was the impression of a baneful American influence; and the original architect was English.

The city was of two minds about its new Ginza. Everyone wanted to look at it, but not many wanted to live in it. In a short story from early in this century, Nagai Kafū described it as a chilling symbol of the life to come.

The initial plans were for shops on the ground floors and residential quarters above, after the pattern of merchant Edo. The new buildings were slow to fill. They were found to be damp, stuffy, vulnerable to mildew, and otherwise ill adapted to the Japanese climate, and the solid walls ran wholly against the Japanese notion of a place to live in. Choice sites along the main street presently found tenants, but the back streets languished, or provided temporary space for sideshows, "bear wrestling" and "dog dances" and the like. Among the landowners, who had not been made to relinquish their rights, few were willing or able to meet the conditions for repaying government subsidies. These were presently relaxed, but as many as a third of the buildings on the back streets remained empty even so. Vacant buildings were in the end let go for token payments, and cheating on the original plans continued apace. Most Edo townsmen could not afford even the traditional sort of fireproof godown, and the least ostentatious of the new brick buildings were, foot for foot, some ten times as expensive. Such fireproofing measures as the city took through the rest of Meiji went no farther than widening streets and requisitioning land for firebreaks when a district had been burned over.

Despite the views of Miss Bird and Loti, the new Ginza must have been rather handsome. It was a huge success as an instance of Civilization and Enlightenment, whatever its failures as a model in fireproofing. Everyone went to look at it, and so was born the custom of Gimbura, "killing time in Ginza," an activity which had its great day between the two world wars.

The new Ginza was also a great success with the printmakers. As usual they show it in brilliant sunlight with the cherries in bloom; and indeed there were cherries, at least in the beginning, along what had become the widest street in the city, and almost the only street wide enough for trolleys. There were maples, pines, and evergreen oaks as well, the pines at intersections, the others between.

It is not known exactly when and why these first trees disappeared, leaving the willow to become the great symbol of Ginza. The middle years of Meiji seem to have been the time. Perhaps the original trees were victims of urbanization, and perhaps, sprawling and brittle and hospitable to bugs, they were not practical. Willows, in any event, took over. Hardy and compact, riffled by cooling breezes in the summer, they were what a busy street and showplace seemed to need. Long a symbol of Edo and its rivers and canals, the willow became a symbol of the newest in Tokyo as well. Eventually the willow too went away. One may go out into the suburbs, near the Tama River, and view aged specimens taken there when, just before the earthquake, the last Ginza willows were removed.

With the new railway station just across a canal to the south, the southern end of what is now Ginza—it was technically not then a part of Ginza—prospered first. From middle into late Meiji it must have been rather like a shopping center, or mall, of a later day. There were two bazaars by the Shimbashi Bridge, each containing numbers of small shops. The youth of Ginza, we have been told by a famous artist who was a native of the district, loved to go strolling there, because from the back windows the Shimbashi geisha district could be seen preparing itself for a night's business. One of the bazaars kept a python in a window. The python seems to have perished in the earthquake. From the late Meiji Period into Taishō, Tokyo Central Station was built to replace Shimbashi as the terminus for trains from the south. It stood at the northern boundary of Kyōbashi Ward, and so Ginza moved back north again to center upon what is now the main Ginza crossing.

At least one building from the period of the new Ginza survives, Elocution Hall (Enzetsukan) on the Mita campus of Keiō University. Fukuzawa Yukichi invented the word *enzetsu*, here rendered as "elocution," because he regarded the art as one that must be cultivated by the Japanese in their efforts to catch up with the world. Elocution Hall, put up in 1875 and now under the protection of the government as a "cultural property" of great merit, was to be the forum for aspiring young elocutionists. It was moved from the original site, near the main entrance to the Keiō campus, after the earthquake. It is a modest building, not such as to attract the attention of printmakers, and a pleasing one. The doors and windows are Western, as is the interior, but the exterior, with its "trepang walls" and tiled roof, is strongly traditional. In its far more monumental way, the Hoterukan must have looked rather thus.

The great Ginza fire of 1872 is rivaled as the most famous of Meiji fires by the Yoshiwara fire of 1911, but neither was the most destructive. The Ginza fire burned over great but not consistently crowded spaces. The Kanda fire of 1881, the one that brought an end to Kiyochika's flourishing years as a printmaker, destroyed more buildings than any other Meiji fire. And not even that rivaled the great fires of Edo, or the Kyoto fire of 1778. Arson was suspected in the 1881 fire, as it was suspected, and sometimes proved, in numbers of other fires. It was a remarkable fire. Not even water stopped it, as water had stopped the Ginza fire. Beginning in Kanda and fanned by winter winds, it burned a swath through Kanda and Nihombashi, jumped the river at Ryōgoku Bridge, and burned an even wider swath through the eastern wards, subsiding only when it came to open country.

In a space of fifteen years, from early into middle Meiji, certain parts of Nihombashi were three times destroyed by fire. Great fires were commonest in the early months of the year, the driest months, when strong winds often came down from the north and west. (The incendiary raids of 1945 took advantage of these facts.) Much of what remained of the Tokugawa castle burned in 1873, and so the emperor spent more than a third of his reign in the Tokugawa mansion where the Akasaka Palace now stands. He did not move back into the palace until 1889. There were Yoshiwara fires in 1871, 1873, 1891, and 1911, and of course in 1923.

But Kanda has in modern times been the best place for fires. Of five great Meiji fires after a central fire department was organized in

The great Yoshiwara fire of 1911

1880, four began in Kanda, two of them within a few weeks of each other in 1881. The great Yoshiwara fire was the fifth. Only one Taishō fire, that of 1923 excepted, was of a magnitude to compete with the great Meiji fires. It too began in Kanda. No other Taishō fire, save again that of 1923, was remotely as large. The flowers of Edo were finally withering.

It was not until early Taishō that the fire department was sufficiently well manned to fight fires without amateur help. The disbanding of the old volunteer brigades did not come until after the earthquake. A ceremonial trace of them yet survives in the *dezomeshiki,* the display of the old panoply and tricks that is a part of the Tokyo New Year. Half the trucks owned by the department were lost in the earthquake, the first of them having been acquired five or six years before.

The Low City lived with the threat of fire. Only the wealthy had fireproof godowns. The lower classes kept emergency baskets ready in conspicuous places, and dug pits under their floors with ingenious arrangements that caused flooding when heated, and so, it was hoped, preserved such valuables as had been put away in time.

The young Tanizaki and his friends found an interesting use for the baskets.

They were oblong and woven of bamboo, about the size of a small trunk, and they were kept where everyone could see them, awaiting an emergency. In the Kairakuen they were kept in a storeroom that had been the Chinese room. For us, as we played at our games, they became the cribs of the courtesans. Three and four of us would take turns in a basket as ladies and their companions. Gen-chan and I were lady and companion any number of times. I do not remember that we did much of anything but lie face to face for a few minutes. Then it would be the turn of another lady and companion to produce staring and snickering.

I think that the origin of the game was probably in reports that Gen-chan had from the cooks about the Susaki quarter. The game delighted us, in any event. Day after day we would play it, the fire-basket game, as we called it.

"Let's have another go at the fire baskets," someone would say.

E. S. Morse, the American zoologist who taught at the imperial university in early Meiji, was a great connoisseur of fires and firefighting methods.

Nearly every house has a staging on the ridge-pole with a few steps leading to it. Here one may go the better to observe the progress of a conflagration. . . . When endangered by the approach of a conflagration the heavy window shutters and the doors of the fireproof building are closed and clay is then plastered over the cracks and chinks. Before closing it up, a number of candles are placed in a safe spot on the floor within and are lighted, thus gradually consuming all the oxygen and rendering ignition less likely.

Morse was initially contemptuous of Tokyo firefighting methods, but moved towards admiration as he became more knowledgeable. Of the first good fire to which he was witness, he said, among other things:

The stream thrown was about the size of a lead pencil and consisted of a series of independent squirts, as there was no air chamber as with our hand engines. The pumps were square instead of cylindrical and everything so dry, having hung in the sun for weeks, that more water spurted up in the air from the cracks than was discharged through the pipe. . . . The fire companies are private and each company has a standard-bearer. . . . These standard-bearers take a position as near the fire as possible, on the roof even of a burning building, and the companies whose standard-bearers are in evidence get a certain amount of money from the owners of the buildings saved.

In a note added for publication, he provided more sophisticated information, to the effect that the chief work of the firemen was not to put fires out but to prevent their spreading, and that the purpose of the little streams of water was not to extinguish the fire but to preserve the firemen.

By 1879, when he ran two miles at five o'clock one April morning to observe a fire, admiration was predominant.

The extent of the conflagration showed how rapidly it had spread, and the wooden buildings partly burned indicated that the work of firemen was not so trivial as foreigners supposed it to be; at least to check the fire in a high gale must have required great effort and skill. The fact is that their houses are so frail that as soon as a fire starts it spreads with the greatest rapidity, and the main work of the firemen, aided by citizens, is in denuding a house of everything that can be stripped from it. . . . It seems ridiculous to see them shoveling off the thick roofing files, the only fireproof covering the house has; but this is to enable them to tear off the roofing boards, and one observes that the fire then does not spring from rafter to rafter. The more one studies the subject the more one realizes that the first impressions of the fireman's work are wrong, and a respect for his skill rapidly increases.

Given the fact that the fire brigades were largely manned by carpenters, a certain conflict of interest might be suspected; but they seem to have done their work bravely and, within the limits of the materials they had to work with, well.

Fire losses declined as Meiji gave way to Taishō. An accompaniment, or so the children of Edo often saw it, was a loss of harmony in traditional architecture. Kafū lamented it, and so did the novelist, playwright, and haiku master Kubota Mantarō, who may be numbered among Kafū's disciples. Kubota was a true son of Edo, born in 1889 in Asakusa (Tanizaki was born in Nihombashi three years earlier) to a family of craftsmen and shopkeepers. He stayed in Asakusa until the fires of 1923 drove him away, and, though he never moved back, spent most of the four decades that remained to him in various parts of the Low City. Sadness for the Low City and what the modern world did to it dominated his writing in all the several forms of which he was master. He had the right pedigree and unswerving devotion to the cause; and so he may be called the most eloquent spokesman for that loquacious band, the sons of Edo. Tanizaki was a better novelist, but he spoke on the whole grouchily of his native Low City. Writing in

1927, Kubota lamented the disappearance of the *hinomi*, the "fire-watcher" or staging noted by Morse on the ridges of Tokyo houses.

> Among the things that have disappeared from all the blocks of Tokyo is the *hinomi*. I do not mean the fire ladder or the firewatch tower. I mean the *hinomi* itself. I do not know about the High City, but in the Low City, and especially on the roofs of merchant houses in busy and prosperous sections, there was always a *hinomi*. It was not only a memento of Edo, so ready with its fires. In the days when the godown style was the ideal in Japanese architecture, the *hinomi* was, along with the board fence, the spikes to turn back robbers, and the eaves drains, an indispensable element giving form to a Japanese house. And such fond dreams as the thought of it does bring, of Tokyo under willows in full leaf.

It may seem silly to mourn for appurtenances that proclaim a building, and indeed a whole city, to be a firetrap. Yet Kubota's remarks, and similar remarks by other mourners for Edo such as Nagai Kafū, have substance. Despite the failure of the city to take advantage of the Ginza model, it gradually made itself more resistant to fire, and the result was a great increase in ugliness. "Fair to look at is the capital of the Tycoon," said Sir Rutherford Alcock, who was in Edo during the last years of the Tycoon, or shogun. No one could call the Tokyo of our day a fair city, though it contains beautiful things. Coming upon a surviving pocket of Edo or Meiji, one sees in the somber harmonies of tile and old wood what has been lost.

The domestic and commercial architecture of Tokugawa Japan varied with the region. Except for warehouses, it was almost always of wooden frame construction, one or two storeys high. The Kansai region favored paints and stains much more than did the Kantō and its greatest city, Edo. In Edo there were several kinds of roofing. The more affluent merchant houses were heavily roofed with dark tiles, while humbler dwellings had thatched or shingled roofs, the best kind of fuel for the fires that were always getting started. The wooden fronts of the unpainted houses and shops of Edo, often with delicate lattices over the windows, turned to rich shades of brown as they aged, and the roofs were of neutral tones to begin with.

Only an eye accustomed to austere subtleties could detect the reposeful variations upon brown and gray which a Low City street must have presented. That is probably why one looks in vain through writings by early foreign visitors for descriptions of what the Low City looked like (as distinguished from its effect upon the other senses). Even E. S. Morse, the most discerning and sympathetic of them, is far better at street cries and the buzz of life and quaint curiosities than he is at the expanses of wood and tile that he must have passed every day. Isabella Bird went through the wards east of the river in her quest for unbeaten tracks. She tells us nothing about them, though they must have been among the urban places of early Meiji where the old harmonies were least disturbed. Perhaps if she had known that they all were to go (and to do so more rapidly than unbeaten tracks), she might have tried a little to describe them.

The very first Western buildings, such as the British legation and the Hoterukan, were not fireproof. They were built by Japanese, accommodating old Japanese techniques to what were presumed to be Western needs and sensibilities. The first period of pure Western building may be held to begin with the new Ginza. It is often called the English period. Thomas Waters gave advice for Ginza, and Josiah Conder, the most famous of foreign architects active in Meiji Japan, put up buildings all over the city. The work of Japanese architects, inconspicuous during the English period, began to appear again in mid-Meiji. The most eminent were Conder's pupils. A Japanese architect designed the first Imperial Hotel, which opened on a part of the present site in 1890. The grandest buildings of late Meiji and early Taishō—the Bank of Japan, the Akasaka Palace, the Imperial Theater, Tokyo Central Station—were by Japanese.

Conder, born in 1852, came to Japan early in 1877, retained by the Ministry of Technology. He taught architecture at the College of Technology and later at the university. A student of Japanese painting, he was especially good at fish.

He was a very important man. No other foreign architect who worked in Japan, not even Frank Lloyd Wright, was as influential as Conder, and probably none will be. He was a highly eclectic and not particularly original architect, but he was enormously successful as a teacher. The grand style in public building derives from him. His most famous work was an early one, the Rokumeikan, which gave its name

The Rokumeikan

to a span of years in mid-Meiji. Begun in 1881 and finished in 1883, the Rokumeikan was a state-owned lodging and gathering place for the cosmopolitan set. It was also, in those days when the "unequal treaties" were the great sore to be healed, a means of demonstrating to the world that the Japanese were as civilized and enlightened as anyone else, and so need not put up with such indignities as extra-territoriality.

The name means "House of the Cry of the Stag." It is a literary allusion, to a poem in the oldest of Chinese anthologies, the *Shih Ching,* and it signifies a hospitable summons to illustrious guests, and the convivial gathering that ensues. The Hama Palace, which had a semi-Western guest house even before the rebuilding of the Ginza, had earlier provided lodging for such guests, among them General Grant; it was in a bad state of repair, however, and otherwise considered un-suited to the needs of foreigners. So the Rokumeikan was put up, on the site of a Satsuma estate in Hibiya, by then government property, across from what was to become Hibiya Park.

It was a two-storey structure of brick, in an Italianate style, most splendid for the time, with about fifteen thousand square feet of floor space. It had a ballroom, a music room, a billiard room, a reading room, suites for illustrious guests, and a bathtub such as had never before been seen in the land: alabaster, six feet long and three feet wide. Water thundered most marvelously, we are told, from the faucets.

Pierre Loti, who attended a Rokumeikan ball on the emperor's birthday in 1885, thought that, all flat, staring white, it resembled a casino at a French spa. He may have been dazed. He was taken by rickshaw, he says, from Shimbashi Station through dark, solitary streets, and arrived at the Rokumeikan about an hour later. One can easily walk the distance in ten minutes.

The great day of the Rokumeikan must be discussed later. It became the Peers Club once its vogue had passed (though the unequal treaties had not yet disappeared), and then the offices of an insurance company. After further changes it was torn down, on the eve of Pearl Harbor, to make way for a cluster of temporary government buildings. A far more delicate structure than the Imperial Hotel (the second one, designed by Frank Lloyd Wright) on the same Satsuma lands, it too survived the earthquake.

Perhaps the best notion of what it was like is to be had from a still-surviving Conder building, the Mitsui Club in Mita near Keiō University. Finished in 1913, the Mitsui Club is larger, but it is similarly provided with wide verandas and colonnades. Pictures suggest that the Rokumeikan, at least its front elevation, was more ornate— busier—than the Mitsui Club. Verandas do not run the whole length of the Mitsui Club as they apparently did that of the Rokumeikan, columns are fewer and farther apart, and the eaves and the roof do not, as with the Rokumeikan, call attention to themselves. Yet the Mitsui Club is probably of all buildings in the city the one most like the lost treasure. The first Imperial also echoed the Rokumeikan. A part of the same panorama, it must have seemed very much what it was, the work of the faithful and reverent disciple.

Conder put up many buildings, only a few of which remain. He supervised the building of the Nikolai Cathedral in Kanda, which was finished in 1891, after the design of a Russian professor. Seriously damaged in the earthquake, the Nikolai is now squatter and solider than it was before the disaster.

The Imperial and the Ryōunkaku, the "cloud scraper" of Asakusa, opened for business within a week of each other. Popularly called the Asakusa Twelve Storeys, the Ryōunkaku was the building that lost its top storeys in the earthquake and was then demolished by army engineers. If the Rokumeikan was the great symbol of the Meiji elite and its cosmopolitanism, the Twelve Storeys was in late Meiji the great symbol of the masses and their pleasures. Asakusa was by that time the busiest center of popular entertainment. The Twelve Storeys symbolized Asakusa. Kubota Mantarō wrote:

> In days of old, a queer object known as the Twelve Storeys reared itself over Asakusa.
>
> From wherever you looked, there it was, that huge, clumsy pile of red bricks. From the roof of every house, from the laundry platform, from the narrowest second-floor window, there it was, waiting for you. From anywhere in the vastness of Tokyo—the embankment across the river at Mukōjima, the observation rise at Ueno, the long flight of stone steps up Atago Hill, there it was, waiting for you, whenever you wanted it.
>
> "Look—the Twelve Storeys."
>
> So we would say, at Mukōjima or Ueno, or on Atago Hill. There was quiet pleasure in the words, the pleasure of finding Asakusa. That was what the Twelve Storeys meant to Asakusa, a new pleasure each time, the pleasure of knowing Asakusa and its temple.
>
> And yet how clumsy, in illustrated guides, in prints of the Eastern Capital . . . how clumsy, above cherries fairly dripping with blossoms.
>
> Those cheap prints bring nostalgia for Asakusa as it was, the Asakusa of memory. In memories from my childhood it is always even thus, in the bosom of spring. The rich sunlight, the gentle winds, the green willow shoots, they speak always and only of spring; and as my eyes mount in pursuit of a wavering dragonfly or a stray balloon, there it is, the Twelve Storeys, dim in mists.

The Twelve Storeys was built by Japanese with the advice of an Englishman named William Barton. Some sources say that it was 320 feet high, some 220. The latter figure seems the more likely. It was in

The Asakusa Twelve Storeys

any event the highest building in the city, almost twice as high (even if the lower figure is accepted) as the Nikolai Cathedral. It contained many interesting and amusing things, and, along with a tower on Atago Hill, was the place to go for a view of the city.

Octagonal, of red brick, the Twelve Storeys had the first elevator in the land, imported from the United States; it took passengers, twenty of them at a time, to the eighth floor. The elevator was thought dangerous, and shut down after two months. On the second to eighth floors, wares from the world over were for sale. There was a Chinese shop with goods from the China of the Empress Dowager and sales girls in Chinese dress. The ninth floor contained diversions of a refined sort, such as art exhibitions. The tenth floor served as an observation lounge, with chairs scattered about. All of the floors were well lighted—the building was described as a tower of light—but the eleventh floor especially so. It had rows of arc lights inside and out. The top floor, also for observation, was provided with telescopes. For all these delights the entrance fee was a few pennies.

The Twelve Storeys may have boasted the first elevator, but the first one to continue operating seems to have been in Nihombashi, some sources say in the Bank of Japan, some in the Mitsui Bank. Nihombashi was itself both progressive and conservative, enlightened and benighted. It divided cleanly in two at the main north-south street, the one that crossed the Nihombashi Bridge. In early Meiji the place for Civilization and Enlightenment would of course have been the Ginza Bricktown. At the end of Meiji it might well have been the western portions of Nihombashi. The Bank of Japan, under construction there for eight years and finished in 1896, was the grandest of piles. To the east was the Mitsui Bank, south of which lay the Mitsukoshi department store, stone-built and several floors tall by the end of Meiji.

The main Nihombashi street passed to the east of them, and across it and a few paces towards the bridge lay the fish market. The conjunction was remarkable; nowhere else in the city was the sudden leap back into the past, or, if one preferred, the leap in the other direction, into the new world, more apparent than here. (For the problem of the fish market, see below, pages 82–83.) The view eastwards from the Mitsukoshi was over an almost unbroken expanse of low wooden buildings and the dark back streets of Tanizaki's boyhood. Change had come to them, in the form, for instance, of rickshaws, but not much else; if one did not like brick, stone, and bright lights, one could turn eastwards up one of the narrow streets and walk to the river and beyond, and be scarcely troubled at all by modern contrivances.

To the west, the new Bank of Japan looked grandly towards the palace ramparts over the almost empty spaces of "Mitsubishi Meadow." The original bank building survived the earthquake and survives today, the southwest portion of a much larger complex. A

Panoramic photograph by Ogawa Isshin,

domed central hall runs east and west and two colonnaded wings extend to the south. It was to have been entirely of stone, but the Nagoya earthquake of 1891 persuaded the architect that brick would be safer. Two other buildings by the same architect survived the earthquake and down to our day—Tokyo Central Station and the Daiei Building, originally Imperial Hemp, a thin triangle somewhat reminiscent of the Flatiron Building in New York.

The Bank of Japan complex is held to mark the beginning of a new phase in Meiji architecture—the design and construction of buildings by Japanese architects, quite without foreign assistance, in the courtly and classical styles of Europe. This is probably true enough in a general way, though not absolutely so. There is a tiny building in front of the National Diet, put up in 1891, and thought to be the earliest stone structure designed by a Japanese. Though scarcely monumental, it is certainly classical. It is no more than four yards square, and looks like a tomb that is trying to look like a Roman temple. It houses the prime bench mark for measuring elevation, a bench mark that was two hundred eighty-six millimeters lower after the 1923 earthquake than before.

taken from atop the City Hall: northeast quadrant

Great changes were coming, meanwhile, to the Mitsubishi Meadow, also known as Gambler's Meadow. The meadow (the Japanese term might also be rendered "wasteland") lay within the old outer moat of the castle, or palace. Such of its buildings as survived the Restoration disturbances served as the bureaucratic center of early Meiji. The offices gradually moved out, and in 1890 the meadow was sold as a whole to the Mitsubishi enterprises. The army, which then owned the land, needed money for installations on the outskirts of the city, and first proposed selling the tract to the royal household. This body, however, was in straitened circumstances, and unable to pay what the army asked. So the land went to Mitsubishi. It is the present Marunouchi district, where the biggest companies strive to have their head offices. When such early visitors as Griffis remarked upon the great expanses of empty lands in the city, Marunouchi (which means something like *intramuros,* "within the walls") must have been among the places they had in mind. The Mitsubishi purchase was considered a folly. If the government did not want the place, who would? In very late Meiji it was rejected as a possible site for a new Sumō wrestling stadium. The children of Edo who provided Sumō with its spectators

Southeast quadrant of panorama from City Hall

could not be expected to go to so desolate and forbidding a place. "It
was a day," wrote the poet Takahama Kyoshi,

> when people spoke of the row-houses, four in number, on the
> Mitsubishi Meadow, otherwise the abode of foxes and badgers.
> Here and there were weed-grown hillocks from aristocratic gar-
> dens. The murder of O-tsuya was much talked about in those
> days. . . .
>
> Marunouchi was a place of darkness and silence, of loneli-
> ness and danger. If one had to pass the Meiji Life Insurance
> building, a black wilderness lay beyond, with only the stars to
> light it. Darkness lay over the land on which Tokyo Central
> Station now stands, and on towards Kyōbashi, where a few
> lights were to be discerned.

The murder of O-tsuya dates the description. It occurred in 1910,
and was indeed talked about, one of the most famous of Meiji crimes.
The corpse of a young lady, identified as Kinoshita O-tsuya, had been
found one November morning near the prefectural offices. Her murderer was apprehended, quite by accident, ten years later.

The Mitsubishi Londontown, Marunouchi

77

Late in Meiji, Ogawa Isshin, one of the more famous of Meiji photographers, took panoramic photographs from the City Hall, on the site of the present prefectural offices in Marunouchi. On most sides of the City Hall appear empty expanses, very unlovely, as if scraped over by some landmover ahead of its time. In a southwesterly direction, scarcely anything lies between the City Hall and the Hibiya crossing, at the southeast corner of the palace plaza. The aspect to the north is even more desolate. There are a few barracks-like buildings, but for the most part the City Hall and the Bank of Japan, off on the western edge of Nihombashi, face each other across an expanse of nothing at all. To the northwest are the first of the new Mitsubishi buildings. Yet at the end of Meiji, Marunouchi still looked very hospitable, on the whole, to foxes, badgers, and gamblers. Only the view to the east towards the Ginza district, beyond the arches for the new elevated railroad, is occupied, most of it in what seems to be a rather traditional way. The remains of Ginza Bricktown do not show.

Mitsubishi was even then filling in the emptiness. In 1894, Conder finished the first of the brick buildings for what came to be known as the Mitsubishi Londontown. More than one architect worked on the district, and suggestions of more than one style were to be detected while Londontown yet survived. The first buildings lay along the street that runs past the prefectural offices from the palace moat. When this thoroughfare had been imposingly lined with brick, there were extensions to the south and then the north, where at the end of Meiji the new Tokyo Central Station was going up. Marunouchi took a quarter of a century being filled, and the newest buildings of Londontown did not last much longer than a quarter-century more. No trace survives today of the original rows of brick. Mitsubishi tore them all down in the years after the Second World War, perhaps a little too hastily. A surviving Conder building would be splendid public relations.

The preeminence of Marunouchi as a business district was assured by the opening of the new station in 1914, at which point it replaced Ginza as "the doorway to Tokyo." Gotō Shimpei, director of the National Railways, he who was to become the mayor with the big kerchief, told the architect to produce something that would startle the world. The brick building, three towers and joining galleries said to be in a French style, is not very startling today. It was once more ornate, however, and grander in relation to its surroundings. The central tower, now topped by a polyhedron, was originally domed; the dome was badly damaged in 1945. In 1914 the station looked off towards the palace over what had been finished of Londontown. Perhaps the most startling thing about it was that it did front in that direction, rather than towards the old Low City, which, thus eloquently told that it might be damned, was separated by tracks and a moat from the station.

This curious orientation has been explained as a show of respect for the palace and His Majesty. Certainly Mitsubishi and its meadow benefited enormously from the arrangement. There was nothing explicitly corrupt about it, but the smell of collusion is strong. So it is that economic miracles are arranged. To many it seemed that the naming of the station was itself an act of arrogance, implying that the other stations of the city, including Shimbashi, were somehow provincial.

Kyōbashi and Nihombashi, east of the station, felt left out of things, and continued to board their trains at Shimbashi. It was friendlier and almost as convenient. In 1920 a decision was finally reached to give Tokyo Central a back or easterly entrance, but at this point the Low City proved uncooperative. Quarreling between Kyōbashi and Nihombashi about the location of the necessary bridge was not settled until after the earthquake, which destroyed most of both wards.

Only after the earthquake were tracks laid from Tokyo Central to Ueno, whence trains depart for the north. By then Tokyo Central was unshakably established as the place where all trains from the south stopped and discharged their crowds. Even today, one cannot take a long-distance express from the north through Tokyo and on to the south and west without changing trains. It is rather as Chicago was back in the days when Americans still traveled by rail. The traveler from San Francisco had to change in Chicago if he wished to go on to New York. The traveler southwards gets off at Ueno and boards again at Tokyo Central. Economic reasons can be offered to explain the tardiness with which Tokyo and Ueno were joined. The right-of-way passes through densely populated regions laid waste by the earthquake and fire, far more heavily used in Meiji than those between Shimbashi and Tokyo Central or north of Ueno; but the effect was to assure that Mitsubishi Meadow would become worth approximately its weight in

Tokyo Station from Nihombashi, about 1915

gold. The governor of Tokyo has recently announced his opposition to a new express line from the north extending all the way to Tokyo Central. Thus a curious gap yet remains in one of the best railway systems in the world.

Another Meiji revolution was that which dispelled the shadows of Edo. It has happened everywhere, of course—dark medieval corners have become rarer the world over—but it happened more rapidly in the Japanese cities than in Europe and America. There are those, Tanizaki among them, who have argued that dark places were central to Japanese aesthetics, and that doing away with them destroyed something of very great importance. In his famous discourse on shadows, a subject dear to him, Tanizaki speculated on the course modern inventions might have taken had the Japanese done the inventing. Shadows would not have been done away with so brusquely.

Edo already had the kerosene lamp. Tokyo acquired gaslights sixty years later than London, and so the gaslit period was that much shorter. A leading Meiji entrepreneur named Shibusawa Eiichi proposed that the first gaslights be in the Yoshiwara. His reasons seem to have been aesthetic and not moral, and certainly it would have been appropriate for that center of the old, shadowy culture to lead the way into the new. But before this could happen the great Ginza fire intervened, and the rebuilt Ginza became the obvious place for the new brightness. In 1874 eighty-five gaslights flared, and became the marvel of the city, from Shiba along the main Ginza street as far north as Kyōbashi. By 1876 there was a line of gaslights all the way from Ginza to Asakusa, and westwards from Ginza towards the palace as well.

The first experiments with electric lighting were not entirely successful. The main attraction at the opening of the Central Telegraph Office in 1878 was an electric bulb, which burned out in fifteen minutes, leaving the assembly in darkness. In 1882 an arc light was successfully installed before the Ginza offices of the Okura enterprises. The crowds seen gazing at it in Meiji prints give not the smallest sign that they share Tanizaki's grief at the extinction of shadows. (It was, to be sure, only much later that he wrote his essay; in his youth he too loved lights.)

The effect upon the arts was profound, and probably most profound upon the theater. By at least 1877 Kabuki was gaslit, and a decade later had its first electric lights. Today it is dazzlingly bright, and to imagine what it was like in the old shadowy days is almost impossible.

Having left shadows behind, Tokyo seemed intent upon becoming the brightest city in the world, and it may well have succeeded. A series of industrial expositions became the ground for testing the limits. "Sift civilization to the bottom of your bag of thrills," wrote the novelist Natsume Sōseki in 1907, "and you have an exposition. Filter your exposition through the dull sands of night and you have blinding illumination. If you possess life in some small measure, then for evidences of it you go to illumination, and you must cry out in astonishment at what you see. The civilized who are drugged with civilization are first aware that they live when they cry out in astonishment." It is the late-Meiji view of someone who was himself becoming weary of Civilization and Enlightenment; but it is not wrong in identifying "illumination" (the English word is used) with the soul of Meiji. Turning up the lights, much more rapidly than they had been turned up in the West, was indeed akin to a quest for evidence of life. Freed from the black Edo night, people gathered where the lights were brightest, and so at nightfall the crowds commenced heading south to Ginza from a still dark Nihombashi.

Tanizaki did not become a devotee of shadows until his middle years. In his boyhood Nihombashi was more amply provided with them than he wished. "Even in the Low City there were few street lights. The darkness was rather intimidating. I would return after dark from my uncle's house a few blocks away, scampering past certain ominous places. They were lonely places of darkness, where young men in student dress would be lurking in wait for pretty boys." Tanizaki himself was abducted by an army officer who had the "Satsuma preference," as it was called, and taken to the Mitsubishi Meadow, where he made a perilous escape.

Like the trolley system, the electric power system advertised the confusion of a city growing and changing too rapidly, and the inadequacies of private enterprise. In late Meiji the city had three power companies, in sometimes violent competition. Charges were not for power consumed but for the number of bulbs, which system of course provided encouragement for keeping all bulbs burning at all times. The same house might have a power supply from more than one company, and there were fistfights among linemen when a house changed from one company to another. Two mayors, one of them the famous parliamentarian Ozaki Yukio, were forced to resign because of their inability to impose order in this situation. Proposals for public ownership came to nothing. Finally, in 1917, an accord was reached dividing the city and the prefecture among the three companies. The city did presently buy a part of the system, and was providing power to extensive regions in the High City at the time of the earthquake.

Enlightenment was not immediately successful in dispelling shadows, and smells proved even more obstinate. In 1923 the central fish market stood where it had for almost three hundred years, right beside the Nihombashi Bridge, almost across the street from the Mitsukoshi Department Store and only a few steps from the Mitsui Bank and the Bank of Japan.

As early as the opening of Shimbashi Station, there were earnest endeavors to beautify the main street leading north through Nihombashi. The market was forbidden to use the street, and every effort was made to keep dealers out of sight. Yet the establishment sent its odors through much of Nihombashi and Kyōbashi. There were only two latrines, at the eastern and western ends of the market, remote from the convenience of busy fish dealers. Fish guts were left for the crowds to trample. Each time there was a cholera epidemic the market was blamed, and a clamor arose to move it where it might have the space (should it choose to use it) to be more sanitary and less smelly. Cholera germs were in fact traced to the market in 1922, and authorities closed it for several days.

It had been proposed in 1889 that the market move eastwards to the river, the move to be accomplished by the end of the century. There was strong opposition. A complex system of traditional rights stood in the way of expeditious removal. Nothing happened. In 1923 almost four hundred persons are thought to have died there in the post-earthquake fires that finally decided the matter. The market re-opened, first in quarters by the bay and a few months later on the site it now occupies in Tsukiji, a short distance south of where the foreign settlement would be had it survived the earthquake. Most of the fish sold in the last years of the Nihombashi market were brought there by land. What came by water had to be reloaded for transport up the canal. The new site, by the harbor and only a short distance from the freightyards where the old Shimbashi terminus had been, was far more convenient. It was just across a canal from the Hama Palace, but the day was long past when eminent foreigners stayed there. The present emperor, an uncomplaining man, was then regent.

Sewers scarcely existed at the end of Meiji. Kanda had a tile-lined ditch for the disposal of kitchen wastes, but body wastes were left to the *owaiya* with his dippers and buckets and carts and his call of *owai owai* as he made his way through the streets. It was still a seller's market at the end of Meiji; the *owaiya* paid for his commodity. The price was falling rapidly, however, because the growth of the city and the retreat of farmlands to greater distances made it more and more difficult for the farmer to reach the inner wards. The problem grew to crisis proportions in the Taishō Period, as the seller's market changed to a buyer's and in some parts of the city it was not possible to get rid of the stuff. Shinjuku, on the western edge of the city, was known as the anus of Tokyo. Every evening there would be a rush hour when great lines of sewage carts formed a traffic jam.

The water supply was more sophisticated. It long had been. The Tokugawa magistracy had done virtually nothing about sewers, and the Meiji governors and mayors did little more, but there was a venerable system of reservoirs and aqueducts. The Low City was still heavily dependent on wells at the end of Meiji, however, making the problem of sewage disposal not merely noisome but dangerous as well. Water from wells was murky and unpalatable, and so water vendors made the rounds of the Low City, buckets hanging from poles on their shoulders, a wooden float in each bucket serving as a simple and ingenious device to keep the water from spilling.

It has been customary, this century and more, for the person who sees the city after an absence to remark upon the dizzying changes. W. E. Griffis, back in Tokyo a few weeks before the Ginza fire and after about a year in the provinces, found the city "so modernized that I scarcely recognize it. . . . Old Yedo has passed away forever." Edo has gone on passing away ever since.

Certainly a comparison of the central Ginza district at the beginning and end of Meiji, or the Mitsubishi Meadow east of the palace, or the western part of Nihombashi, tells of devastating (if one wishes to call it that) change. Scarcely anything present at the beginning of the period, apart from streets, canals, and rivers (or some of them), is present at the end. Not only the visitor, but the native or old resident could remark upon the devastation.

"Bridges were rebuilt, there were evictions after fires, narrow streets were widened," said the novelist Tayama Katai in 1917. "Day by day Edo was destroyed."

Some streets were indeed widened, especially towards the end of Meiji, to make way for the trolley and to provide firebreaks. Others disappeared. The back alleys, the *uradana* of Edo, had been altogether too crowded and dark, and when it became possible to spread out even a little the townsmen quickly did so. Photographs and other graphic materials inform us that the extreme closeness of Edo was early, and happily, dispensed with. The most straitened classes, when they could put together the means, would rather be on a street, however narrow, that led somewhere than on a closed alley.

Yet even today, after numerous minor disasters and two huge ones, the Tokyo street pattern is remarkably like that of Edo. On the eve of the earthquake the traveler could still complain that the city was alternately a sea of mud and a cloud of dust. The surfaced street was still a novelty. In certain heavily commercial parts of the Low City the proportion of streets to total area actually declined in the last two decades of Meiji. Such widening as occurred was not enough to compensate for the loss of back alleys.

In 1915 the mayor found a curious excuse for inaction in the matter of parks, an excuse that tells much of life along the narrow streets. More than nine-tenths of the city was still wooden, he said, and most of the wooden houses were but one storey high, each with its own little park. So public parks were not needed as in the cities of the West. It is good bureaucratic evasion, of course, but there must have been truth in it. Most of the streets had to be only wide enough for rickshaws to pass, and an occasional quarrel between runners when they could not was rather fun. The Edo townsman had long been accustomed to thinking of only the central portion of the street as public in any event. The rest could be devoted to greenery, especially to such plants as the morning glory, which gave a delicious sense of the season and did not require much room. The back streets may indeed have been like little parks, or fairs. Edo had always been the greenest of the large cities, and the morning glory might have been as good a symbol as the abacus of the Low City and its concerns.

Improved transportation had by the end of Meiji brought the Low City and the High City closer together. The aristocratic wife of Edo scarcely ever went into the plebeian city, though instances are recorded of well-born ladies who attained notoriety by becoming addicted to the theater and actors. Now they commonly went shopping in Ginza or Nihombashi. Kabuki became an object of wealthy High City attention. Its base was more general. It was no longer the particular pride and treasure of the Low City.

In another sense, the division between high and low was accentuated. Class distinctions, measured in money and not pedigree, became clearer. The wealthy moved away from the Low City. Still in Tanizaki's childhood, the mansion of the entrepreneur Shibusawa Eiichi was an object of wonderment, looking somewhat Moorish on a Nihombashi canal. The great flood of 1910 destroyed many of the riverside villas of the wealthy—which were not rebuilt—but the last

The Shibusawa mansion, Nihombashi

such place did not disappear until after the Second World War. The process was one of gradual evacuation, leaving the Low City with vestiges of a professional middle class, but no one from the old military and mercantile elite or the new industrial elite. Wealth went away and the self-contained culture of the Low City went too.

This is not to say that the Low City and the High City became alike. The *Shitamachi jōchō,* the "mood of the Low City," still existed, in the row upon row of wooden buildings and in the sense of neighborhood as community. But the creative energies had waned. The arts of Edo became respectable, and the lesser plebeian ranks, stranded in the Low City when the wealthy moved away, were not up to creating anything of a disreputability delicate and intricate enough to match the tradition. It was as in the old castle towns that had been cultural centers of some note: the new and original things were being done elsewhere.

In early Meiji, as industrialization got underway, factories were scattered over the city. By the end of Meiji a pattern had emerged: three-quarters of the factories were in the bay-shore wards, Kyōbashi and Shiba, and the two wards east of the river. Tokyo lacked the prominence in manufacturing that it had, by the end of Meiji, in finance, management, and (vague word) culture. Yet Meiji may be seen as a period of concentration, and the time when this one city emerged as a place of towering importance. Edo was important, having in its last century pulled ahead of its Kansai rivals, culturally at least. Tokyo by the end of Meiji was far more important.

On the eve of the earthquake the city had about a sixteenth of the population of the country and about two-fifths of the economic capital. Osaka had almost as many corporations as Tokyo, but less than half as much capital. A quarter of the total bank deposits were in Tokyo. Within the city, the wealth was concentrated in three wards: Kōjimachi, which contained the palace and the Mitsubishi Meadow, and Kyōbashi and Nihombashi to the east. Four-fifths of all Japanese companies with capitalization of five million yen and more had their headquarters in one or another of three wards.

In one curious cultural respect Tokyo lagged behind the nation. There was far greater reliance upon private education at the primary level than in the nation at large. In 1879 Tokyo contained more than half the private elementary schools in the country. Despite its large population, it had fewer public schools than any other prefecture except Okinawa. The "temple schools" of Edo had the chief responsibility for primary education in early and middle Meiji. It was only towards the turn of the century that the number of pupils in public schools overtook the number in private schools. The reason would seem to be that the Meiji government could not do everything at once, and the system of private elementary education was so well developed in Edo that it could be made to do for a time. Ahead at the end of Edo, Tokyo was consequently neglected. The public schools had the greater prestige. Higuchi Ichiyō's novella *Growing Up,* about a group of children on the edge of the Yoshiwara, informs us of the inferiority and resentment which the ordinary child felt towards the privileged ones in the public schools.

In higher education, Tokyo prevailed. The western part of Kanda was by the end of Meiji all students and universities, and so was a large part of Hongō. In more general cultural matters, the century since the Meiji Restoration may be seen as one of progressive impoverishment of the provinces, until eventually they were left with little but television, most of it emanating from Tokyo. This process was far advanced by 1923; Tokyo was big-time as Edo had not been. While the cities of the Kansai might preserve their own popular arts and polite accomplishments (and for reasons which no one understands have produced most of the Japanese Nobel laureates), it was in Tokyo that opinions and tastes were formed. It was because Tokyo was so much the center of things that Tanizaki's decision to stay in the Kansai after the earthquake was so startling. All other important literary refugees quickly returned to Tokyo, and even Tanizaki in his last years was edging in that direction.

When, in 1878, the fifteen wards were established, they more than contained the city. They incorporated farmland as well. At the turn of the century two-thirds of the city's paddy lands were in Asakusa Ward and the two wards east of the Sumida. Half the dry farmlands were in Shiba and Koishikawa, the southern and northern fringes of the High City. Farmland had virtually disappeared by the end of Meiji. Attrition was especially rapid late in the period. In 1912, the last year of Meiji, there was only one measure of paddy land within the fifteen wards for every two hundred fifty that had been present but a decade before, and one measure of dry farmland for every three hundred.

The situation was similar with fishing and marine produce. The last authentic "Asakusa laver" (an edible seaweed) had been produced early in the Tokugawa Period. In early Meiji most of the nation's laver still came from outlying parts of Tokyo Prefecture. By the end of the period the prefecture produced none at all, save for the Izu Islands and beyond. The largest fishing community was at Haneda, beyond the southern limits of the city. *Sushi* is still described in restaurants as being *Edo-mae*, "from in front of Edo"—that is, from Tokyo Bay—but very little of it in fact was by the end of Meiji. None at all is today.

So a great deal changed in Meiji, and a good deal remained at the end of Meiji for the earthquake to destroy. In 1910, or whatever the chosen year, one could have joined all the sons of Edo in lamenting the demise of their city, and one could as well have rejoiced at all the little warrens of unenlightenment still scattered over the Low City. It is not possible to weigh change and tradition and decide which is the heavier.

To rejoice in what remained might, in the end, have been the less discommoding course. Recovering from his shock on perhaps the seventh or eighth of September, 1923, many a son of Edo must have lamented that he had not paid better attention to what had until so recently been all around him.

3

THE DOUBLE LIFE

Civilization and Enlightenment could be puzzling, and they could be startling too.

In Japan one always hears about "the double life," not as suggestive a subject as it may at first seem to be, and indeed one that can become somewhat tiresome. It refers to the Japanese way of being both foreign and domestic, of wearing shoes and sleeping on floors. The double life is at best an expense and an inconvenience, we are told, and at worst a torment, leading to crises of identity and such things.

Looking about one and seeing the calm, matter-of-fact way in which the Japanese live the double life, one can dismiss the issue as intellectual sound and fury. The world has been racked by changes, such as the change from the rural eighteenth century to the urban twentieth, and, compared to them, the double life does not seem so very much to be tormented by. Yet there can be no doubt that it lies beyond the experience of the West. The West went its own way, whether wisely or not, one step following another. Such places as Tokyo had to—or felt that they had to—go someone else's way.

The playwright Hasegawa Shigure came home one day and found that she had a new mother. Had her old mother been evicted and a new one brought in to replace her, the change might have been less startling.

What Shigure found was the old mother redone. "She performed the usual maternal functions without the smallest change, but she had a different face. Her eyebrows had always been shaved, so that only a faint blue-black sheen was where they might have been. Her teeth had been cleanly black. The mother I now saw before me had the stubbly beginnings of eyebrows, and her teeth were a startling, gleaming white. It was the more disturbing because something else was new. The new face was all smiles, as the old one had not been."

The women of Edo shaved their eyebrows and blackened their teeth. Tanizaki, when in his late years he became an advocate of darkness, developed theories about the effect of the shadows of Edo upon the spectral feminine visages created by these practices. Whatever may be the aesthetic merits of tooth-blackening, it was what people were used to. Then came a persuasive sign from on high that it was out of keeping with the new day. The empress ceased blackening her teeth in 1873. The ladies of the court quickly followed her lead, and the new way spread downwards, taking the better part of a century to reach the last peasant women in the remotest corners of the land. If the Queen and the Princess of Wales were suddenly to blacken their teeth, the public shock might be similar.

E. S. Morse did not record that his rickshaw runner was other than good-natured at having to stop at the city limits and cover his nakedness. The relationship between tradition and change in Japan has always been complicated by the fact that change itself is a tradition. Even in the years of the deepest Tokugawa isolation there had been foreign fads, such as one for calicos, originally brought in as sugar sacks, and later much in vogue as kimono fabrics. There had always been great respect for foreign things, which needed no justification. The runner probably felt no more imposed upon by this new vestmental requirement than by the requirement that he be cheerful and reasonably honest. There was, moreover, a certain sense of proportion. Hasegawa Shigure's mother was shamed by the neighbors into thinking that she may have gone too far. She did not return to tooth-blackening, but she did return to a traditional coiffure. The pompadour that had been a part of her new image was a subject of hostile criticism. The neighborhood was not yet ready for it.

If they sought to do what was expected of them, however, the lower orders must have occasionally wondered just what the right thing was. So many acts that had seemed most natural were suddenly uncivilized. A tabulation survives of misdemeanors committed in the city during 1876. "Urinating in a place other than a latrine" accounts for almost half of them. Quarreling and nudity take care of most of the remaining five or six thousand. Not many people were inconvenienced by other proscriptions, but they suggest all the same that one had to tread carefully. Cutting the hair without permission seems to have been an exclusively feminine offense. There is a single instance of "performing mixed Sumō, snake shows, etc." The same pair of miscreants was presumably guilty of both, etc. There are eight instances of transvestism, a curious offense, since it had long been a part of Kabuki, and does not seem to have troubled people greatly in more private quarters. Hasegawa Shigure tells in her reminiscences of a strange lady who turned up for music lessons in Nihombashi and proved to be a man. The police were not summoned, apparently, nor was the person required to discontinue his lessons.

Mixed bathing was banned by the prefecture in 1869. Indifference to the order may be inferred, for it was banned again in 1870 and 1872. Bathhouses were required to have curtains at their doors, blocking the view from the street. Despite these encumbrances, the houses were very successful at keeping up with the times. Few plebeian dwellings in the Low City had their own baths. Almost everyone went to a public bath, which was a place not only for cleansing but for companionship. The second floors of many bathhouses offered, at a small fee, places for games and for sipping tea poured by pretty girls. These facilities were very popular with students. From mid-Meiji, the nature of bathhouses seems to have become increasingly complex and dubious. The bathing function lost importance as private domestic baths grew more common, while second floors were sometimes converted to "archery ranges" (the pretty girls being available for special services) and drinking places. The bathhouse had earlier been a sort of community center for plebeian Edo, a relief from crowding and noise, or, perhaps, a place that provided those elements in a form somewhat more appealing than the clamor of home and family. Now it was a new and rather less innocent variety of pleasure center.

In the fiction of late Edo the barbershop, like the bathhouse, had been a place for watching the world go by. The new world spelled change here too. Western dress was initially expensive, but the Western haircut was not. The male masses took to it immediately; the other masses, as the example of Hasegawa Shigure's mother tells us, more slowly. The Meiji word for the most advanced way of cutting the hair was *zangiri* or *jangiri*, meaning something like "random cropping." The old styles, for aristocrat and commoner alike, had required shaving a part of the head and letting the remainder grow long, so that it might be pulled into a topknot. Already in 1873, the sixth year of Meiji, a newspaper was reporting that about a third of the men in the city had cropped heads.

"If you thump a *jangiri* head," went a popular ditty of the day, "it sounds back 'Civilization and Enlightenment.'" The more traditional heads echoed in a more conservative way, and some even carried overtones suggesting a revocation of the Restoration and a return to the old order.

The first new-style barbershop opened in 1869. It was in Ginza, which had new things even before the fire. The barber had learned his trade in Yokohama, and his first customer is said to have been the chief of a fire brigade. This seems appropriate. Firemen were among the more traditional of people, noted for verve and gallantry, and figuring prominently in the fiction and drama of Edo. So it often seems in Meiji: tradition and change were not at odds; the one demanded the other.

By 1880, two-thirds of the men in the city had randomly cropped heads. The figure had reached 90 percent a scant six years later, and by 1888 or 1889 only the rare eccentric still wore his hair in the old fashion.

The inroads of the Western barber were far more rapid than those of the Western tailor. It was not until the day of the flapper that women really began to cut their hair and let it down. Liberated Meiji women went in for a pompadour known as "eaves," from its way of projecting outwards in a sheltering sweep. A few geisha and courtesans adopted Western dress from mid-Meiji, and several wore what was known as the "shampoo coiffure," from its resemblance to hair let down for washing and not put back up again. The first beauty school was opened early in the Taishō Period, by a French lady named Marie-Louise. Others quickly followed.

The English expression "high-collar" came into vogue from about the turn of the century. At first it was derisive, signifying the ex-

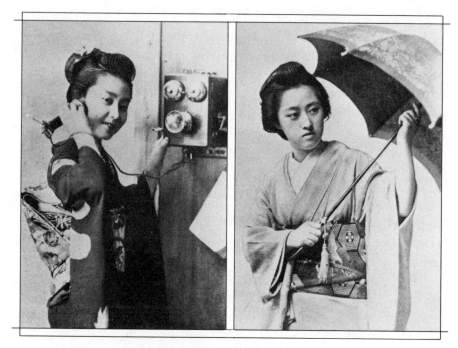

Up-to-date geisha, by Ogawa Isshin, 1902

tremely and affectedly foreign. A lady's coiffure was high-collar if it was thought to be too sweeping and eaveslike. A suggestion of dandyism still clings to the expression.

Some rather surprising things were high-collar, in the broad sense of innovative. Items and institutions which one might think to be very old and very Japanese have their origins in Meiji, under the influence of Civilization and Enlightenment. The word *banzai* is an old one, but the shouting of it on felicitous occasions seems to have occurred first with the promulgation of the Meiji constitution, in 1889. The popularity of Shinto weddings also dates from Meiji. The first marriage broker set up business in Asakusa in 1877. It may be that the police box, so much a part of Japan since Meiji, has its origins in certain Edo practices, but just as probably it began with the guards at the gates of the legations and the foreign settlements. The first private detective agency is believed to have been founded in 1891. Private detectives now seem to be everywhere, and they are so sophisticated that their relatively recent origins are cause for wonderment.

Traffic on the left side of the street also appears to have been a

Meiji innovation. There had not been much vehicular traffic in Edo, but bridge signs give evidence that such as there was had been expected to pass on the right. In early Meiji, police orders—probably under the influence of the British, at the forefront of Civilization and Enlightenment in so many ways—required carriages to pass on the left.

Reading a line of horizontal print from left to right was a Meiji innovation. Not imposed by authority, the practice gradually and uncertainly came to prevail. Two adjoining Nihombashi financial establishments might have signs reading in contradictory fashion, one in the old direction, right to left, the other in the new. On the same train the description of the route would read right to left and the no-smoking sign left to right.

Beer, which has now replaced sake as the national drink, even as baseball has replaced Sumō as the national sport, made its appearance early in Meiji. The first brewery was in Tokyo, just south of the Hibiya parade grounds, not far from where the Rokumeikan and the Imperial Hotel later arose. The first beer hall opened in Kyōbashi on the Fourth of July in 1899, celebrating the end of the "unequal treaties."

Until very recently, the system of house numbers was so chaotic that ancient uncodified custom seemed the most likely explanation. In fact, however, there were no house numbers at all until Meiji. The sense of place centered upon the *machi* or *chō*, which might be rendered "neighborhood." A few streets had popular names and today a few have official names, but the neighborhood continues to be the central element in an address. Before Meiji there was nothing else. If more detailed information was required as to the site of a dwelling, only description could be offered—"two houses from the retired sealmaker in the second back alley," and the like. House numbers were observed by early travelers to the West, and thought desirable, and assigned helter-skelter as new houses went up and old houses wished numbers too.

The want of system has been remedied somewhat in recent years, so that Number 2 in a certain neighborhood will usually be found between Number 1 and Number 3; yet the consciousness of place continues to be by tract or expanse and not by line. Though it provides its pleasures, and sometimes one has a delicious sense of adventure in looking for an address, a system of numbers along a line is without question more efficient than one of numbers scattered over an area. The chaos of the Meiji method was a product of Civilization and Enlightenment, however, and not of benighted tradition, which eschewed house numbers.

What is now the most ubiquitous of Japanese accessories, the calling card, is a Western importation. The first ones are believed to have been brought from Europe in 1862 by a Tokugawa diplomatic mission.

In the 1903 edition of their guide to Japan, Basil Hall Chamberlain and W. B. Mason describe Tokyo as having "a tranquil and semi-rural aspect owing to the abundance of trees and foliage." Compared to most Japanese cities, and especially Osaka, Tokyo is indeed a city of greenery. Yet the planting of trees along streets is a modern innovation. In the premodern city there had been some public trees (as they might be called) along waterways. The Yanagiwara, the "Willowfield" along the Kanda River, even predated the Tokugawa hegemony. Virtually all the trees and grasses of the old city were in pots or behind walls, however, and the pines, cherries, maples, and oaks of Ginza were the first genuine street trees.

Western things tended to make their first appearance in the treaty ports. Yet many an innovation was first seen in Tokyo. Yokohama may have had the first lemonade and ice cream, but Tokyo had the first butter and the first Western soup.

The first artificial limb in the land was bestowed in Yokohama upon a Tokyo Kabuki actor, the third Sawamura Tanosuke. Dr. J. C. Hepburn, a pioneer medical missionary and the deviser of the Hepburn system of Romanization (still in use despite modifications in detail), amputated a gangrenous leg and then sent to America for a wooden one, which arrived and was fitted in the last full year before Meiji. Tanosuke lost his other leg and a hand before he finally died, in 1878. He went on acting to the end.

Men were in most respects quicker to go high-collar than women. It was so in the cutting of the topknot, and it was so as well in the discarding of traditional dress. The phenomenon is to be observed elsewhere in Asia. It has to do, probably, with the decorative functions assigned to women, and also with somewhat magical aspects assigned to Western panoply and appurtenances. Whether or not the business suit is more businesslike than the kimono, people are bound to think it is, because the wearer has been better at business.

There may have been a few geisha with bustles and flounces and the shampoo coiffure, and these were the proper accouterments for a well-placed lady of the upper classes on her way to the Rokumeikan. Yet even for upper-class ladies the emphasis in the late years of the century shifted from Western dress to "improvement" of the Japanese kimono. Though hot-weather dress became Westernized more quickly than dress for the cooler seasons, most lady strollers in Ginza still wore Japanese dress on the eve of the earthquake. Some two-thirds of the men were in foreign dress, which was very expensive in the early years, and attainable only by the wealthy and the bureaucracy (for which it was mandatory). The military and the police were the first to go Western. The change had begun before the end of the shogunate. By 1881, there were two hundred tailoring and dressmaking establishments in the city, more than half of them in Nihombashi.

The emperor's buttons and the empress's bracelets and bodkins arrived from France in 1872. Traditional court dress was abolished by the Council of State that same year, though most court officials were still in traditional dress at the opening of the Yokohama railroad. Willingness to wear Western dress was more prevalent among men than among women, and among the upper classes than the lower.

Even at the height of the Rokumeikan era (for a description of that building see pages 68–69), when the world was being shown that the Japanese could do the Western thing as well as anyone else, there seems to have been more determination than ardor. Newspaper accounts inform us that the dance floor at some of the more celebrated events was dominated by foreigners, and Pierre Loti informs us that Japanese ladies, when coaxed out upon the floor, were correct but wooden.

Rokumeikan parties did not have much to do with the life of the city. They belonged in the realm of politics and the highest society, and if the sort of person who took his pleasures at Asakusa ever set foot in the place, it was doubtless as a servant or a delivery boy. Such affairs do not belong to the story of what happened to Edo and all its townsmen. Yet the Rokumeikan era was such an extraordinary episode, or series of episodes, that to dismiss it as political and really too high-class would be to risk letting the Meiji spirit, at its most ardent there in Tokyo whether of the city or not, disappear in an excessively rigid schema.

The building itself is gone, and historical treatment of the era runs towards dryness. The life of the place is best sensed in the works of woodcut artists who, not themselves of high society, can have attended few if any Rokumeikan soirees. They make the best years of the Rokumeikan, and especially the ladies in their bright, bright dresses, seem utterly charming. Had one lived through those years, however, and been among the lucky few on the invitation lists, one might well have found the Rokumeikan hard work, no more charming than the doings of the Ladies' Benevolent Society today. The flounces and bustles might not be so much fun had they been photographed rather than made into prints. They came when the art of the Ukiyoe was having its last show of vigor, and lent themselves well to the bold pigments favored by Meiji artists.

The Rokumeikan seems to have been the idea of Inoue Kaoru. When Inoue became foreign minister in 1879, treaty reform was among the great issues. He was of the Nagato clan, which with the Satsuma clan had been the principal maker of the Restoration. In 1881 his good friend and fellow Nagato clansman, Itō Hirobumi, emerged as the most influential figure on the Council of State. Both were young men as politicians go, Itō in his late thirties, Inoue in his early forties. They had gone together some years before the Restoration to study in England. When, in 1885, Itō became the first prime minister with the title that office still bears, Inoue was his foreign minister. They saw Europeanization as the best way to get rid of the unequal treaties, and most particularly of extraterritoriality. Among the details of the movement was the Rokumeikan.

Whatever other ideas he may have had, Inoue is best remembered for conceiving of the Rokumeikan. The charm of the place, in addition to the bustles and flounces, lies largely in an element of fantasy. What politician, one asks, could possibly have thought that such a hard-headed person as the British minister would be so moved by a few Westernized balls at the Rokumeikan that he would recommend treaty revision to the home office? Yet that is what the Rokumeikan was about. In the episode is all the eagerness and wishfulness of young Meiji.

Records are not consistent as to the number of guests invited by Inoue for his opening night. There may have been upwards of a thousand, with several hundred foreigners among them. The façade was a great expanse of branches and flowers, dotted with flags and the royal crest. The garden glittered rather than blazed, with myriads of little lights, each shining chiefly upon a miniature stag. In the hallway were two stags formed from leafy branches. The great staircase was solidly embanked with chrysanthemums. Wishing to seem European in every respect possible, Inoue had the orchestra play to what would have been a fashionable hour in a European capital, but well beyond the hour when the son of Edo would have headed for home or settled in for the night. Accordingly, there was a special train to accommodate guests from Yokohama.

Almost everything for which the Rokumeikan provided the setting was new. Invitations addressed jointly to husbands and wives were an astonishing innovation—the son of Edo would not have known what to say. The Rokumeikan saw garden parties and evening receptions, and in 1884 there was a big charity bazaar. This too was very new. The old order had managed charities differently; it might have been thought proper to give largesse of some sort to a deserving individual who was personally known to the donor, but the trouble of a bazaar to benefit faceless strangers would have seemed purposeless. The 1884 bazaar lasted three days, and ten thousand tickets were sold. At the end of it all, the head of the Mitsubishi enterprises bought the unsold wares. The chief organizer was a princess (by marriage) belonging to a cadet branch of the royal family, and many another great lady of the land was on the committee.

Whether done easily or not, dancing was the main thing to do at the Rokumeikan. Ladies and gentlemen were expected to appear in foreign dress, so much less constricting than Japanese dress, and so flattering to the foreigner. Beginning late in 1884, ladies and gentlemen gathered for regular and studiously organized practice in the waltz, the quadrille, and the like. Two noble Japanese ladies were the organizers, and the teachers were of foreign extraction.

The grand climax of the Rokumeikan era did not occur at the Rokumeikan itself, but serves well by way of summing up. In 1885 Itō Hirobumi, still prime minister, gave a huge masked ball at his Western mansion. Again, reports on the number of guests vary widely, ranging from four hundred to over a thousand. Foreign dress was not required, and numbers of eminent Japanese guests took advantage of this fact. Itō himself was a Venetian nobleman, but Inoue was a Japanese buffoon, and the Home Minister a Japanese horseman. The president of the university came as the poet Saigyō, who had lived some seven centuries earlier.

Itō was involved shortly afterwards in an amorous scandal, an affair with a noble lady who was another man's wife. The Itō cabinet became known—and the appellation is no more flattering in Japanese than in English—as "the dancing cabinet." Itō held on as prime minister until 1888, but the fresh bloom of the Rokumeikan was passing. The antiquarian example of the university president seems to suggest that not everyone who went there was enthusiastic.

Strongly elitist from the outset, the Rokumeikan became the target of growing criticism, some of it spiteful and emotional, some of it soundly realistic. There were incidents, the *Normanton* incident of 1886 most prominent among them. The *Normanton* was a British freighter that sank off the Japanese coast. All the survivors were British, and all twenty-three Japanese passengers drowned. The captain was tried by consular court in Kobe and acquitted. He was later sentenced to a short prison term by the Yokohama consulate, but the sentence did not still public outrage. Extraterritoriality was becoming intolerable. The Rokumeikan and all its assemblies were accomplishing nothing towards the necessary goal.

The end of the decade approached, and it came to seem that the Rokumeikan had no friends anywhere. Itō's political career did not end with the scandal and his resignation, but Inoue never really came into his own. Demagogues of the radical right and leaders of the "people's rights" movement on the left were at one in thinking that the Rokumeikan must go. In 1889 it was sold to the Peers Club, and so began the way into obscurity and extinction that has been described.

The name will not be forgotten. During its brief period of prominence the Rokumeikan was among the genuinely interesting curiosities the city contained. It has fascinated such disparate writers as Akutagawa Ryūnosuke and Mishima Yukio.

Though the enthusiasm with which the grand men of the land went out courting Europe and America had passed, the vogue for big parties did not pass. Three thousand five hundred guests were present at a party given by a shipowner in 1908, at what had been the Kōrakuen estate of the Mito Tokugawa family. Another shipowner gave a remarkable party in 1917, by which time the art of party-giving had advanced beyond mere imitation of the West. He had been tiger-hunting in Korea, and his two hundred guests, assembled at the Imperial Hotel, were invited to sample tiger meat.

Government offices were first provided with chairs in 1871. Later that year it became unnecessary to remove the shoes before gaining admission. Shoes were quickly popular with both sexes. Schoolgirls in full Japanese dress except for what appear to be buttoned shoes are common in Meiji prints. Clara Whitney, an American girl who lived in Tokyo from 1875, was distressed to see, at the funeral in 1877 of the widow of the fourteenth shogun, a band of professional mourners in traditional dress and foreign shoes. In early Meiji there was a vogue for squeaky shoes. To produce a happy effect, strips of "singing leather" could be purchased and inserted into the shoes.

Student uniforms of the Western style were adopted for men in mid-Meiji, and so came the choke collars and the blackness relieved only by brass buttons that prevailed through the Second World War. At the outset, school uniforms were not compulsory. Rowdiness was given as the reason for the change. Curiously, there had been a period earlier in Meiji when students were *forbidden* to wear foreign dress. Rowdyism seems to have been the reason then too, and the fact that foreigners were distressed to see students wandering about in foreign underwear.

It was not until the Taishō Period that the masses of students, young and older, changed to Western dress. A graduation picture for a well-known private elementary school shows all pupils in Japanese dress at the end of Meiji. A picture for the same school at the beginning of Shōwa (the present reign) shows most of the boys and about half the girls in Western dress. The middy blouse that continues to be a standard for girl students on the lower levels did not come into vogue until after the earthquake.

At the end of Meiji, the old way of dress yet prevailed among students, though the enlightened view held that it was constricting and inconsistent with modern individualism. When male students chose Western costume, they often wore it with a difference. A flamboyant messiness became the mark of the elite, and a word was coined for it, a hybrid. The first syllable of *bankara* is taken from a Chinese word connoting barbarity, and the remainder from "high-collar," signifying the up-to-date and cosmopolitan. The expression, still used though uniforms have virtually disappeared from higher education, means something like "sloppily modern."

High-collar aspects of food had been present since early Meiji, especially the eating of meat, a practice frowned upon by Buddhist orthodoxy. It is recorded that Sumō wrestlers of the Tokugawa Period ate all manner of strange things, such as monkeys, but the populace at large observed Buddhist taboos. The beef-pot was among the radical Meiji departures, and among its symbols as well. Pigs, horses, and dairy products, almost unknown before Meiji, now entered the Japanese diet. So too did bread, which was not thought of as a staple until about the time of the earthquake. In Meiji it was a confection. A Japanized version, a bun filled with bean jam, was inexpensive and very popular among students.

The city had a slaughterhouse from late Tokugawa, first in the hills of Shiba, then, because of local opposition, on the more secluded Omori coast, beyond the "red line" that defined the jurisdiction of the city magistrates. The students at Fukuzawa's Keiō University seem to have been inveterate eaters of beef, as was most appropriate to that Westernizing place. Yet they had their inhibitions. Reluctant to be seen in butcher shops, customers would receive their orders through inconspicuous windows. When a butcher entered the Keiō gates to make deliveries, he would be greeted with the clicking of flints that was an ancient cleansing and propitiatory ritual.

Chinese cuisine was also new to the city, though it had long been present in Nagasaki. It is so ubiquitous today, and in many ways so Japanized, that one might think it most venerable. The first Chinese restaurant in Tokyo opened for business only in 1883. It was the Kairakuen in Nihombashi, where Tanizaki and his friends played at whores and cribs. Where the beef-pot seems to have caught on without special sponsorship, the Kairakuen, like the Rokumeikan, had wealthy and powerful promoters, who thought Chinese cooking a necessity in any city worthy of the name.

There were pig fanciers. Pigs commanded high prices. The tiny creatures known as Nanking mice also enjoyed a vogue. But the rabbit vogue was more durable and more intense, a rage of a vogue indeed. Though it spread all over the country, its beginnings were in Tokyo, with two foreigners, an Englishman and an American, who, situated in the Tsukiji foreign settlement, offered rabbits for sale. They also offered to make plain to the ignorant exactly what a rabbit connoisseur looked for in a particularly desirable beast. The rabbits were to be patted and admired, as dogs and cats are, and not eaten. A society of rabbit fanciers was formed. Rabbits with the right points brought huge prices, far greater, by weight, than those for pigs. Large floppy ears were much esteemed, as was the *sarasa,* or calico coat. A person in Shitaya was fined and jailed for staining a white rabbit with persimmon juice.

Imports from distant lands increased the rabbit count, and encouraged speculation and profiteering. In 1873, a year in which the population of domestic rabbits in the central wards reached almost a hundred thousand, authorities banned a meeting of the society of rabbit fanciers. Later that year they banned the breeding of the rabbits themselves, and imposed a tax to discourage possession. The vogue thereupon died down, though foreigners were observed thereafter selling French rabbits in Asakusa. Newspapers regarded the consular courts as too lenient, and so the rankling issue of extraterritoriality came into the matter. So did one of the great social problems of early Meiji, because the lower ranks of the military aristocracy—who had great difficulty adjusting to the new day—were the chief losers from the profiteering.

The enthusiasm for foreign things waned somewhat in mid-Meiji. In the realm of personal grooming there was a certain vogue for "improving" Japanese things rather than discarding them for the Western. This nationalist reaction was by implication anti-Western, of course, but it was not accompanied by the sort of antiforeign violence that had been common in late Tokugawa. There were such incidents in early Meiji, but usually under special circumstances. When, in 1870, two Englishmen who taught at the university were wounded by swordsmen, W. E. Griffis was on hand to help treat them. Initially he shared the anger and fear of the foreign community, but eventually he learned of details that shocked his missionary sensibilities and caused him to put the blame rather on the Englishmen. They had been out womanizing. What happened to them need no more concern the God-fearing citizen of Tokyo than a similar incident at the contemporary Five Points slum need concern a proper citizen of New York. Two men from southwestern clans were executed for the assaults, some have thought on insufficient evidence. Sir Harry Parkes, the formidable British minister, was about to depart for home, and it was thought necessary (or so it has been averred) that something memorable be done for the occasion. One of the two condemned men retracted his confession, which did not in any event agree with the evidence presented by the wounds.

Out of fashion for some decades after Prince Itō's masked ball, dancing became wild and uncontrolled, by police standards, in the years after the First World War. Another new institution of the Rokumeikan period, the coffee house, also left its early primness behind. A Chinese opened the first one near Ueno Park in 1888. Descriptions of it suggest that it may have been a sort of gymnasium or health club, with coffee offered as an invigorating potion. The transcription of "coffee" had a sort of devil-may-care quality about it. Today the word is generally written with two characters that have only phonetic value, but the founder of the Coffee House chose a pair signifying "pros and cons," or perhaps "for better or for worse." The English word has continued to designate the beverage, while the French came to signify a place where stylish and affluent gentlemen (without their wives) went to be entertained by pretty and accommodating young ladies. It was among the symbols of the Taishō high life.

Though sea bathing was not completely unknown in Meiji, ladies' bathing garments became good business only in Taishō. Immersion in natural bodies of cold water has long been a religious observance, but it was not until recent times that the Japanese came to think it pleasurable. When Nagai Kafū describes a summer beach of late Meiji it is notable for its loneliness, even a beach which now would be an impenetrable mass of bodies on a hot Sunday afternoon. In his memoirs Tanizaki describes an excursion to the Shiba coast, to a beach situated almost exactly where the expressway now passes the Shiba Detached Palace. The purpose of the outing seems to have been more for clamdigging than for bathing. In late Meiji there was an advertising campaign to promote the district and induce people to come bathing in its waters (then still clean enough for bathing, even though the south shore of the bay was becoming a district of factories and docks). Among the points made in favor of sea bathing was that it was held in high esteem by foreigners.

Eminent foreigners began coming to Tokyo at an early date. They were on the whole treated hospitably. An exception was the czarevitch of Russia, who was wounded by a sword-swinging policeman, though not in Tokyo, when he paid a visit to Japan in 1891. The very earliest was the Duke of Edinburgh, who came in 1869. Others included German and Italian princes, Archduke Franz Ferdinand, and a head of state, the King of Hawaii. William H. Seward called in 1870. The Meiji government felt more immediately threatened by Russia than by any other nation. Seward suggested an Alaskan solution to the Russian problem: buy them out. Pierre Loti was probably the most distinguished literary visitor of Meiji, but such attention as he received—his invitation to the Rokumeikan, for instance—had less to do with his writing than with his diplomatic status as a naval attaché.

The eminent foreigners most lionized were without question General and Mrs. Ulysses S. Grant. On a round-the-world journey, they reached Nagasaki by cruiser in June, 1879, and were in Tokyo for two months, from early July to early September. They were to have visited Kyoto and Osaka, but this part of their schedule was canceled because of a cholera epidemic. The guard along the way from Yokohama was commanded by Nogi Maresuke, who became, in the Russo-Japanese War, the leading military immortal of modern times, and demonstrated the extent of his loyalty to the throne by committing suicide on the day of the Meiji emperor's funeral. For the Grants there was a reception at Shimbashi Station, before which a display of hydrangeas formed the initials "U.S.G." Japanese and American flags decorated every door along the way to the Hama Palace, where the party stayed, and where the governor honored them with yet another reception. Receptions were held during the following weeks at the College of Technology and Ueno. The former is said to have been the first soiree essayed by the Japanese, whose ways of entertaining had been of a different sort. There were parades and visits to schools and factories, the sort of thing one gets on a visit to the New China today. The general planted a cypress tree in Ueno. It came through the holocausts of 1923 and

A parade during General Grant's visit in 1879. Woodcut by Kunichika
(The Metropolitan Museum of Art; gift of Lincoln Kirstein, 1962)

1945, and yet survives, providing the background for an equestrian statue of the founder of the Japanese Red Cross. Mrs. Grant planted a magnolia, which survives as well. There was classical theater, both Kabuki and Nō, and there was the most festive of summer observances, the "opening of the Sumida" in July. The general viewed it in comfort from an aristocratic villa, it being a day when there were still such villas on the river. The crowds were twice as large as for any earlier year in Meiji, despite the fact that the weather was bad. Fireworks and crowds got rained upon. All manner of pyrotechnical glories were arranged in red, white, and blue. The general indicated great admiration.

The general and the emperor saw a good deal of each other. The general paid a courtesy call on the Fourth of July, the day after his arrival. They had breakfast together after a troop review on July 7, and met again at the great Ueno reception in August. Also in August, they had a long and relatively informal meeting in the Hama Palace. The general argued the virtues of democracy, though with a caution against too hasty adoption of this best of systems. He expressed the hope that the Japanese would be tactful and considerate of Chinese sensibilities as they took over the Ryūkyū Islands, claimed by both countries. A few days before his departure, he took his leave of the emperor.

Though overall the visit was a huge success, there were a few unpleasant incidents. Clara Whitney overheard a catty Japanese lady remark "that General Grant is treated so much like a god here that a temple should be erected immediately." Towards the end of his stay there were rumors of an assassination plot, but they proved to be the inventions of a jealous Englishman. The 1879 cholera epidemic, by no means the only such epidemic in Meiji, had led to the building of the first isolation hospitals in the city. Rumors spread similar to earlier ones about telegraph poles (see p. 49): the hospitals were for purposes of snatching livers, General Grant being ready to pay a handsome price for a liver.

These were minor details, however. On the whole, the city seems to have loved the general and the general the city.

The high point of the visit, for the historian of the event if not for the general himself, was his evening at the Kabuki. He went to the Shintomiza near Ginza, the most advanced theater in the city. Carpets and lacquered chairs had been carried in from the Hama Palace. Three royal princes were in attendance, as was the prime minister. The play was called *The Latter Three Years' War in the North*. Minamoto Yoshiie, the victorious general in that war (a historical event), resembled the visiting general in a most complimentary manner: he behaved with great courtliness and magnanimity towards his defeated adversary.

The theater manager, accompanied by Danjūrō, the most famous actor of the day, stepped forth in frock coat during an entr'acte to thank the general for a curtain he had donated. The climax was a dance performed against a backdrop of flags and lanterns. Some of the musicians wore red and white stripes, others stars on a blue ground. Then appeared a row of Yanagibashi geisha, each in a kimono of red and white stripes drawn down over one shoulder to reveal a star-spangled singlet. Japanese and American flags decorated their fans.

"Ah, the old flag, the glorious Stars and Stripes! . . ." Clara Whitney wrote in her diary. "It made the prettiest costume imaginable. . . . We looked with strong emotion upon this graceful tribute to our country's flag and felt grateful to our Japanese friends for their kindness displayed not only to General Grant but to our honored country."

.   .   .

Next to General and Mrs. Grant, the foreigner who got the most attention from the newspapers and the printmakers was probably an Englishman named Spencer, who came in 1890, bringing balloons with
which he performed stunts, once in Yokohama and twice in Tokyo.
The emperor was present at the first Tokyo performance. Parachuting
from his balloon, Spencer almost hit the royal tent, and injured himself slightly in his efforts to avoid it. He drew huge crowds at Ueno a
few days later, and this time landed in a paddy field. An American
named Baldwin tried to outdo him the following month, with aerial
acrobatics and a threatening smoky balloon. Spencer is the one who is
remembered, to the extent that he was given credit by the printmakers
for stunts that apparently were Baldwin's. The following year the great
actor Kikugorō appeared on the Kabuki stage as Spencer, in a play by
Mokuami. Coached by a nephew of Fukuzawa Yukichi, he even
essayed a speech in English. There was a vogue for balloon candies,
balloon bodkins, and, of course, balloon prints. Since the Japanese had
been launching military balloons for more than a decade, it must have
been the parachuting and stunting that so interested people—or perhaps they enjoyed seeing a foreigner in a dangerous predicament.

W. E. Griffis, who felt that those two grievously wounded Englishmen (see page 103) deserved what they got, said that the same judg-
ment applied to all attacks upon foreigners of which he was aware. It
may be true. The attack on the czarevitch may not seem to fit the
generalization as well as it might, but the assailant could have argued
that Russia itself was behaving provocatively. Violence was also directed at Salvation Army workers, and much the same justification
might have been offered—the army itself was provocative.

An American colonel of the Salvation Army arrived and set up an
office in the summer of 1900. Very soon afterwards he published a
tract called *Triumphant Voice (Toki no Koe)*, addressed to the ladies of
the Yoshiwara. It exhorted them to flee their bondage, and offered help
to those who responded positively. The brothel keepers attempted to
buy up all copies. A Japanese worker for the Salvation Army was
pummeled by a Yoshiwara bully boy as he hawked *Triumphant Voice*.
Two men tried to rescue a lady from the Susaki quarter, and they too
were attacked. This charitable endeavor attracted the attention and
support of the newspapers. A reporter succeeded in rescuing a
Yoshiwara lady, whereupon fleeing the quarters became something of a
fad. The Salvation Army announced that during the last months of

1900 there were more than a thousand refugees in Tokyo alone. The figure is not easy to substantiate, but publicity was enormous. The vogue presently passed, and the Salvation Army was not afterwards able to match this initial success.

The "double life," that mixture of the imported and the domestic, was certainly present from early Meiji and indeed from late Tokugawa, for people to enjoy and to be tormented by. Eminent foreigners came, objects of admiration and emulation, and once Civilization and Enlightenment had been accepted as worthy, it must have been difficult to see pinching shoes and injunctions to urinate indoors as other than important. Through most of Meiji, however, the cosmopolitan part of the double life was the part added, the frills attached somewhat self-consciously and discarded when a person wanted to be comfortable. The big change, the domestication of the foreign, began in late Meiji, at about the time of the Russo-Japanese War, and the advertising man and the retail merchant may have been responsible for it. Perhaps it would have occurred without their aggressive urgings. Yet the old dry-goods store became the modern department store in late Meiji, and in the change we may see how the double life itself was changing. Civilization and Enlightenment were no longer much talked of in late Meiji, but it was hard for anyone, in the dingiest alley east of the river, not to know what the Mitsukoshi and the Shirokiya were offering this season.

Advertising is a modern institution. The canny merchant of Edo had been aware of its merits, and there are well-known stories of Kabuki actors who promoted lines of dress. Edo was a closed world, however, in which vogues, led by the theater and the pleasure quarters, spread like contagions. People knew their stores, and stores knew their people. Even the largest and richest were highly specialized. Faster transportation led to the development of a wide clientele, gradually becoming something like national. At the same time came the idea of offering everything to everyone.

Through most of Meiji, the old way prevailed. The big shops specialized in dry goods. The customer removed his footwear before stepping up to the matted floor of the main sales room. There was no window shopping. If the customer did not know precisely what he wanted, the clerk had to guess, and bring likely items from a godown.

Aristocratic ladies from the High City did not go shopping in the Low City. Clerks came to them from the big "silk stores," or from smaller establishments that would today call themselves boutiques.

The Mitsui dry-goods store, presently to become Mitsukoshi, had a fixed schedule of prices from early in its history. Haggling seems to have been common in early Meiji all the same, and a mark of cultural differences. The clans of the far southwest had made the Meiji revolution, and were the new establishment. Their ways were frequently not the ways of Edo and Tokyo. Their men took haggling as a matter of course, and the shopkeepers of Edo resisted it or acceded to it as their business instincts advised them. At least one old and well-established dry-goods store bankrupted itself by the practice. Mitsui held to its fixed schedule, and survived.

The last decades of Meiji saw the advent of the department store. In many of its details it represented the emergence of a Western institution and the retreat of the traditional to the lesser realm of the specialty store. Certainly there was imitation. The big Mitsukoshi store of the Taishō era, the one that burned so brightly after the earth-

Mitsukoshi's famous glass display cases

quake, was an imitation of Wanamaker's. If the department store symbolized the new city, however, it remained a Japanese sort of symbol. Department stores sold their wares by drawing crowds with culture and entertainment as well as merchandise. They were heirs to the shrine and temple markets, shopping centers ahead of their time.

Mitsukoshi and Shirokiya, at opposite approaches to the Nihombashi bridge, led the way into the great mercantile transformation. Edo methods predominated until about the turn of the century. They did not disappear even then, but the big dealers quickly moved on to mass sales of myriad commodities.

Mitsui, or Mitsukoshi, had entered Edo from the provinces in the seventeenth century. Shirokiya had opened for business in Nihombashi a few years earlier. Mitsukoshi has fared better than Shirokiya in the present century, but it would be facile to see in this the commonly averred victory of the provincial trader over the son of Edo. Both enterprises had been a part of Edo from its earliest years. Mitsukoshi was better at advertising and "image-making" than Shirokiya. Though purveying almost everything to almost everyone, it has preserved a certain air of doing so with elegance. In late Meiji, standing face to face across the bridge to which all roads led, the two sought to outdo each other with bold new innovations. Shortly after the Russo-Japanese War of 1904–1905 Mitsui added a second floor, with showcases. These were innovations so startling that they were for a time resisted. Edo had done its shopping on platforms perhaps two or three feet from the ground, with no wares on display.

Although Mitsukoshi was ahead in the matter of showcases and elevated shopping, Shirokiya was ahead in other respects. In 1886 it became the first of the old silk stores to sell Western clothes. It had one of the first telephones in the city, which, however, was kept out of sight, in a stairwell, lest it disturb people. It provided the country with its first shop girls. All the clerks in the old dry-goods stores had been men. From about the time it became Mitsukoshi, which was registered as the legal name in 1904, Mitsui began selling hats, leather goods, and sundries. Then, having withdrawn to a back street because the main north-south street through Nihombashi was being widened, Mitsukoshi reopened on the old site in 1908, with the makings of a department store. Shirokiya replied with a new building, four storeys and a tower, in 1911. It had game rooms and the first of the exhibition

Shirokiya Department Store, Nihombashi, after 1911

halls that give the modern Japanese department store certain aspects of a museum and amusement park. In 1914 Mitsukoshi completed a grand expansion, into the building that burned after the earthquake. The new Mitsukoshi was a five-storey Renaissance building, not the highest in the city, but the largest, it was said, east of Suez, and very modern, with elevators, central heating, a roof garden, and even an escalator.

The Mitsukoshi of 1914 was not a very interesting building, at least from the outside, but the Shirokiya must have been a delight, built as it was in an eclectic style that looked ahead to the more fanciful effusions of Taishō. The building of late Meiji does not survive, but in photographs it seems the more advanced and certainly the more interesting of the two. Yet Shirokiya was less successful than its rival in keeping up with the times.

Mainly, Mitsukoshi was the better at the big sell. Already at the turn of the century, a life-size picture of a pretty girl stood in Shimbashi Station inviting everyone to Mitsukoshi. Early in Taishō the store joined the Imperial Theater in a famous advertising campaign. The slogan was the only one still remembered from the early years of Japanese advertising: "Today the Imperial, tomorrow Mitsukoshi." Inviting the public to spend alternate days at the two establishments, it was very successful. In the Taishō period Mitsukoshi had a boys' band known to everyone. It is said to have been the first nonofficial band in the nation. The boys wore red and green kilts.

Despite all this innovation, the department stores were far from as big at the end of Meiji as they have become since. The old market was still healthy. Neighborhood stores offered most commodities and had most of the plebeian trade, the big Nihombashi stores still being a little too high-collar. Yet the department stores worked the beginnings of a huge cultural shift, so that the city of late Meiji seems far more familiar than the city of late Tokugawa. They were not the only enterprises of their kind in the city. Kanda and Ueno each had one, both of them to advance upon Ginza after the earthquake.

The problem of what to do with footwear was not solved until after the earthquake, and the delay was in some measure responsible for the slowness of the big stores to attract a mass clientele. Footwear was checked at the door in traditional fashion, sometimes tens of thousands of items per day, and replaced by specially furnished slippers. On the day of the dedication of the new Nihombashi bridge, still in use, Mitsukoshi misplaced five hundred pairs of footwear. For this reason among others the department store was a little like the Ginza brick-town: everyone wanted a look at it, but it would not do for everyday. It was on the standard tour for *onobori*, country people in for a look at the capital. The presence of Mitsukoshi, indeed, along with certain patriotic sites now out of fashion, is what chiefly distinguishes the Meiji Tokyo tour from that of today.

There was another kind of shopping center, also new in Meiji, and the vexing problem of footwear has been offered to explain its very great popularity from late Meiji into Taishō. The word *kankōba* is a Meiji neologism that seems on the surface to mean, with exhortatory intent, "place for the encouragement of industry." It actually signifies something like "bazaar" or "emporium." Numbers of small shops would gather under a roof or an arcade and call themselves a *kankōba*. In the years when the old dry-goods stores were making themselves over into department stores, the bazaars were much more popular,

Matsuzakaya Department Store in Ueno

possibly because the customer did not have to remove his shoes or clogs. The great day of the bazaar was late Meiji. When the department stores finally emerged as a playground for the whole family, on whatever level of society, bazaars went into a decline.

The first bazaar was publicly owned. It opened in 1878, selling products left over from the First Industrial Exposition, held at Ueno the preceding year. Its location was for the day a remote one, at the northern end of what would become the Mitsubishi Meadow, just east of the palace. Two bazaars dominated the busy south end of Ginza, near which the main railway station stood until early Taishō. The building of the present Tokyo Central Station displaced the crowds and sent the bazaars into a decline. In the fourth decade of Meiji, however, there were three bazaars in Kanda and seven in Ginza. By 1902 there were twenty-seven scattered over the city. Nine years later there were only eleven, and in 1913, the first full year of Taishō, only six.

No establishment has called itself a *kankōba* since the 1930s, but the *kankōba* must have been not unlike the shopping centers that are a threat to the Nihombashi stores today. For all the newness of the word, the *kankōba* also had much in common with the neighborhood shopping district of Edo. There is continuity in these things, and what seems newest may in fact be tradition reemerging.

· · ·

The department stores and the bazaars were in it to make money, but they also provided pleasure and entertainment. So it was too with the expositions. People were supposed to be inspired and work more energetically for the nation and Civilization and Enlightenment, but expositions could also be fun.

The Japanese learned early about them. The shogunate and the Satsuma clan sent exhibits to the Paris fair of 1867, and the Meiji government to Vienna in 1873 and the Centennial Exposition in Philadelphia. The Japanese experimented with domestic fairs early in Meiji, one of them in the Yoshiwara. The grand exhibition that called itself the First National Industrial Exposition occurred at Ueno in 1877, from late summer to early winter. The chief minister was chairman of the planning committee. He was a man of Satsuma, and the Satsuma Rebellion was just then in progress; and so the import of the exposition was highly political, to demonstrate that the new day had arrived and meant to stay, in spite of dissension. The emperor and empress came on opening day and again in October, a month before the closing. The buildings were temporary ones in a flamboyantly Western style, with an art gallery at the center and flanking structures dedicated to farming and machinery and to natural products. Some of the items on display seemed scarcely what the Japanese most needed—a windmill, for instance, thirty feet high, straight from the drylands of America. Almost a hundred thousand items were exhibited by upwards of sixteen thousand exhibitors. The total number of visitors was not much less than the population of the city.

Other national exhibitions were scattered across Meiji. As a result of the second, in 1881, Tokyo acquired its first permanent museum, a brick structure designed by Josiah Conder, begun in 1878 and not quite finished in time for the exposition. The fourth and fifth expositions, just before and after the turn of the century, were held in Kyoto and Osaka. The sixth, in 1907, at Ueno once more, remains the grandest of the Tokyo series. Coming just after the Russo-Japanese War, it had patriotic significance, and therapeutic and economic value as well. Economic depression followed the war, and a need was felt to increase consumption. The main buildings, Gothic, in the park proper, were built around a huge fountain, on six levels, surmounted by Bacchus and bathed in lights of red, blue, and purple. Although the architecture was for the most part exotic, the prestige of Japanese painting had so recovered that the ceiling of the art pavilion was decorated with a

dragon at the hands of the painter Hashimoto Gahō, who was associated with such fundamentalist evangelizers for the traditional arts as
Ernest Fenollosa and Okakura Tenshin.

A water chute led down to the lower level, on the shores of
Shinobazu Pond, where special exhibitions told of foreign lands and
a growing empire. There was a Taiwan pavilion and a Ryūkyū pavilion,
the latter controversial, because ladies from the pleasure quarters were
present to receive visitors and make them feel at home. They were
considered an affront to the dignity of the Ryūkyūs, whose newspapers
protested.

It was the Sixth Exposition that inspired Natsume Sōseki's famous
remarks about illumination (see page 81). Indeed, all the expositions
were makers of taste. The more fanciful architectural styles of Taishō
derive quite clearly from two expositions, held at Ueno early and midway through the reign.

Ueno, the place for expositions, is one of five public parks, the first
in the city, established in 1873. The public park is another Meiji
novelty introduced under the influence of the West. The old city had
not been wanting in places for people to go and be with other people,
but the idea of a tract maintained by the city solely for recreation was a
new one. We have seen that at least one mayor thought such places
unnecessary. He had a good case. The city already possessed myriads
of gardens, large and small, and temples, shrines, cemeteries, and
other places for viewing the flowers and grasses of the seasons.

The fact that one such place, in the far south of the city, was
chosen by the shogunate as the site for the British legation was among
the reasons for public satisfaction at the destruction of the unfinished
building. A succession of temples occupied most of the land from what
is now Ueno Park to the Sumida.

There were fewer such public spaces as time went by; and so the
principle that the city had a responsibility in the matter was an important departure. The grandest of Edo temples are far less grand today.
Had public parks not come into being, the loss of open space as religious establishments dwindled might have been almost complete.

A foreigner is given credit for saving Ueno. Almost anything might
have happened to the tract left empty by the "Ueno War," the subjuga-
tion in 1868 of holdouts from the old regime. Before that incident it
had been occupied by the more northerly of the two Tokugawa funeral

temples, the Kan-eiji. With branch temples, the Kan-eiji (named for the era in early Edo when it was founded) extended over the whole of "the mountain"—the heights to the north and east of Shinobazu Pond—and low-lying regions to the east as well, where Ueno Station now stands. Six of the fifteen shoguns are buried on the Kan-eiji grounds. The grave of Keiki, the last, is nearby in the Yanaka cemetery. The attacking forces destroyed virtually the whole of the great complex. What is the main hall of the Kan-eiji today was moved in 1879 from the provinces to the site of a lesser temple. A gate is the only relic of the central complex, although a few seventeenth-century buildings, among the oldest in the city, still survive in the park. The public had been admitted to the Kan-eiji during the daytime hours. The precincts were, then as now, famous for their cherry blossoms.

After the fighting of 1868, Ueno was a desolate but promising expanse, more grandly wooded than it is today. The Ministry of Education wanted it for a medical school. The army, the most successful appropriator of land in early Meiji, thought that it would be a good location for a military hospital. It was at this point that the foreign person offered an opinion.

Dr. E. A. F. Bauduin, a Dutchman, had come to Japan in 1862. He was a medical doctor, and during his career in Japan served as a consultant on medical education in Nagasaki and Edo, and at the university in Tokyo. The Ministry of Education summoned him from Nagasaki for consultations in the matter of making the Ueno site a medical school. Quite contrary to expectations, he argued instead that Ueno would make a splendid park, and that the medical school could just as well go in some other place, such as the Maeda estate in Hongō, now the main campus of Tokyo University.

This view prevailed. In 1873, Ueno became one of the first five Tokyo parks. The others were the grounds of the Asakusa Kannon, the Tokugawa cemetery at Shiba, some shrine grounds east of the river, and a hill in the northern suburbs long famous for cherry blossoms. Of the four parks in the city proper it was the only one that was not otherwise occupied, so to speak, and it has had a different career than the others. It was transferred to the royal household in 1890, and returned to the city in 1924, to honor the marriage of the present emperor. Today it is officially called Ueno Royal Park. Shinobazu Pond to the west, a remnant of marshlands that had once spread over most of the Low City, was annexed to the park in 1885.

Ueno has not entirely escaped the incursions of commerce. Though the scores of little stalls that had established themselves in the old temple precincts were closed or moved elsewhere, the huge Seiyōken restaurant is the chief eyesore on an otherwise pleasing skyline. (An 1881 poster informs us that the restaurant is in Ueno Parque.) The original park now includes the campus of an art and music college. The Tokugawa tombs were detached from the park in 1885.

Yet Ueno has remained very much a park, less greedily gnawed at than Asakusa and Shiba have been. For a decade in mid-Meiji, until 1894, there was a horseracing track around Shinobazu Pond, a genteel one, with a royal stand. The emperor was present at the opening. The purpose, most Meiji-like, was not pleasure or gambling but the promotion of horsemanship in the interests of national defense. Woodcuts, not always reliable in such matters, seem to inform us that the horses ran clockwise.

Ueno Park had the first art museum in the land, the first zoo, the first electric trolley, a feature of one of the industrial expositions, and, in 1920, the first May Day observances. (There have been 53 as of 1982; a decade's worth were lost to "Fascism.") In a city that contains few old buildings, Ueno has the largest concentration of moderately old ones. It was saved by royal patronage, and, ironically, by the fact that its holocaust came early. The arrangements of early Meiji prevailed through the holocausts of 1923 and 1945.

Besides Edo survivals, the park, broadly defined to include the campus of the art college, contains the oldest brick building in the city. It has just passed its centennial. The oldest concert hall, of wood, is chronically threatened with dismemberment. The oldest building in the National Museum complex, in a domed Renaissance style, was a gift of the Tokyo citizenry, put up to honor the wedding of the crown prince. The present emperor was already a lad of seven when it was finished. The planning, collecting of funds, and building took time. What has become the great symbol of the park, recognized all over the land, is also a relic of Meiji. The bronze statue of Saigō Takamori, on the heights above the railway station, was unveiled in 1898. The original plans had called for putting it in the palace plaza, but it was presently decided that Saigō, leader of the Satsuma Rebellion, at the end of which, in 1877, he killed himself, had not yet been adequately rehabilitated. His widow did not like the statue. Never, she said, had she seen him so poorly dressed.

Huge numbers of people went to Ueno for the industrial expositions, and soon after it became a park it was again what it had been in Edo, a famous place for viewing cherry blossoms. Under the old regime the blossoms had been somewhat overwhelmed by Tokugawa mortuary grandeur, however, and singing and dancing, without which a proper blossom-viewing is scarcely imaginable, had been frowned upon. A certain solemnity seems to have hung over the new royal park as well. Blossom-viewing places on the Sumida and on the heights to the north of Ueno were noisier and less inhibited. Indeed, whether or not because of the royal association, Ueno seems early to have become a place of edification rather than fun.

Asakusa was very different. The novelist Saitō Ryokuu made an interesting and poetic comparison of the two, Asakusa and Ueno. Ryokuu's case was similar to Nagai Kafū's: born in the provinces in 1867 or 1868 and brought to Tokyo as a boy of perhaps nine (the facts of his early life are unclear), and so not a son of Edo, he outdid the latter in his fondness for the Edo tradition. His way of showing it was different from Kafū's. He preferred satire to lyricism, and falls in the proper if not entirely likeable tradition of Edo satirists whose favorite subject is rustic ineptitude in the great pleasure palaces of the metropolis. He is not much read today. His language is difficult and his manner is out of vogue, and it may be that he was the wrong sex. Women writers in a similarly antique mode still have their devoted followings.

Some of his pronouncements deserve to be remembered. Of Ueno and Asakusa he said: "Ueno is for the eyes, a park with a view. Asakusa is for the mouth, a park for eating and drinking. Ueno puts a stop to things. From Asakusa you go on to other things. In Ueno even a Kagura dance is dour and gloomy, in Asakusa a prayer is cheerful. The vespers at Ueno urge you to go home, the matins at Asakusa urge you to come on over. When you go to Ueno you feel that the day's work is not yet finished. When you go to Asakusa you feel that you have shaken off tomorrow's work. Ueno is silent, mute. Asakusa chatters on and on."

Ueno was the largest of the five original parks. Of the other four, only Asukayama, the cherry-viewing place in the northern suburbs, has managed to do as well over the years as Ueno in looking like a park. The notion of what a park should be was a confused one. The Edo equivalent had been the grounds of temple and shrine. The park system of 1873 tended to perpetuate this concept, merely furnishing certain tracts a new and enlightened name. Ueno was almost empty at the outset and presently became royal, and ended up rather similar to the city parks of the West.

Asakusa, on the other hand, resembles nothing in the West at all. It was the third largest of the original five, more than half as large as Shiba and Ueno, and several times as large as the two smaller ones. What remains of the Edo temple gardens is now closed to the public, and of what is open there is very little that resembles public park or garden. The old park has in legal fact ceased to be a park. A decree under the Occupation, which liked to encourage religious institutions provided they were not contaminated by patriotism, returned the park lands to the temple. Yet the technicalities by which it ceased to be a park had as little effect on its career as those by which it had become a park in the first place.

The original Asakusa Park was expanded in 1876 to include the gardens and firebreak to the west. There was further expansion in 1882, and the following year "the paddies," as the firebreak was called, were excavated to make two ornamental lakes. The reclaimed wetlands were designated the sixth of the seven districts into which the park was divided. In the Meiji and Taishō periods, and indeed down to Pearl Harbor, "Sixth District" meant the music halls and the movie palaces and the other things that drew mass audiences. The Sixth District had its first theater in 1886, and, in 1903, Electricity Hall, the first permanent movie theater in the land. Among the other things were a miniature Mount Fuji, sixty-eight feet high, for the ascent of which a small fee was charged, and a rope bridge across the lakes, to give a sense of deep mountains. The Fuji was damaged in a typhoon and torn down the year the Twelve Storeys, much higher, was completed, on land just north of the park limits. Among those who crossed the bridge was Sir Edwin Arnold, the British journalist best remembered as the author of *The Light of Asia*. Several urchins tried to shake him and a lady companion into one of the lakes. The workmanship of the bridge reminded him of the Incas.

By the turn of the century, the Sixth District was a jumble of show houses and archery stalls—the great pleasure warren of a pleasure-loving city. It may be that the change was not fundamental, for the "back mountain" of the Asakusa Kannon had already been something of the sort. The Sixth District was noisier, brighter, and gaudier, however, and its influence extended all through the park. Remnants of the old Asakusa, shrinking back into it all, spoke wistfully to the few who took notice.

Kubota Mantarō, poet, novelist, playwright, and native of Asakusa, wrote of the change wrought by the cinema:

> Suddenly, it was everywhere. It swept away all else, and took control of the park. The life of the place, the color, quite changed. The "new tide" was violent and relentless. In the districts along the western ditch, by the Kōryūji Temple, somnolence had reigned. It quite departed. The old shops, dealers in tools and scrap and rags, the hair dresser's and the bodkin and bangle places—they all went away, as did the water in the ditch. New shops put up their brazen signs: Western restaurants, beef and horse places, short-order places, milk parlors. Yet even in those days, there were still houses with latticed fronts, little shops of uniform design, nurseries with bamboo fences, workmen from the fire brigades. They were still to be observed, holding their own, in a few corners, in the quiet, reposed, somehow sad alleys of the back districts, in the deep shade of the blackberry brambles behind the grand hall.

Asakusa had its gay and busy time, which passed. The lakes grew dank and gaseous in the years after the surrender, and were filled in. The crowds ceased to come, probably more because of changes in the entertainment business and new transportation patterns than because of what had happened to the park. It might be argued that Asakusa would have fared better if it had not become an entertainment center. If the old park had gone on looking like a park, then Asakusa, like Ueno, might still have its lures. As to that, no one can say—and it may be that if we could say, we would not wish the story of Asakusa to be different. It was perhaps the place where the Low City had its last good time. Nowhere today is there quite the same good-natured abandon to be found, and if people who remember it from thirty years ago may properly lament the change, the laments of those who remember it from twice that long ago are, quite as properly, several times as intense.

It is another story. Asakusa is an instance of what can happen to a public park when no one is looking, though the more relevant point may be that it never really was a park. As an episode in intellectual history, it illustrates the ease with which words can be imported, and the slowness with which substance comes straggling along afterwards. In 1873 Tokyo could face the other capitals of the world and announce that it too had public parks; but it was not until two decades later, when the city acquired land suitable for a central park (if that was what was wished) that the possibility of actually planning and building a park seemed real. The double life, in other words, was gradually reaching down to fundamentals. What had happened at Ueno had happened more by accident than forethought, and not much at all had happened at Asakusa—except that the purveyors of pleasure had had their cheerful and energetic way.

Since the rise of Marunouchi, Hibiya Park, along with the public portion of the palace grounds abutting it on the north, has been the central park of the city—perhaps more important, because of easy access to Ginza, than Ueno. In early Meiji it was not a place where a townsman would have chosen to go for a pleasant walk, and it did not become a public park until thirty years after the original five. Lying within the outer ramparts of the castle, it was at the end of the Tokugawa regime occupied by mansions of the military aristocracy. While the castle grounds nearby were being put to somewhat helter-skelter use by the new government and ultimately, after their time of providing homes for foxes and badgers, were left as public gardens or turned over to the commercial developers, Hibiya was a parade ground. It was cleared for the purpose in 1871, and there, a year later, the emperor first reviewed troops. It seems to have been fearfully dusty even after the Rokumeikan and the Imperial Hotel were built to the east, for a scorched-earth policy was deemed in accord with modern military methods. In 1893 the army, which had acquired more suitable spots on the western fringes of the city, announced its intention of turning Hibiya over to the city by stages. Hibiya Park was opened in 1903.

Initially it was thought that the present Hibiya park lands would become the bureaucratic center. Planning to that effect began after the burning of the palace in 1872. There was no hesitation about rebuilding the palace on the site of the old castle, and in 1886 a government planning office proposed a concentration of government buildings on the parade grounds. The advice of the Germans was invited. Two eminent architects arrived and drew up plans for a complex of highly ornate buildings. A big hole was dug, at great expense, before it was concluded that the soil would not really bear the weight of all that *echt* Western brick and stone, and that lands farther to the west might be more suitable. Though German prestige slid, we may be grateful for the results. Without the excavation Tokyo might lack a central park (as Osaka does). The German plans, modified in the direction of simplicity, found use in the government complex that did presently come to be. The original plans have been described as seven parts Nikkō (with reference to the most florid of the Tokugawa tombs) and three parts Western.

Some liked the new park, some did not. Nagai Kafū, on his return from France in 1908, found it repellently formal. It became so favored a trysting place, however, that the Kōjimachi police station felt compelled to take action. On the summer night in 1908 when a dozen or so policemen were first sent into the park, they apprehended about the same number of miscreant couples, who were fined. Hibiya is usually referred to as the first genuinely Western park in the city and in Japan. That is what Kafū so disliked about it—he did not think that Westernization worked in any thing or person Japanese but himself.

In fact a good deal of the park is fairly Japanese, and it contains relics of all the eras—trees said to be as old as the city, a fragment of the castle escarpment and moat, a bandstand that was in the original park, a bronze fountain only slightly later. The bandstand has lost its original cupola and the park has changed in matters of detail; yet of all the major parks it is the one that has changed least. Perhaps the fact that it was Western in concept as well as in name may be given credit for this stability.

The area officially devoted to parks grew slightly through Meiji and Taishō, but remained low compared to the cities of the West with which comparison is always being made. (It is high compared to Osaka.) In the last years of Taishō, the total of open spaces, including temples, shrines, and cemeteries, offered each resident of the city only one four-hundredth as much as was available to the resident of Washington. Even New York, whose residents were straitened in comparison with those of London and Paris, boasted forty times the per-capita park area that Tokyo did.

Yet there is truth in the excuse given by that Taishō mayor for the shortage of tracts officially designated as parks. While public parks were not pointless, they may have seemed much less of a necessity than they did in Western cities. Besides the tiny plots of greenery before rows of Low City houses, there continued to be a remarkable amount of unused space, especially in the High City, but in the Low City as well.

Kafū could be lyrical on the subject of vacant lots.

I love weeds. I have the same fondness for them as for the violets and dandelions of spring, the bell flowers and maiden flowers of autumn. I love the weeds that flourish in vacant lots, the weeds that grow on roofs, the weeds beside the road and beside the ditch. A vacant lot is a garden of weeds. The plumes of the mosquito-net grass, as delicate as glossed silk; the plumes of foxtail, soft as fur; the warm rose-pink of knotgrass blossoms; the fresh blue-white of the plantain; chickweed in flower, finer and whiter than sand: having come upon them does one not linger over them and find them difficult to give up? They are not sung of in courtly poetry, one does not find them in the paintings of Sōtatsu and Kōrin. They are first mentioned in the haiku and in the comic verse of plebeian Edo. I will never cease to love Utamaro's "Selection of Insects." An Ukiyoe artist sketched lowly grasses and insects quite ignored by Sinified painters and the schools of Kyoto. The example informs us how great was the achievement of haiku and comic verse and the Ukiyoe. They found a subject dismissed by aristocratic art and they made it art in its own right.

Far more than the plantings in all the new parks around the outer moat and behind the Nikolai Cathedral, I am drawn to the weeds one comes upon in vacant lots.

An important addition was made in Meiji to the lists of shrines, some of them not so very different from parks. Kudan Hill, to the west of the Kanda flats and northwest of castle and palace, was once higher than it is now. It once looked down over the swampy lands which the shogunate early filled in to accommodate merchants and artisans. The top half or so was cut off to reclaim the swamps. Barracks occupied the flattened top in the last Tokugawa years. In 1869 it became the site of a *shōkonsha,* a nationally administered "shrine to which the spirits of the dead are invited," or, in a venerable tradition, a place where the dead, and the living as well, are feasted and entertained. The specific purpose of several such shrines scattered over the country was to honor those who had died in line of duty "since the Kaei Period." This is a little misleading. Commodore Perry came in the Kaei Period, and there may seem to be an implication that he was resisted with loss of life, which he was not. The real intent was to honor those who died in the Restoration disturbances. As other conflicts and other casualties occurred, the rosters expanded. They include three Englishmen who died in the battle of Tsushima, at the climax of the Russo-Japanese War, as well as other surprises. Not many now remember that Japanese lives were lost in the Boxer Rebellion. It is of interest that Tokyo names on the growing rosters ran consistently below the national average. The son of Edo was not as eager as others to die for his country.

In 1879 the Kudan *shōkonsha* became the Yasukuni Jinja, "Shrine for the Repose of the Nation." It was in the Edo tradition, combining reverence and pleasure. There was horseracing on the grounds before the Shinobazu track was built. In 1896, the grandest equestrian year, 268 horses participated in the autumn festival. The last meet took place in 1898, and the track was obliterated in 1901. The shrine continued to be used for a great variety of shows, artistic and amusing, such as Sumō tournaments and Nō performances. A Nō stage built in 1902 survives on the shrine grounds, and a lighthouse from early Meiji. The latter served to guide fishing boats—for there were in those days fishing boats within sight of the hill.

A military exhibition hall was put up in 1882, a grim, Gothic place. It contained a machine gun made by Pratt and Whitney and presented to the emperor by General Grant. The Yasukuni had ten million visitors annually during and just after the Russo-Japanese War. Though the figure fell off thereafter, it continued to be in the millions. The shrine was more of a park, as that term is known in the West, than Asakusa. To those Japanese of a traditional religious bent it may have seemed strange that expanses of protective greenery extended to the southeast, southwest, and northwest of the palace—Hibiya Park, the Sannō Shrine (a very old one) and the Yasukuni Shrine—while the businessmen of the Mitsubishi Meadow were custodians of the most crucial direction, the northeast, "the devil's gate."

Tokyo grew the most rapidly of the large Japanese cities. At the close of Meiji, there can have been few foxes and badgers left in the Mitsubishi Meadow, lined all up and down with brick, and not many weeds can have survived either. Yet the fact remains that Tokyo was, by comparison with the other large cities of Japan, even Kyoto, the emperor's ancient capital, a place of greenery. Tanizaki's wife, a native of Osaka, asked what most struck her on her first visit to Tokyo, replied without hesitation that it was the abundance of trees. The paddies had by the end of Meiji withdrawn from the gate of the Yoshiwara, and they have been pushed farther and farther in the years since; but it was still a city of low buildings, less dense in its denser regions than late Edo had been. So it has continued to be. Perhaps, indeed, it contains the most valuable unused land in the world—the most luxurious space a weed, and even an occasional fox or badger, could possibly have.

There is another sense in which the city was still, at the end of Meiji, near nature, and still is today. The rhythm of the fields and of the seasons continued to be felt all through it. Everywhere in Japan Shinto observances follow the seasons. (It may be that in the United States only the harvest festival, Thanksgiving, is similarly bound to nature.) In deciding which among the great Japanese cities is, in this sense, most "natural," subjective impression must prevail, for there are no measuring devices. When Tanizaki's Makioka sisters, from an old Osaka family, wish to go on a cherry-blossom excursion, they go to

Kyoto. They might have found blossoms scattered over Osaka, of course, but Osaka, more than Tokyo, is a place of buildings and sterile surfaces. From one of the high buildings, it is an ashen city. Having arrived in Kyoto, the sisters seem to have only one favored blossom-viewing spot near the center of the city, the grounds of a modern shrine. All the others are on the outskirts, not in the old city at all.

One is left with a strong impression that Tokyo has remained nearer its natural origins, and nearer agrarian rhythms, than the great cities of the Kansai. This fastest-growing city did remarkably well at preserving a sense of the fields and the moods of the seasons. At the end of Meiji the Tokyo resident who wished to revel under the blossoms of April might have gone to Asukayama, that one among the five original parks that lay beyond the city limits, but he could have found blossoms enough for himself and several hundred thousand other people as well at Ueno or along the banks of the Sumida. Nothing comparable was to be had so near at hand in Osaka or Kyoto.

Places famous in early Meiji for this and that flower or grass of the seasons did less well at the end of Meiji. Industrial fumes ate at the cherries along the Sumida, and clams, the digging of which was a part of the homage paid to summer, were disappearing from the shores of Shiba and Fukagawa. (The laver seaweed of Asakusa, famed in Edo and before, had long since disappeared.) Even as the city grew bigger and dirtier, however, new places for enjoying the grasses and flowers came to be.

Every guide to the city contains lists of places to be visited for seasonal things. Going slightly against the natural pattern, these things begin with snow, not a flower or a grass, and not commonly available in quantity until later in the spring. The ornamental plants of midwinter are the camellia and a bright-leafed variety of cabbage, but neither seems to have been thought worth going distances to view. The Sumida embankment was the traditional place for snow viewing. There were other spots, and in the course of Meiji a new one, the Yasukuni Shrine, joined the list. Probably snow has been deemed a thing worth viewing because, like the cherry blossom, it so quickly goes away—on the Tokyo side of Honshu, at any rate.

At the beginning of Meiji, the grasses and flowers of the seasons were probably to be found in the greatest variety east of the Sumida. One did not have to go far east to leave the old city behind, and, having entered a pastoral (more properly, agrarian) village, one looked back towards the river and the hills of the High City, with Fuji rising grandly beyond them. These pleasures diminished towards the end of Meiji, as the regions east of the river fell victim to economic progress. Kafū seems prescient when, in a story from very late Meiji, he takes a gentleman and a geisha to view some famous peonies in Honjo, east of the river. They are disappointed, and the disappointment seems to tell us what the future holds for the peonies and indeed all these regions east of the river. Yet as the peony lost ground in Honjo it gained elsewhere: famous peony places have been established nearer the center of the city.

Another generous disposition of blossom-viewing and grass-viewing places lay along the ridge that divided the Low City from the High City. From here one looked eastwards towards the river and the fields. At the southern end of the ridge was the site of the British legation that never came to be. Ueno and Asukayama, famous spots for cherry blossoms, both stood on the ridge.

The viewing places along the ridge fared better in Meiji than did those east of the river. Ueno gradually ceased to intimidate, as it had under the shoguns, and so moved ahead of Asukayama and the Sumida embankment as the favored place for the noisiest rites of spring. The part of the ridge that lay between Ueno and Asukayama, inside and outside the city limits, was the great Edo center for nurseries, for potted chrysanthemums and morning glories and the like. The pattern has prevailed through the present century. These establishments have been pushed farther and farther out, so that not many survive today in Tokyo Prefecture, but the northern suburbs are still the place for them.

Early in the spring came the plum blossom. To admire it in early Meiji one went to Asakusa and Kameido, a slight distance beyond Honjo, east of the Sumida. Kameido is also recommended for wisteria in May. The Kameido wisteria have survived, but there are plums no longer, either in Kameido or in Asakusa. The plum is the personal blossom, so to speak, of Sugawara Michizane, a tragic and quickly deified statesman of the tenth century, who is the tutelary god of the Kameido Shrine. If his flower has gone from Kameido, a plum orchard has since been planted at another of his holy places, the Yushima Shrine in Hongō. So it is that the flowers and grasses cling to existence, losing here and gaining there. Towards the end of *The River Sumida* Kafū has his sad hero go walking with an uncle to Kameido, and the poignancy of the scene comes in large measure from an awareness already present, then in late Meiji, of what progress is doing to the district. It lies in the path of economic miracles.

In April came the cherry, which might be called the city's very own blossom. It has long been made much of, for the swiftness of its blooming and of its falling appeals to the highly cultivated national sense of evanescence. In the years of the Tokugawa hegemony the cherry became the occasion for that noisiest of springtime rites. Goten Hill, overlooking the bay at the southern edge of the Meiji city, is no longer found on early Meiji lists of blossom-viewing places. That was where the British legation had been put up and so promptly burned down. The most popular Meiji sites for the cherry blossom were Asukayama, remotest of the original five parks; Ueno; and the Sumida embankment. Two of the three have declined as the city and progress have engulfed them, while Ueno, nearest of the three to the center, thrives. It still draws the biggest crowds in the city and doubtless in all of Japan.

The peach and the pear come at about the same time, slightly later in the spring. They are dutifully included in Meiji lists of things to see, but the Japanese have not made as much of them as the Chinese, whose proverb has the world beating a path to a door with a blooming peach or pear. It would be easy to say that they are too showy for Japanese taste, but the chrysanthemum and the peony, both of them showy flowers, are much admired. Perhaps observance of the passing seasons was becoming less detailed, and the peach and the pear are among the lost details. There were no famous places within the city limits for viewing either of the two. In the case of the pear, one was asked to go to a place near Yokohama (the place where, in 1862, Satsuma soldiers killed an Englishman, prompting the British to shell Kagoshima). There were other flowers of spring and early summer—wisteria, azaleas, peonies, and *yamabuki*, a yellow-flowering shrub related to the rose.

Certain pleasures of the seasons were not centered upon flowers and grasses, or upon a specific flower or grass. For plucking the new shoots and herbs of spring, the regions east of the river and the western suburbs were especially recommended. For the new greenery of spring there were Ueno and the western suburbs. For the clams of summer there were the shores of the bay, at Susaki and Shibaura, where Tanizaki and his family went digging. Insects were admired, and birds. Fireflies, now quite gone from the city save for the caged ones released at garden parties, were to be found along the Kanda River, just below Kafū's birthplace. They were also present in the paddy lands around the Yoshiwara, to the north of Ueno, and along the banks of the Sumida, where no wild fireflies have been observed for a very long time. Birds were enjoyed less by the eye than by the ear. Two places in the city are called Uguisudani, Warbler Valley, one in Shitaya and the other in Koishikawa. *Horeites diphone*, the warbler in question, may still be heard in both places. For the cuckoo there was a listening point in Kanda, near the heart of the old Low City, and another near the Maeda estate in Hongō, to which the university presently moved. For the voice of the wild goose one went beyond the Sumida, and also to the Yoshiwara paddies and to Susaki, beside the bay in Fukagawa. For singing autumn insects, the western suburbs were recommended.

In high summer came morning glories, lotuses, and irises. The Meiji emperor's own favorite iris garden, on the grounds of what is now the Meiji Shrine, was opened to the public a few years after his death. The morning glory has long had a most particular place in the life of the Low City. It was the omnipresent sign of summer, in all the tiny garden plots and along the plebeian lanes, a favorite subject, as principal and as background, in the popular art of Edo. The place to go for Meiji morning glories was Iriya, to the east of Ueno Park. It still is the place to go, but it has suffered vicissitudes in the century since its morning glories first came into prominence. In early Meiji, Iriya was still paddy land, and among the paddies were extensive nurseries. One looked across them to the Yoshiwara, the great houses of which kept villas in the district. The last of the nurseries left Iriya, no longer on the outskirts of the city, in 1912, and so too, of course, did excursions for viewing and purchasing morning glories. They have returned in the last quarter of a century. For the morning-glory fair in early July, however, the plants must be brought in from what are now the northern outskirts of the city.

A famous lotus-viewing spot was lost in the course of Meiji. Tameike Pond in Akasaka was allowed to become silted in, and pres-

Shinobazu Pond, Ueno

ently built over. Shinobazu Pond, the other Meiji place for viewing and listening to lotuses (some say that the delicate pop with which a lotus opens is imagined, others say that they have heard it), survived Meiji, despite expositions and horse racing, and yet survives, despite the years of war and defeat, during which it was converted to barley fields. In Meiji and down to the recent past there were extensive commercial tracts of lotus east of the river, grown for the edible roots. They too were recommended in Meiji for lotus-viewing, and today they have almost disappeared.

The eastern suburbs were, again, the place to go for "the seven grasses of autumn," some of them actually shrubs and only one a grass as that term is commonly understood in the West. The chrysanthemum, not one of the autumn seven, was featured separately. Dangozaka, "Dumpling Slope," just north of the university in Hongō, was a famous chrysanthemum center that came and went in Meiji. Chrysanthemum dolls—chrysanthemums trained to human shape—were first displayed there in 1878. They figure in some famous Meiji novels, but by the end of Meiji were found elsewhere, first at the new Sumō

stadium east of the river, and later in the southern and western sub-
urbs. (Also, occasionally, in a department store.) The grounds of the
Asakusa Kannon Temple were famous for chrysanthemums early in
Meiji, but are no longer.

Asuka Hill, noted for its cherry blossoms, was the best place near
the city for autumn colors. At the end of the year there were hibernal
moors to be viewed, for the wasted moor ended the cycle, as snow had
begun it. Had nature been followed literally, the sequence could as
well have been the reverse; but an ancient tradition called for the
wasted and sere at the end of the cycle of grasses and flowers. For
the best among sere expanses, one went to Waseda, in the western
suburbs.

It is not surprising, though it is sad, that so many famous places of
early Meiji for the things of the seasons are missing from late-Meiji
lists. Gone, for instance, are the night cherries of the Yoshiwara, popular in the dim light of early Meiji. It is more surprising that many
places remain, in a larger, smokier city. A guide published by the city
in 1907 gives a discouraging report on the Sumida cherries, even then
being gnawed by industrial fumes and obscured by billboards. Yet it
has a ten-page list of excursions to famous places in and near the city.
Arranged by season, the list begins with felicitous New Year excursions, "all through the city," and ends with New Year markets,
"Nihombashi, Ginza, etc." Snow-viewing tides the cycle over from one
year to the next, and the Sumida embankment is still preeminent
among places for indulging. Most if not quite all of the flowers and
grasses are covered, from the plum (twenty-nine places recommended,
all in the city and the suburbs, with a new place, the Yasukuni Shrine,
at the head) to wasted moors (none left in the fifteen wards—only the
western and northern suburbs). The twenty-three places for viewing
cherry blossoms are headed, as they would have been at the end of
Edo, by Ueno and the Sumida embankment. The sixty-page section on
"pleasures" includes cemeteries and graves. They are chiefly for those
of an antiquarian bent, of course, but a Japanese cemetery can also be
pleasant for observing the passage of the seasons.

A person of leisure and some energy could have filled most of his
days with the round of annual and monthly observances. The same
guide contains a five-page list of monthly feast days at shrines and
temples, and only on the thirty-first day of a month would there have

been nowhere to go. In this too, tradition survives. No month in the lunar calendar had thirty-one days, and no thirty-first day in the solar calendar has been assigned a feast. Besides monthly feast days, most shrines had annual festivals, boisterous to the point of violence, centering upon the *mikoshi* "god-seats," portable shrines borne through the streets and alleys over which the honored god held sway. The god-seat sort of festival was among the great loves of the son of Edo, who, it was said, would happily pawn his wife to raise the necessary funds. Some of the god-seats were huge. Weaving down narrow streets on the shoulders of manic bearers who numbered as many as a hundred, they could go out of control and crash into a shopfront. Sometimes this happened on purpose. In Asakusa, especially, such assaults were welcomed: it was thought that if a god in his seat came crashing through the front of a shop, the devils must depart through the rear.

Some shrines and temples had annual markets, perhaps the most remarkable of them being the Bird Fair, the Tori no Ichi, on the days in November that fell on the zodiacal sign of the bird. It was held at several "eagle shrines" throughout the city, the most famous and popular of them just outside the Yoshiwara. Bird days occur either twice or three times in a month, and when they occurred in November the throngs at the Yoshiwara were enormous. They threatened the pillars of heaven and the sinews of earth, said Higuchi Ichiyō in the best of her short stories. It was believed that years in which November contained three bird days were also years in which "the flowers of Edo," the conflagrations, flourished.

Though obviously the motives were mixed for crowds so great and boisterous, it was essentially a shopkeepers' fair, and a part of the townsman's culture. The day of the bird was chosen from among the twelve because the Japanese love a pun. *Tori,* "bird," also means "taking in" or "reaping," and ornamental rakes were purchased at the market, as a means of assuring a profitable year. The rake merchants added a pleasant twist: to insure the flow of profits, a larger rake must be purchased every year. Bird fairs have declined in recent years, largely because the traditional business of the Yoshiwara has been outlawed. They have not, however, disappeared.

But many observances that must have been very amusing *are* gone. One no longer hears, for example, of "the watch of the twenty-sixth night." On that night in the Seventh Month under the lunar calendar (which would generally be August under the solar), people would gather along the coasts and in the high places of the city, waiting for the moon to rise. If it emerged in a triple image, presently falling back into a single one, it presaged uncommonly good luck. The watch lasted almost until dawn, since the twenty-sixth is very near the end of the lunar cycle. Devices were therefore at hand for enhancing the possibility of the triple image.

Annual observances were closely tied to the agrarian cycle even when they did not have to do specifically with the flowers, the grasses, the birds, and the insects. A sense of the fields has survived, despite the expansive ways of the city that had driven wasted moors from the fifteen wards by the end of Meiji, and eaten up most of the paddy and barley lands. Spring began in two ways, the lunar and the solar. The lunar way is now hardly noticed, but the solar way survives, with spring beginning, to the accompaniment of appropriate ritual, midway between the winter solstice and the vernal equinox. So it was that the city was awaiting the Two Hundred Tenth Day when the earthquake came.

Lists of "great festivals," the boisterous shrine affairs centering upon god-seats, always come in threes. The Kanda festival and the Sannō festival in Akasaka, to the southwest of the palace, are to be found on most Edo and Meiji lists of the big three.

The Sannō festival has fared badly in this century. Certainly it was among the great festivals of Edo, accorded condescending notice by Lord Tokugawa himself. The Sannō was the shrine to which baby Tokugawas were taken to be presented to the company of gods. It seemed to lose vigor as Tameike Pond, above which the shrine stood, silted in and was developed. Akasaka became a wealthy residential district and a place of chic entertainment, much patronized by the bureaucracy. The affluent bourgeoisie and the bureaucracy do not have much truck with shrine festivals, affairs of the Low City and the lower classes.

The Kanda festival had a troubled time in Meiji, for curious reasons, telling of conservatism and traditionalism. Two gods had in theory been worshipped at the Kanda Shrine. One of them was a proper mythological deity whose name scarcely anyone knew. The other was Taira Masakado, a tenth-century general who led a rebellion in the Kantō region. Unlike most Japanese rebels, he attempted to set himself up as emperor; the usual way has been to take the power but not the position. In 1874 the shrine priesthood, in somewhat sycophantic deference to the emperor cult of the new day, petitioned the governor to have Masakado removed, and another proper mythological entity brought from the Kashima Shrine in Ibaragi Prefecture. The festival languished. The demotion of Masakado, for whom a secondary shrine was presently built, is thought to have been responsible—this despite the fact that the arrival of the new deity, the other proper one, was boisterous. Resentment does seem to have been strong. Everyone had thought of the Kanda Shrine as belonging to Masakado, and he had a devoted following in his own East Country, whose inhabitants had for centuries been victims of Kyoto snobbishness. By 1884 old divisions and resentments were thought to have sufficiently healed that a good old-fashioned festival might be held. It was, and there was a typhoon on the second day, which the newspapers attributed to Masakado's anger. The press was frivolous, but one reads serious intent behind it. The Kanda festival never quite came into its own again.

If some observances disappeared in Meiji, others emerged into prominence, some quite new, some revivals, some revisions of the old. New Year celebrations culminated in a military parade, something new, and a review of the fire brigades, something old given a new turn. The latter had been banned for a time as dangerous. The danger was to the firemen who, dressed in traditional uniforms, did daring things high upon ladders. The old brigades were losing their practical significance, although it was not completely gone until after the earthquake. The New Year review was becoming show and no more, albeit exciting show, and aesthetically pleasing as well. It has survived, and seems in no danger now of disappearing.

Observances now so much a part of the landscape that they seem as venerable as the landscape itself frequently turn out to be no older than Meiji. The practice of taking small children to Shinto shrines in mid-November is an instance. Its origins are very old indeed, for it grew from the primitive custom of taking infants to a shrine at a certain age to confirm that a precarious bit of life had taken hold. It had been mainly an upper-class ritual in Edo, and did not begin to gain popularity in the Low City until mid-Meiji. The flying carp of Boys' Day must unfortunately be associated with militarism. They came into great vogue from about the time of the Sino-Japanese War. Boys' Day,

May 5, is now Children's Day, and the first day of summer by the old reckoning. Girls' Day, March 3, is not a holiday.

Some of the god-seat festivals were very famous and drew great crowds, but they were essentially local affairs, gatherings of the clan (the word *ujiko*, "member of the congregation," has that literal significance) to honor its Shinto god. There were other Shinto festivals of a more generally animistic nature, affairs for the whole city. The two biggest occurred in the summer, in the Sixth Month under the old calendar, transferred to July under the new. Both honored and propitiated the gods of nature, Mount Fuji in the one case and the Sumida River in the other, upon the commencement of the busy summer season, when both would be popular and a great deal would be asked of them.

The Sumida and Fuji were not the only river and mountain that had their summer "openings," but they were the most famous and popular. Besides honoring animistic deities, the observances had practical significance. The opening of the Sumida meant the beginning of the hot weather, and of the pleasures associated with seeking coolness upon the waters. The opening of Fuji, or any other mountain, was the signal for the summer crowds, less of a religious and more of a hedonistic bent as time went on, to start climbing. It was not considered safe earlier in the season, because of slides and storms. Both openings are still observed, the Fuji one now at the end of June, the Sumida one at a shifting date in July. Boating upon the Sumida is not the pleasure it once was, of course. The throngs upon Fuji are ever huger.

In the Edo and early Meiji periods there was a strongly religious element in an ascent of Fuji. The mountain cult was important from late Edo. The opening of the mountain was and is observed at several Fuji shrines through the city. Some may be recognized by artificial hillocks meant to be small likenesses of Fuji. Believers could with merit ascend one of them if an ascent of the real mountain was impractical. The most popular of the Fuji shrines is just north of Asakusa, to the east of the Yoshiwara. Several days in early summer (a single day is not incentive enough for moving the giant trees and rocks that are offered for sale) there are garden fairs north of Asakusa, and great crowds.

The Sumida had always had a special significance for the city. All the wards of the Low City but one either bordered it or fell but a few paces short of it, and the elegant pleasures of Edo could scarcely have done without it. The summer opening, at Ryōgoku Bridge, was a time of boats and splendid crowds and fireworks. Purveyed by two venerable and famous makers, each of which had its claque, they were of two kinds, stationary displays near water level, and rockets. General Grant joined the crowds in 1879. E. S. Morse was there earlier, and described what he saw with delight:

> At the river the sight was entrancing, the wide river as far as the eye could reach being thickly covered with boats and pleasure barges of all descriptions. We had permission to pass through the grounds of a daimyo, and his servants brought chairs to the edge of the river for our accommodation. After sitting for a few minutes we concluded to see the sights nearer, and at that moment a boat came slowly along the bank, the man soliciting patronage. We got aboard and were sculled into the midst of the crowds. It would be difficult to imagine a stranger scene than the one presented to us; hundreds of boats of all sizes,—great, square-bottomed boats; fine barges, many with awnings and canopies, all illuminated with bright-colored lanterns fringing the edge of the awnings. . . . It was a startling sight when we got near the place to see that the fireworks were being discharged from a large boat by a dozen naked men, firing off Roman candles and set pieces of a complex nature. It was a sight never to be forgotten: the men's bodies glistening in the light with the showers of sparks dropping like rain upon them, and, looking back, the swarms of boats, undulating up and down, illuminated by the brilliancy of the display; the new moon gradually setting, the stars shining with unusual brightness, the river dark, though reflecting the ten thousand lantern lights of all sizes and colors, and broken into rivulets by the oscillations of the boats.

Clara Whitney went too, and had mixed feelings:

> The Sumida stretched out before us, and for nearly a mile up and down it was covered by myriads of boats, from the clumsy canal boat to the gay little gondola dancing like a cockle shell on

the tiny wavelets. . . . Millions of lanterns covered the river as far as we could see until the sober Sumida looked like a sea of sparkling light. . . . It was altogether a very pretty sight—the brilliantly lighted houses, the illuminated river, the gay fireworks, and crowds of lanterns held aloft to prevent their being extinguished. . . . Like a stream of humanity they passed our perch and Mama and I spoke with sadness of their lost and hopeless condition spiritually.

There were, of course, changes in the festive pattern through Meiji and on into Taishō. New Year celebrations were less elaborate at the end of Meiji than at the beginning. Certain customs quite disappeared, such as the use of "treasure boats" to assure a good outcome for the "first dream of the year," which in turn was held to augur good or ill for the whole year. Treasure boats were paintings of sailing-boats manned by the Seven Gods of Good Luck or other bearers of good fortune. A treasure boat under a pillow, early in the New Year, assured the best sort of dreams. Conservative merchants paid particular heed to such matters, and so the simplification of the New Year may be taken as a sign of emergent modernism in commercial affairs. Meiji New Year celebrations lasted down to the "Bone New Year" on the twentieth of January, so designated because only bones remained from the feasts prepared late in the old year. They have gradually been shortened, so that little now happens after the fourth or fifth. In late Meiji there was still a three-day "Little New Year" centering on the fifteenth. The fifteenth is now Adults' Day, vaguely associated with the New Year in that it felicitates the coming of age. Under the old system New Year's Day was, so to speak, everyone's birthday. Reckoning of age was not by the "full count," from birthday to birthday, as it usually is today, but by the number of years in which one had lived. So everyone became a year older on New Year's Day.

Still, with all the changes, the flowers and grasses, the god-seats and the shrine fairs, survived. New Year celebrations became less prolonged and detailed. The advent of spring became less apparent in the eastern suburbs as industrial mists replaced natural ones. Nurseries were driven farther and farther north, and presently across the river into another prefecture. Yet the city remained close to nature as has no other great city in the world. In midsummer, for the festival of the dead, people returned in huge numbers to their villages, and those who could not go had village dances in the city. It was the double life at its best. Civilization and Enlightenment had to come, perhaps, but they did not require giving up the old sense of the earth. It is a part of Japanese modernization which other nations might wish to emulate, along with managerial methods and quality control and that sort of thing. No one can possibly have attended all the observances that survived from Edo through Meiji. It is a pity that no record-keeper seems to have established who attended the most.

The moods of a place will change, whatever its conscious or unconscious conservatism. The exotic and daring becomes commonplace, and other exotic and daring things await the transformation. Tolerance grows, the sense of novelty is dulled, and revolutions are accomplished without the aid of insistent revolutionaries. The old way did not go, but more and more it yielded to the new. The shift was increasingly pronounced in the last years of Meiji, after two ventures in foreign warfare.

If a native who departed Tokyo in 1870, at an age mature enough for clear observation and recollection, had returned for the first time forty years later, he would have found much to surprise him. He might also have been surprised at how little change there was in much of the city. The western part of Nihombashi and Kanda had their grand new banks, department stores, and universities, while fires played over the wooden clutter to the east. So too with trendier, more high-collar Kyōbashi: the new Ginza went as far as the Kyōbashi bridge, where the shadows of Edo took over.

He would have found ample changes, certainly: the new Ginza, the government complex to the south of the palace, the financial and managerial complex to the east. Scarcely a trace remained of the aristocratic dwellings that had stood between the outer and inner moats of the castle. He would have found department stores in place of the old "silk stores" (though he would still have found silk stores in large numbers as well), and an elevated railway pushing into the heart of the city, through what had been the abode of daimyo, badger, and fox.

He might have been more aware of a change in mood, and had more trouble defining it.

There was great insecurity in the early years of Meiji. Nagai Kafū describes it well in an autobiographical story titled "The Fox." The time is the aftermath of the Satsuma Rebellion. The place is Koishi-kawa, the northwest corner of the High City, above the Kōrakuen estate of the Mito Tokugawa family.

> The talk was uniformly cruel and gory, of conspirators, of assassinations, of armed robbers. The air was saturated with doubt and suspicion. At a house the status of whose owner called for a moderately imposing gate, or a mercantile house with impressive godowns, a murderous blade could at any time come flashing through the floor mats, the culprit having stolen under the veranda and lain in wait for sounds of sleep. I do not remember that anyone, not my father or my mother, gave spe-cific instructions, but roustabouts who frequented our house were set to keeping guard. As I lay in my nurse's arms through the cold winter night, the wooden clappers of the guards would echo across the silent grounds, sharp and cold.

Some of the disorder was mere brigandage, but most of it was obviously reactionary, directed at the merchant and politician of the new day, and reflecting a wish to return to the old seclusion. Of a piece with the reactionary radicalism of the 1930s, it suggests the gasps and convulsions of the dying. Already the Rokumeikan Period was approaching, and the high-water mark of Civilization and Enlighten-ment. The serving women in the Nagai house read illustrated roman-ces of the old Edo variety, and we know that their children would not. At the beginning of the Rokumeikan Period the revolution known as the Restoration was not yet complete and thorough. The violence was nationalistic in a sense, stirred by a longing for the secluded island past, but it suggests an afterglow rather than a kindling.

The Meiji Period was sprinkled with violence. It was there in the agitation for "people's rights" and the jingoism that inevitably came with the first great international adventure, the Sino-Japanese War of 1894–1895. The *sōshi* bully-boys of the eighties and nineties were a strange though markedly Japanese combination of the expansive and the narrow. They favored "people's rights" and they were very self-righteous and exclusive. "The Dynamite Song," "The Chinks," and

"Let's Get 'Em" were among their favorite militant songs. Not many voices were raised against the xenophobia, directed this time at fellow Orientals, save for those of a few faltering Christians. The disquiet of Kafū's boyhood was probably more serious, in that people lived in greater danger, but it was less baneful, something that looked to the past and was certain to die. The mood of the city at the end of the century was more modern.

Despite economic depression, it would seem to have been festive during the Sino-Japanese War. We hear for the first time of roistering at Roppongi, on the southern outskirts of the city, and so have the beginnings of what is now the most blatantly electronic of the city's pleasure centers. Roppongi prospered because of the army barracks it contained. What is now the noisiest playground of self-indulgent pacifism had its beginnings in militarism. The Ukiyoe print, also more than a little militarist and nationalist, had its last day of prosperity. Anything having to do with the war would sell. The great problem was the censors, who were slow to clear works for printing. Great crowds gathered before the print shops, and pickpockets thrived. The Kyōbashi police, with jurisdiction over the Ginza district, sent out special pickpocket patrols. No Japanese festive occasion is without its amusing curiosities. A Kyōbashi haberdashery had a big sale of cod-pieces, strongly recommended for soldiers about to be exposed to the rigors of the Chinese climate.

There was ugliness in the "Chink"-baiting and perhaps a touch of arrogance in the new confidence, and one may regret that Roppongi ever got started, to drain youth and money from less metallic pleasure centers. Yet, despite casualties and depression, the war must have been rather fun for the city.

The Russo-Japanese War of 1904–1905 was a more somber affair. The boisterous war songs of the Sino-Japanese War were missing. Nor were the makers of popular art as active. Pounds and tons of prints survive from the Sino-Japanese War; there is very little from the Russo-Japanese War. It may be said that the Ukiyoe died as a popular form in the inter-bellum decade. Dark spy rumors spread abroad. Archbishop Nikolai, from whom the Russian cathedral in Kanda derives its popular name, felt constrained to request police protection, for the first time in a career that went back to the last years of Edo.

The rioting that followed the Portsmouth Treaty in 1905 was a new thing. It was explicitly nationalist, and it seemed to demand something almost the opposite of what had been demanded by the violence of Kafū's boyhood. Japan had arrived, after having worked hard through the Meiji reign, and now must push its advantage. The politicians—the violence said—had too easily accepted the Portsmouth terms. The war itself had of course been the first serious engagement with a Western power. That it should have been followed by a burst of something like chauvinism is not surprising. Yet rioting could more understandably have been set off by the Triple Intervention that followed the Sino-Japanese War and took away some of the spoils. The early grievance was the greater one, and it produced no riots. The mood of the city in 1905 was even more modern.

On September 5, 1905, the day the Portsmouth Treaty was signed, a protest rally gathered in Hibiya Park. For the next two days rioting was widespread, and from the evening of the fifth to the evening of the sixth it seemed out of control. The rioters were free to do as they wished (or so it is said), and the police were powerless to stop them. Tokyo was, albeit briefly, a city without government. There were attacks on police boxes, on government offices, on the houses of notables, on a newspaper, and on the American legation. (Today the American embassy is an automatic target when anything happens anywhere, but what happened in 1905 was unprecedented, having to do with Theodore Roosevelt's offices as peacemaker.) Ten Christian churches were destroyed, all of them in the Low City. Casualties ran to upwards of a thousand, not quite half of them policemen and firemen. The largest number occurred in Kōjimachi Ward, where it all began, and where the largest concentration of government buildings was situated. Some distance behind, but with enough casualties that the three wards together accounted for about a third of the total, were two wards in the Low City, Asakusa and Honjo, opposite each other on the banks of the Sumida. It would be hard to say that everyone who participated did so for political reasons. Honjo might possibly be called a place of the new proletariat, now awakening to its political mission, but Asakusa is harder to explain. It was not rich, but it was dominated by conservative artisans and shopkeepers.

In some ways the violence was surprisingly polite. None was directed at the Rokumeikan or the Imperial Hotel, both of them symbols of Westernization and right across the street from Hibiya Park. Too much can be made of the attack on the American legation. It was unprecedented, but mild, no more than some shouting and heaving of stones. So it may be said that the violence, though widespread and energetic, was neither as political nor as threatening as it could have been. There was an element of the festive and the sporting in it all. There usually is when violence breaks out in this city.

Yet the Russo-Japanese War does seem to mark a turning point. Edo had not completely disappeared in the distance, but the pace of the departure began to increase. Our old child of Edo, back in 1910 after forty years, might well have been more surprised at the changes had he gone away then and come back a decade later. The end of a reign is conventionally taken as the end of a cultural phase, but the division between Meiji and Taishō would have been clearer if the Meiji emperor had died just after the Russo-Japanese War, in perhaps the fortieth year of his reign.

The Russo-Japanese War was followed by economic depression and, for the city, the only loss in population between the Restoration disturbances and the earthquake. Kōjimachi Ward, surrounding the palace, lost population in 1908, and the following year the regions to the north and east were seriously affected. When next a war came along, it brought no surge of patriotism; the main fighting was far away, and Japan had little to do with it. In an earlier day, however, there would have been huge pride in being among the victors. The city and the nation were getting more modern all the time.

4

THE DECAY
OF THE DECADENT

People like to think themselves different from other people; generally they like to think themselves superior. In the centuries of the Tokugawa seclusion, the Japanese had little occasion to assert differences between themselves and the rest of the world, nor would they have had much to go on, were such assertion desired. So the emphasis was on asserting differences among various kinds of Japanese. The son of Edo insisted on what made him different from the Osakan. He did it more energetically than the Osakan did the converse, and in this fact we may possibly find evidence that he felt inferior. Osaka was at the knee of His Majesty, whereas Edo was merely at the knee of Lord Tokugawa. Today it is Osaka that is more concerned with differences.

Aphorisms were composed characterizing the great Tokugawa cities. Some are clever and contain a measure of truth. Perhaps the best holds that the son of Kyoto ruined himself over dress, the son of Osaka ruined himself over food, and the son of Edo ruined himself looking at things.

This may seem inconsistent with other descriptions we have heard of the son of Edo, such as the one holding that he would pawn his wife to raise funds for a festival. There is no real inconsistency, however. What is meant is that Edo delighted in performances, all kinds of performances, including festivals and fairs. Performances were central to Edo culture, and at the top of the hierarchy, the focus of Edo connoisseurship, was the Kabuki theater. On a level scarcely lower were the licensed pleasure quarters. So intimately were the two related that it is difficult to assign either to the higher or the lower status. The great Kabuki actors set tastes and were popular heroes, and the Kabuki was for anyone (except perhaps the self-consciously aristocratic) who had enough money. The pleasure quarters, at their most elaborate, were only for male persons of taste and affluence, but the best of what its devotees got was very similar to what was to be had at the Kabuki. The difference between the two might be likened to the difference between a performance of a symphony or opera on the one hand and a chamber concert on the other.

It has been common among cultural historians to describe the culture of late Tokugawa as decadent. It definitely seemed so to the bureaucratic elite of the shogunate, and to eager propagandists for Civilization and Enlightenment as well. That it was unapologetically sensual and wanting in ideas seemed to them deplorable. They may not have been prudes, exactly, but they did want things to be edifying, intellectual, and uplifting, and to serve an easily definable purpose, such as the strengthening of the state and the elevating of the commonweal. If certain parts of the Edo heritage could be put to these purposes, very well. Everything else might expect righteous disapproval.

There is a certain narrow sense in which anything so centered upon carnal pleasure ought indeed to be described as decadent. However refined may have been the trappings of the theater and of its twin the pleasure quarter, sex lay behind them, and, worse, the purveying of sex. Perhaps something of the sort may also be said about the romantic love of the West. The high culture of Edo, in any event, the best that the merchant made of and for his city, is not to be understood except in terms of the theater and the pleasure quarters. What happened in these decadent realms is therefore central to the story of what happened to the Meiji city.

We have seen that General and Mrs. Grant visited the Kabuki in the summer of 1879. Probably the general did not know that he was participating in the movement to improve the Kabuki. It had already been elevated a considerable distance. Had he come as a guest of the shogunate, no one would have dreamed of taking him off to the far reaches of the city, where the theaters then were, and having disrepu-

table actors, however highly esteemed they might be by the townsmen
of Edo, perform for him and his Julia. His aristocratic hosts would not
have admitted to having seen a performance themselves, though some
of them might on occasion have stolen off to the edge of the city to see
what it was like. It belonged to the townsman's world, which was
different from theirs. Making it a part of high culture, which is what
"improvement" meant, had the effect of taking it from the townsman
and his world.

The Shintomiza, which the Grants visited, was managed by Morita
Kanya, the most innovative of early Meiji impresarios. The Kabuki had
been removed from the center of the city to Asakusa in that last seizure
of Tokugawa puritanism, a quarter of a century before the Restoration.
There, remote, the three major theaters still stood when the Restoration came. All three were soon to depart, and none survives. The
Nakamuraza, which stayed closest to the old grounds, was the first to
disappear. It was still in Asakusa Ward, near the Yanagibashi geisha
quarter, when in 1893 it was destroyed by fire one last time. The
Ichimuraza stayed longest on the Asakusa grounds, and survived until
1932, when one of repeated burnings proved to be its last.

The Moritaza left Asakusa most swiftly and with the most determi-
nation, and led the way into the new day. It took the new name
Shintomiza from the section of Kyōbashi, just east of Ginza, to which
Kanya moved it.

He had long harbored ambitions to return his theater to the center
of the city. He thought to make the move in stealth, because he wanted
none of his Asakusa colleagues to come tagging after him. He preferred
to be as far as possible from the old crowd, and especially from such
sponsors of the Kabuki as the fish wholesalers, who were likely to
oppose his reforming zeal. The Shintomi district was his choice for a
new site because it was near Ginza and because it was available, nothing of importance having come along to take the place of the defunct
New Shimabara licensed quarter. There were bureaucratic difficulties. His petition would be approved, he was told, only if it was presented jointly by all three theaters. By guile and determination he was
able to obtain the seals of the other two managers. He moved just after
the great Ginza fire, the rebuilding from which put Ginza at the forefront of Civilization and Enlightenment.

The first Shintomiza looks traditional enough in photographs, but certain architectural details, such as a copper-roofed tower, were a wonder and a pleasure to the Kabuki devotee. In the pit (though they are not apparent in woodcuts) were several dozen chairs, for the comfort of those who chose to attend in Western dress. Kanya's first Shintomiza burned in 1876. The theater visited by General Grant was opened in 1878.

Kanya was an enthusiastic improver—in content, in techniques, and in managerial methods. He introduced bright new lights, and theater evenings. Kabuki had been staged only during daylight hours, on moral grounds, it seems, and also for the practical reason that the fire hazard increased as darkness came on. With the opening of his second Shintomiza he greatly reduced the number of theater teahouses, with a view to eliminating them altogether. The teahouse functioned as a caterer and ticket agency, monopolizing the better seats. Kanya's endeavor to get rid of the teahouses was in the end a complete success, although it took time. Only complete control of the box office would

The Shintomiza

permit a rationalization of managerial methods. With little exaggeration, it might be said that he looked ahead to the impersonal efficiency of the computer. Old customs can be slow to disappear, however, when people find them a little expensive and time-consuming, but not unpleasant. That they should die was probably more important to entrepreneurs like Kanya than to the Low City Kabuki devotee. (Traces of the old system survive, even today, in box-office arrangements for Sumō wrestling.) In his boyhood Tanizaki Junichirō was taken to a more modern and rationally organized theater, the Kabukiza, and it still had teahouses. Tanizaki was born in 1886, almost a decade after the opening of the second Shintomiza.

> I remember how my heart raced as we set out by rickshaw, my mother and I, southwards from Nihombashi towards Tsukiji. My mother still called the Shintomi district Shimabara, from the licensed quarter of early Meiji. We crossed Sakura Bridge, passed Shimabara, where the Shintomiza then stood, and turned from Tsukiji Bridge to follow the Tsukiji canal. From Kamei Bridge we could see the dome of the Kabukiza, which was finished in 1889. This would have been perhaps four or five years later. There were eleven theater teahouses attached to the Kabukiza. Always when a play was on they had awnings draped from their roofs. We had our rickshaw pull up at the Kikuoka, where we would rest for a time. Urged on by a maid, we would slip into straw sandals and hurry over the boardwalks to the theater. I remember how strangely cold the smooth floor of the theater was as I slipped from the sandals. A cold blast of air always came through the wooden doors of a theater. It struck at the skirt and sleeves of a festive kimono, and was at one's throat and stomach like peppermint. There was a softness in it, as on a good day in the plum-blossom season. I would shiver, pleasantly.

Kanya spent a great deal of money on important officials and foreign visitors. On opening day of the second Shintomiza in 1878 all manner of notables, dressed in swallowtails, were set out upon the stage on chairs. The prime minister and the governor were among them, and so were most of the actors to whom the future belonged.

As an innovator, Kanya experimented boldly to bring modern elements into the Kabuki repertoire. The ninth Danjūrō became famous for his "living history," which sought to introduce literal reality into the properties and costumes of historical plays, while the fifth Kikugorō was renowned for his "cropped-head pieces"—plays with modern settings, distinguished by enlightened haircuts. Among Kikugorō's roles were the celebrated murderesses Takahashi O-den and Hanai O-ume, and Spencer the balloon man. Kanya even experimented with foreign performers and settings. Clara Whitney witnessed his most ambitious attempt at the cosmopolitan, *A Strange Tale of Castaways,* in 1879. A foreign lady from Yokohama trilled, "delightful on the high notes. But the best parts were spoiled because the Japanese, who thought it was something unusually funny, would laugh aloud. . . . I was quite out of patience." The experiment was a financial disaster, and Kanya's enthusiasm for Western things waned thereafter.

Kikugorō's balloon ascent did not join the Kabuki repertoire, but Kanya's experiments in stagecraft had a profound effect on the form. Near-darkness had prevailed in Edo, and he started it on its way to the almost blinding illumination of our time. The second Shintomiza had gaslights, but it may be that Kanya was not the very first to use them. E. S. Morse thus describes a visit to a theater, probably one of the two that still remained in Asakusa, in 1877:

> Coming up the raised aisle from the entrance, several actors stride along in a regular stage strut and swagger, the grandest of all having his face illuminated by a candle on the end of a long-handled pole held by a boy who moved along too and kept the candle constantly before the actor's face no matter how he turned. . . . There were five footlights, simply gas tubes standing up like sticks, three feet high, and unprotected by shade or screen, a very recent innovation; for before they had these flaring gas jets it was customary for each actor to have a boy with a candle to illuminate his face.

Conservative actors still attempt to follow old forms as they are recorded in Edo prints and manuscripts; but bright lights have changed Kabuki utterly. Kanya also introduced evening performances, permitted because the bright new lights were regarded as less of a fire hazard than the dim old lights had been. From Edo into Meiji, theaters sometimes opened as early as seven in the morning, to pack in as much as possible before dusk. We can but imagine how heavily the shadows hung over the old Kabuki, natural light and candles doing little to dispel them. Perhaps Kabuki was improved by the efforts of people such as Kanya, perhaps it was not; but certainly it was changed.

Kanya was a zealous reformer in another sense. The "movement for the improvement of the theater" had two aims in his most active years: to abolish what was thought to be the coarseness and vulgarity of late Edo, and to make the Kabuki socially acceptable, a fit genre for upper-class viewing, let the lower classes follow along as they could and would.

As early as 1872, there were bureaucratic utterances informing the Kabuki that it must cease being frivolous and salacious and start being edifying. Danjūrō—to his great discredit, many will say—was a leading exponent of improvement. Wearing striped pants and morning coat at the opening of the second Shintomiza, he read a statement on behalf of his fellow actors: "The theater of recent years has drunk up filth and reeked of the coarse and the mean. It has discredited the beautiful principle of rewarding good and chastising evil, it has fallen into mannerisms and distortions, it has been going steadily downhill. Perhaps at no time has the tendency been more marked than now. I, Danjūrō, am deeply grieved by these facts, and, in consultation with my colleagues, I have resolved to clean away the decay."

Improvement became an organized movement during the Rokumeikan Period, shortly after *The Mikado* was first performed in London. There seems to have been a link between the two events. *The Mikado* was the talk of the Rokumeikan set, which thought it a national insult. Proper retaliation, it seems, was the creation of a dramatic form that foreigners *had* to admire, in spite of themselves. The Society for Improving the Theater had among its founders the foreign minister and the education minister. The wantonness of the old Kabuki must be eliminated. An edifying drama, fit for noble ladies, domestic and foreign, must take its place.

These purifying endeavors had little permanent effect on the Kabuki repertoire. Danjūrō presently moved away from "living history," which had never been popular. Many found it incomprehensible. The novelist Mori Ogai advised the spectator to stuff his ears with cotton upon entering the theater. Danjūrō was all right to look at, he said, but dreadful to listen to.

Yet for better or for worse, the endeavor to make Kabuki socially acceptable did succeed. The emperor's presence always conferred the badge of respectability; he dutifully viewed what he was told to, and one form of entertainment after another received the badge. He went to see Sumō wrestling in 1884 at the Hama Palace; the grand match was, most fittingly for all, a draw. He viewed certain offerings of the variety halls—and in 1887 he attended a presentation of Kabuki, at the foreign minister's residence. Kanya was in charge of the arrangements, and Danjūrō headed the cast. The first performance, at which the emperor was present, lasted through the afternoon. The emperor did not leave until almost midnight. Danjūrō grumbled to Kanya that no actor could be expected to perform well with a truncated *hanamichi* (the processional way by which actors approach the stage through the pit), but of course he could not, on such an occasion, decline to go on. (Actors grumbled similarly, but likewise went on, when Kabuki came to New York in 1960.) On the second day the empress had her viewing, and on two succeeding days other members of the royal family, including the empress dowager, had theirs. The emperor was taciturn in his reaction, declaring merely that he found Kabuki unusual, but the empress wept so profusely at a play about the murder of a child that Kanya, alarmed, urged the actors to try understatement.

In Edo and the Tokyo of Meiji, the most highly esteemed Kabuki actors had enormous popularity and influence. They set styles, such as that for a certain kind of umbrella, which quite swept the place. Huge crowds, of which Tanizaki himself was sometimes a part, turned out for the funerals of famous actors.

Still in late Meiji, after the turn of the century, the Kabuki was, along with the licensed quarters, the form on which the high world of the Low City centered. At the end of Meiji a lumber merchant from east of the river, as in Osanai's novel *The Bank of the Big River* (see page 54), could still be a patron of the arts. One would not come upon his kind today. If modern actors have patrons, they are from the entrepreneurial aristocracy of the High City. In this fact is the measure of the success of the improvers in "improving" Kabuki and its actors, making them artists in an art acceptable to the elite. In the process, old ties were cut. The Kabuki and the demimonde are still close, but the demimonde too has cut its ties with the Low City. One would not be likely to find a person from east of the river among the big spenders.

Danjūrō is often reproved for obsequiousness and for indifference to the plebeian culture that produced Kabuki. Whether or not he is to be blamed for what happened, one may see the dispersal of the old mercantile culture in the changing sociology of the theater.

Morita Kanya's day of prosperity had already passed when Spencer came and Kikugorō took his balloon ride. It was at the Kabukiza that he took it. Opened in 1889, on the site east of Ginza where it still stands, the Kabukiza had a generally Western exterior, in a quiet Renaissance style. Some details suggest a wish to incorporate traditional elements as well. A fan-shaped composition on the central pediment looks in photographs like the ridge piece of a shrine or godown. Inside, the chief difference from the Shintomiza was in size: the Kabukiza was much larger. The great day of the former did not return and, immediately upon its opening, the Kabukiza became what it has been for almost a century, the chief seat of Tokyo Kabuki. Managerial methods

The Kabukiza, in a 1902 lithograph

were ever more modern, though the old teahouses were allowed in limited numbers, and yet humbler establishments as well, street stalls for which Ginza was still famous in the years after the surrender.

The improvers still were not satisfied. Even after the opening of the Kabukiza, they lacked a place where a gentleman might enjoy, in gentlemanly company, the traditional theater. So, in the last full year of Meiji, the Imperial Theater was opened beside the palace moat, on the western edge of Mitsubishi Meadow. Plans were begun in 1906. Shibusawa Eiichi, most energetic and versatile of Meiji entrepreneurs, was chairman. He was born in 1840, in what is now a part of metropolitan Tokyo. To the true son of Nihombashi he may have been a bumpkin, but his case further demonstrates that Osaka people were not the only successful ones in emergent Tokyo. He was everywhere, doing everything, among the organizers of the Bank of Japan, the First National Bank (the first incorporated bank in the land), the Oji Paper Company, Japan Mail Lines (N.Y.K.), and the private railway company that put through the first line to the far north. His was the somewhat Moorish house (see page 85) that seemed so strange to the young Tanizaki and other children of Nihombashi. Among the other organizers of the Imperial Theater were Prince Saionji and Prince Itō.

The first Imperial, which survived the disaster of 1945, was a highly Gallic structure of marble, hung with tapestries, and provided with seventeen hundred Western-style seats. Initially it had a resident Kabuki troupe, but it never really caught on as a place for Kabuki. The High City liked it better than did the Low City, which had a happy simile: seated in the Imperial, one felt like a cenotaph in a family shrine. The Imperial was the place for gala performances when, in the years before the earthquake, celebrities like Pavlova began appearing.

Theater was meanwhile becoming a big business, one which Osaka dominated. The theater and journalism, indeed, provide the best instances of the conquest of Tokyo by Osaka capital that is commonly averred and not easy to prove. It may be that Osaka money did best in fields of high risk and low capitalization. The Shōchiku company of Osaka bought the Shintomiza and another Tokyo theater in late Meiji, and in 1912 the Kabukiza. Shōchiku has dominated Kabuki ever since—but of course Kabuki has become a progressively smaller part of the city's entertainment business.

The large theaters were not the only theaters, nor was Asakusa bereft of Kabuki with the departure of the three major establishments. The name Miyatoza inspires great nostalgia, for that theater is held by many a connoisseur to have been the true heir to the Edo theater. It stood for forty years north of the Asakusa temple and park, very near the site of the big three. In 1896 a bankrupt theater was reopened under the name Miyatoza and new management, that of the enterprising Kanya. Miyato is an old name for the Sumida River. By the end of the century the important names in Meiji Kabuki were much too important to be associated with such a place, but many lesser and more traditional actors played there, as did most of the actors to be important in Taishō. The Miyatoza was destroyed in 1923, as the flames advanced upon the Asakusa Kannon but were held back by Danjūrō's statue (see page 7). It was rebuilt, and did not finally close until 1937. The lovelorn hero of Kafū's novella *The River Sumida* goes to the Miyatoza in search of forgetfulness. Asakusa has had nothing like it since. Nor, indeed, has Tokyo.

In 1873 the city issued regulations limiting the number of "proper theaters" to ten. These were theaters that had the appurtenances of grand Kabuki: *hanamichi* processional ways, revolving stages, drawn (as opposed to dropped) curtains, and teahouses. Smaller "Kabuki huts" were also permitted. By the end of Meiji the accumulated count of proper theaters, as one went and another came, was more than double the prescribed ten. The theater was a risky, unstable business, but some survived all the same. Except when rebuilding after fires, the Ichimuraza and the Moritaza stayed in business through the whole of Meiji. Two Kabuki theaters founded in Meiji yet survive, the Meijiza in Nihombashi and the Kabukiza. Neither is in its original building. The origins of the former lie in the years of the first Shintomiza, and so it has passed its centennial.

Kabuki was made proper and even elegant. In a sense, too, a kind of democratization was at work. The affluent bourgeoise from the High City does not at all mind being seen at a Kabuki opening with a Low City geisha a few seats away. The one is not demeaned and the other is perhaps somewhat elevated. Yet the form, as an institution, a play of social forces, has changed utterly; and because it was so crucial to the culture of the city, that has changed as well. The change was of course gradual. Yet something important happened when the Meiji emperor viewed Kabuki and so bestowed upon it the ultimate cachet.

Something important happened again when the Imperial Theater was opened, and the gentry finally had a place where they could watch the old theater comfortably, among people who knew them and whom they knew. The Low City had lost an element of its culture that had but a few decades before been of supreme importance. Other people and places gained, but the loss of something that harms scarcely anyone, and has a refining and even ennobling effect upon many, is sad. In later days the son of Edo may have ruined himself watching baseball. That seems a comedown, somehow, from ruining himself watching Kabuki.

Kabuki was the liveliest of the arts cultivated by the Edo townsman. It was expensive, however, and did not attract people as did the Yose, or variety halls. The term *Yose,* which has been rendered above as "vaudeville," is in fact an abbreviation of a word signifying "a place that brings in the crowds." The heart of it was the monologue, sometimes serious and edifying, sometimes comic. It was the genuinely popular theater.

The average admission for Kabuki ran seven and eight times that for Yose, not including the levies of the teahouses. The cheapest possible day at the Kabuki was twice as expensive as the average for Yose. Attendance at Yose consistently ran four and five times as high as attendance at the Kabuki theaters; and yet total revenues were smaller. The less affluent son of Edo, when he wished to be away from the noise and clutter of home, went to either a bathhouse or a Yose theater.

"There were no electric trolleys and no busses and taxis," wrote the playwright Osanai Kaoru late in his life. "Only horse trolleys ran along the main streets of the Low City. It was a very rare occasion indeed when the Tokyo person set out for Ginza or Asakusa after dark. He would for the most part range no farther than the night stalls in the neighborhood or perhaps a temple or shrine fair. Yose was his one real diversion. It was a bore to stay at home every night, and he could hardly go on a constant round of calls. Even the stroll among the night stalls was denied him on a rainy evening. So what he had left was Yose."

The sedentary father of a geisha in Osanai's *The Bank of the Big*

River goes off every afternoon to the serious, edifying sort of Yose. The playwright Hasegawa Shigure, who grew up in Nihombashi, describes a person in her neighborhood who spent his mornings at the bathhouse and in the afternoon had a good rest in a Yose hall.

The number of such places fluctuated through Meiji, but it was never under a hundred in the fifteen wards, and sometimes it ran as high as two hundred. The greatest concentration was in the less affluent wards of the Low City. In Shiba there were seventeen houses in 1882, and sixteen are listed in a guide published by the city in 1907. In Kanda there were twenty-two and seventeen, respectively.

The best Yose monologues may claim to be literature. Sanyūtei Enchō, the most famous of Meiji performers, is held by the literary historians to have been a pioneer in the creation of a modern colloquial prose style. Born in 1839 in the Yushima section of Hongō, the son of that Entarō who gave his name to the horse-drawn trolley and part of it to the taxi, he was active to the end of the nineteenth century. Like the great Danjūrō of the Kabuki, Enchō has had his critics, and for a similar reason: he too harbored a penchant for "improving," for making his genre acceptable to high society. He did edifying historical pieces (one of them about Queen Elizabeth) and adaptations from Western literature, clearly in an attempt to raise it to the level of high culture, suitable for noble gentlemen and ladies, and for the international set as well—to achieve for Yose, in short, what such improvers as Danjūrō were achieving for Kabuki. Perhaps he was also like Danjūrō in that his popularity did not quite match his fame. He was very good at publicizing himself. Recent scholarship has cast doubt upon the theory that he too was summoned to perform in the royal presence. The chronology does not accord, it seems, with what is known of the emperor's round of engagements. Perhaps, late in his life, Enchō made the story up, and no one saw any reason to doubt him.

Yose did not become excessively proper despite Enchō's efforts. It was not, like Kabuki, taken over by the upper classes and made over into an assembly at which a person of the lesser classes, an artisan or a shopkeeper, was likely to feel uncomfortable. Today it is performed in the National Theater (at rather unfriendly hours), but it survives in the Low City as well. When the writer Nagai Kafū—in rebellion against the High City and intent upon losing himself in low, traditional places—sought to become a Yose performer, a spy tattled upon him, and he was dragged home and presently sent into exile beyond the ocean. It is true that the family's reactions to his plans for a career as a Kabuki playwright were no more positive, but it seems likely that, had he persisted and avoided exile, his chances would have been better in improved Kabuki than in still benighted Yose.

Enchō's achievements were considerable all the same. His was only the biggest name among the many that made for Yose its last golden age. It began to decline from about the turn of the century, although it may be said that the Meiji flowering was in any event not as fine as that of late Edo. The puritanical reformers of the mid-nineteenth century, identifying pleasure with decay, had allowed only one Yose house for every thirty that earlier dotted the city. The Meiji total never reached the highest Edo total, upwards of five hundred. Edo is said, with only slight exaggeration, to have had a Yose house for every block.

Though it has declined grievously since late Meiji, enough remains that we may imagine what Yose was like in the best years of Edo and Meiji. By any standard it was superior to the popular entertainment of our day. A good storyteller, whether of the edifying or the amusing sort, was a virtuoso mimic. The *katsuben* narrator for the silent movies, a remarkable and uniquely Japanese performer, may be seen as successor to the Yose man of the great days. He too took (and still does, vestigially, in the surviving Yose halls) all the parts, distinguishing among them with most remarkable skill. Mass entertainment has come to be dominated by the popular singer and the talk man, neither of whom tries to be other than himself, occasionally interesting and often not. It is perhaps inevitable that this should happen as the mass has grown and the tightness of the Low City been dissipated. The story of decline is a sad one all the same.

The few houses that survive today (there are no more than a half-dozen in the city) are large by Meiji standards, holding several hundred people. The typical Meiji house was cozier, more neighborly, perhaps occupying the space up some back alley that had once accommodated a private house or two, now lost to fire or wind or rot. The great masters of Meiji Yose are said to have striven for small, intimate audiences. A hundred was the ideal size. Fewer than a hundred led to an appearance of unpopularity, and more than a hundred to a loss of rapport. When a theater became too popular, the leading performers would turn their duties over to disciples and wait for more manageable circumstances.

·   ·   ·

The son of plebeian Edo and Tokyo had many things besides Kabuki and Yose to look at and go bankrupt over. The grounds of the larger shrines and temples were often pleasure centers. The Asakusa Kannon, busiest of them all, was one vast and miscellaneous emporium for the performing arts. As Basil Hall Chamberlain and W. B. Mason observed in the 1891 edition of their guide to Japan:

> On no account should a visit to this popular temple and the grounds (*Kōenchi*) surrounding it be omitted; for it is the great holiday resort of the middle and lower classes, and nothing is more striking than the juxtaposition of piety and pleasure, of gorgeous altars and grotesque ex-votos, of pretty costumes and dingy idols, the clatter of clogs, cocks and hens and pigeons strutting about among the worshippers, children playing, soldiers smoking, believers chaffering with dealers of charms, ancient art, modern advertisements—in fine, a spectacle than which surely nothing more motley was ever witnessed within a religious edifice.

And again:

> The grounds of Asakusa are the quaintest and liveliest place in Tokyo. Here are raree shows, penny gaffs, performing monkeys, cheap photographers, street artists, jugglers, wrestlers, life-sized figures in clay, venders of toys and lollipops of every sort, and, circulating amidst all these cheap attractions, a seething crowd of busy holiday-makers.

The skill of jugglers, acrobats, magicians, paper cutters and folders, and the like was so remarkable that Japanese performers had already traveled abroad, to acclaim, before the Restoration. There are records of fat women and peacocks, pleasing to the child of Edo, from the very earliest years of the city. In the last decades of the shogunate, Asakusa was the most thriving pleasure center, for it had the Yoshiwara and the theaters in addition to its great temple. There were other centers, near the two Tokugawa mortuary temples at Ueno and Shiba, for instance, and across the river in Honjo, where the Ekōin Temple, erected in memory of those lost in the great fire of 1657, had become a place for cheering departed spirits as well as for remembering them. Asakusa, Ueno, and Ryōgoku, where the Ekōin is situated, had the most thriving of the *hirokōji*, the "broad alleys," originally cleared as firebreaks and scattered through the city. The broad alleys of Ueno and Ryōgoku did not fare well in Meiji, as Asakusa prospered more and more. The stalls and shows were presently moved from the immediate environs of the temple to the western edge of what had become Asakusa Park.

Some of the shows seem to have been inelegant, even grotesque. At Ryōgoku there was a man greatly skilled at breaking wind. For some years a spider man turned up on all the big Asakusa feast days. He had the head of an aged adult, a body some two feet tall, and the arms and legs of an infant. He was very popular. Also at Asakusa was a woman who smoked with her navel. The painter Kishida Ryūsei, born in 1891, described a puppet show in the Ginza of his boyhood, in which a she-devil slashed open the stomach of a pregnant woman and ate the foetus—or rather, being a doll, not up to the ingestion, announced that she would take it home for dinner. (It was Ryūsei who—see page 62—informed us of that particular Ginza pleasure, peeping in upon Shimbashi geisha as they made ready for a night.)

Many of the shows were free, some of them to aid in the hawking of medicines and the like, while some were willing to accept whatever pennies the viewer felt like tossing down. The larger shrines had stages for Kagura, "god performances," which also were free, and sometimes, as Tanizaki's reminiscences inform us, not very godly.

Kagura has all but disappeared from the shrines of Tokyo, festive performances are probably even rarer. The modern child would probably think it stupid beyond description, but I am filled with almost unbearable longing for the very feel of them, those naïve dances to drum and flute, the dancers masked as fool and as clown, on a long spring day in Nihombashi. . . .

The troupes would also perform for this and that banquet, but the one I saw most frequently offered skits on the grounds of the Meitoku Inari Shrine, very near our house, on the eighth of every month, the feast day, in the evening. A genuine "god dance" would sometimes be offered to the presiding deity, but more commonly there were skits. The performers were ama-

teurs with other occupations. One of them functioned as head
of the company, and even had a stage name, Suzume. All the
others referred to him as "the master."

About then, which is to say the autumn of 1897, there occurred in Ochanomizu the murder of Kono, a very famous one
that will doubtless be remembered by other old persons my age.
A man from Fukushima named Matsudaira Noriyoshi, aged
forty-one, who lived in Ushigome, murdered his common-law
wife, Kono, who had been a serving woman in a geisha quarter
and had accumulated a little money. He murdered her on the
night of April 26, the Bishamon Fair, and mutilated her face to
prevent identification. Wrapping the naked body in a straw mat
and tying it with ropes, he set it rolling down the slope at
Ochanomizu towards the Kanda River. It stopped some five
feet short and was immediately found. There was an enormous
stir. Noriyoshi was soon apprehended. The newspapers of
course made a huge thing of the incident, and in this and that
shop and in stalls on the day of the Suitengū fair I often saw
card-sized pictures of Kono's mutilated face among the usual
pictures of actors and geisha. Kono was forty, a year younger
than Noriyoshi. The line where her eyebrows had been shaved
was "iridescent," it was said, and she was "like a cherry still in
fresh leaf." That the new avant-garde theater should take the
incident up was inevitable. Already in June at the Ichimuraza
the troupe headed by Ii Yōhō and Yamaguchi Sadao presented a
"sensational" (or so it was proclaimed) version, along with *A
Comical Tour of Hell*. . . . It was perhaps a month later that I
saw the Suzume troupe do the affair on the Kagura stage of the
Meitoku Inari, in imitation of Yamaguchi and Kawai, who were
the murderer and his victim at the Ichimuraza. . . . Noriyoshi
. . . throttled her. Then, with the greatest concentration, he
carved several trenches on her face, and, lifting her head by the
hair, showed it to all of us. It seems strange that such a play
should have been done on the grand Kagura stage of a shrine,
and it does not seem strange at all, for it was a day when Kono's
face, on display in all the stalls, upset no one.

All the best-loved crimes of Meiji became material for the theater,
and all of them, probably because the dramatic possibilities were

heightened, involved women. A murdered woman, such as Kono, made good theater and good popular fiction, and a murderess was even better.

There was, for example, Harada Kinu, known as "O-kinu of the storm in the night," a reference to her last haiku, composed as she set out for the Kotsukappara execution grounds:

A storm in the night.
Dawn comes, nothing remains.
A flower's dream.

She was beheaded early in the spring of 1872. Heads of criminals were still put on display, in the old fashion. On his first trip from Yokohama to Tokyo, W. E. Griffis saw some, near the southern limits of the city. The newspapers reported that O-kinu's head possessed a weird, unearthly beauty. The concubine of a minor daimyo, she was left to fend for herself after the Restoration. She became the mistress of a pawnbroker and fell in love with a Kabuki actor, whom, in accepted style, she purchased. The affair proved to be more than a dalliance. One winter morning in 1871 she fed the pawnbroker rat poison, that she might live with the actor. She did so until apprehended. One may pity O-kinu, for she belonged to the class that suffered most in the revolution called Restoration.

The most famous of Meiji murderesses, vastly popular on stage and in fiction, was Takahashi O-den, who was beheaded in the Ichigaya prison in 1879 by the executioner who dispatched O-kinu. She too came from the lower ranks of the military class. The story of her misdeeds has probably been exaggerated by writers of popular fiction. She is charged with more than one poisoning before she committed the crime that took her to Ichigaya. Evidence in support of the charges is slight, and she was convicted only of slitting the throat of a used-clothes merchant in an Asakusa inn. She did it for the sincerest of motives: after the Restoration she had made her way chiefly by prostitution, and she robbed the merchant to pay the debts of her chief patron. Hers was the last case assigned to the famous executioner. He did it badly, wounding her before the final cut. There were horrible screams, according to newspaper accounts.

O-den, too, composed a final poem:

I wish to be no longer in this hapless world.
Make haste to take me over, O ford of the River of Death.

Her grave may be visited in the Yanaka Cemetery, where the poem is cut upon the stone. The little plot of earth is a sad one, beside a public lavatory, clinging precariously to the edge of the cemetery, given only cursory notice in guides that account for all the famous graves, such as that of Kafū's grandfather. The stone is not unimposing, however, and it is replete with bittersweet irony. It was erected in 1881 from contributions by most of the famous theatrical and journalistic persons of the day, and the man who collected the funds was Kanagaki Robun. Robun had rushed into woodcut print with a sensational story of her life a scant month after her execution. (He did a quickie on General Grant before the general had even departed the city.)

Among these dangerous women the most romantic was Hanai O-ume, the only one of the three who survived to enjoy her fame. It is generally agreed that she was less criminal than victim. She too came from the low ranks of the military class. After service as a geisha in Yanagibashi and Shimbashi, she opened a place of her own, near the river in Nihombashi. She was tormented by a former employee, Minekichi by name (it is a name with a nice ring to it), who wanted to

The execution of Takahashi O-den. From an 1879 woodcut

take over both her and her business. One night early in the summer of 1887, answering a summons to meet him on the bank of the canal that ran through her part of Nihombashi, she stabbed him thrice with his own butcher knife, beneath the willows, in a gentle rain. A troublesome and less than romantic detail is that she, and not he, may at the outset have been in possession of the knife. She was sentenced to life imprisonment and freed in 1903. In her last years she joined a troupe of traveling players; her most popular role was that of herself in her finest moment. She died in 1916, in a Yotsuya slum.

The performers who played murderer and victim in the drama described by Tanizaki were both men. So it will be seen that many conventions of Kabuki were retained by the "avant-garde" theater of the day, in spite of its aim to make the theater more Western and realistic. Men still played female roles.

In 1890 the chief of the Tokyo prefectural police let it be known that men and women might appear on the stage together. One of the two great Kabuki actors, improver Danjūrō, supported the policy, and the other, Kikugorō, opposed it. The Kabuki stage continued to be exclusively masculine. The new policy was revolutionary all the same, in a day when so many mixed things, such as bathing and wrestling, were held to accord ill with Enlightenment.

Women had never been absent from the performing arts. They had quite dominated the parlor varieties found at their best in the pleasure quarters. There were well-known actresses in late Meiji, and full-blown celebrities, symbols of their day, in Taishō. *Musumegidayū*, Osaka theater music (*gidayū*) performed by pretty girls (*musume*), was enormously popular in Meiji, especially among students, who seem to have found it erotic. In 1900, when the vogue was at its peak, there were more than a thousand *musumegidayū* performers in Tokyo.

Music was less disposed than other arts to go Western. The *musumegidayū* vogue passed, not so much because it was overtaken by Western forms as because other traditional forms came into fashion. Yet already in Meiji are to be found the beginnings of modern popular music, which, with its volatile trendiness, may be distinguished from folk music and from the various forms of stage music, popular or otherwise, as well.

The street minstrel known as the *enkashi* had his beginnings in the Tokyo of mid-Meiji and was still to be seen for perhaps a half-dozen years after the earthquake. He was such a part of late Meiji and of Taishō that he can scarcely be omitted from graphic and dramatic attempts to convey the mood of the day. The word *enkashi* may be written in two ways, one of them conveying merely "singer," the other something like "singer of amorous songs." The *enkashi* was Western at top and at bottom—bowler hat and shoes—and always accompanied himself on a violin. The remainder of his dress was Japanese. He would stand on a street corner and sing topical songs in return for pennies. The repertoire was in part amorous, but it was also strongly political and satirical. There were war songs and there were songs of a righteous nature criticizing the customs and manners of the day. Perhaps the nearest thing to a hit was called "The Voice of the Pine." In a satirical vein, it criticized the decadent ways of girl students, and might have been called anti-amorous. Fujiwara Yoshie, later to become the most famous of Japanese opera singers, got his start as an *enkashi*, in attendance upon the man who did the voice of the pine.

Three things to ruin oneself in the viewing of—the theater, cherry blossoms, and Sumō wrestling—were held to be the great delights of Meiji Tokyo. Sumō is a very ancient sport, its origins traceable, according to the earliest chronicles, to prehistory. It is more complex and sophisticated than at first sight it seems to be. The rules are simple: when a wrestler touches the ground with any part of himself save the soles of his feet, or when he is forced from the ring, he loses. It may seem that size is the only important thing, for the wrestlers in recent centuries have been huge. The hugest on record, however, have not been the most successful. There are delicate skills having to do with balance and timing.

Early in Meiji, change touched Sumō. Like so many things of Edo, it was meant for masculine enjoyment. In the last years of Edo, women were admitted to the audience only on the final day of a tournament. There seem to have been religious reasons for this exclusion, having to do vaguely with ritual purity. From 1872 women were admitted on every day except the first, and from 1877 they were admitted every day. The Sumō ring continues, however, to be sexist. No woman may step inside. When, recently, a boxer with a lady manager fought in the Sumō stadium, the manager was required to manage from a distance.

Sumō, as we have seen, was made respectable by a royal viewing. This happened in 1884, at the Hama Palace. Sumō had seemed in early Meiji to be declining, but in late Meiji it enjoyed popularity as never before. This was probably due less to royal notice than to the emergence of two uncommonly skilled wrestlers, one of whom fought to the famous draw in the royal presence.

In 1909 Sumō acquired the biggest sports arena in the city and indeed in the whole Orient, a great improvement over the shelters in which tournaments had earlier been held; they were so flimsy that competition had to be called off in bad weather. The new arena was named Kokugikan, "Hall of the National Accomplishment," and Sumō has since been thought of as that, although baseball might in recent years have better claimed the sobriquet. Before construction was begun in 1907 there was a lengthy hunt for a site. Marunouchi, the Mitsubishi Meadow, was considered, but rejected as too remote from the traditional Sumō base in the Low City. The promoters finally decided on an old tournament site at the Ekōin, east of the river. The Meiji building was gutted by fire in 1917, badly damaged in the earthquake, and afterwards rebuilt on the same site.

Sumō was modernized in another way. The "human rights" of wrestlers became a burning issue. Some thought the old authoritarian methods of training and management inappropriate to the new enlightened age. The Tokyo band of professional wrestlers, based at the Ekōin, split over the issue in 1873. The rebellious faction, advocating human rights, withdrew to Nagoya. Back in Tokyo soon after, it held its tournaments at Akihabara, south of Ueno. In 1878 the police intervened, being of the view that two rival bands in the same city had disruptive possibilities. The factions were brought together under a system of government licensing, although a number of wrestlers of advanced views refused to participate.

The rebels became the establishment, and were themselves presently the victims of a strike. This occurred in 1895. The immediate occasion was a contested decision, but the authoritarian ways of the people in control were the real issue. The strike succeeded in that the head of the family, who had been among the rebels of the earlier day, was shorn of his powers. Sumō has continued to be very conservative all the same. Managerial methods, long similar to those of the theater, have remained close to their origins.

Early in Meiji (the precise date is a subject of scholarly dispute) there occurred an event of great moment. Few events have affected the lives of more Japanese. A stick and several hard balls arrived in Yokohama, bringing baseball to Japan. The first games were somewhat aristocratic. They were played on the grounds of a mansion on the southern outskirts of Tokyo belonging to the Tayasu, an important branch of the Tokugawa clan. The early years of Japanese baseball were dominated by the Shimbashi Club, named from the railway station and yards. It included numbers of Americans in the employ of the government. The work of the catcher seems to have been hazardous, for neither mitt nor protector had come with the stick and balls.

By mid-Meiji there were several clubs here and there around the city, and school teams as well. The last years of the century were dominated by the First Higher School, most elitist of institutions. Baseball was still somewhat elegant and high-collar, but it was on the way to becoming business as well. Waseda and Keiō universities, whose teams are today not quite amateur, had their first engagement in 1903. The mood in the stands grew so murderous towards the end of their 1906 series that they did not meet again until late in the following reign.

An international game, believed to have been the first, took place in 1896 between a team of Japanese schoolboys and an American team from Yokohama. The Japanese won. A Japanese university team went to the United States in 1905, and two years later the first foreign team, semiprofessionals from Hawaii, came to Japan. On that occasion an admission fee was charged for the first time.

In 1890 there was an international incident, demonstrating even earlier than the Waseda-Keiō fanaticism how important baseball had become to the Japanese. During a game between Meiji Gakuin and the First Higher School an excited American dashed onto the field. He proved to be a missionary from the Meiji Gakuin faculty. After a pummeling by students from the First Higher School, he was arrested for disturbing the peace. A consular trial seemed in prospect, extraterritoriality yet prevailing. The view of the arbiter that both sides were at fault was accepted, however, and so the matter ended. It was long before the two schools were once again on friendly terms.

Baseball was something very new, a team sport. Traditional sporting encounters had been man-to-man. One can only speculate upon why baseball, among all the possible foreign importations, was chosen to become (as indeed it did) the national accomplishment. A prophet in early Meiji might have given cricket the better chance, for anglomania was strong. Today cricket is almost the only major foreign sport that does not interest Japanese at all.

Having had its beginnings in Tokyo, Japanese baseball is now everywhere. Like so many things, it continues to be dominated by Tokyo. The Tokyo Giants have a nationwide following that is rivaled by no Osaka team, and a Waseda-Keiō series still arouses passions such as are aroused by no other amateur (if somewhat professional) encounter.

Sumō became "the national accomplishment" in late Meiji, but its great popularity had to do less with nationalism than with the attributes and accomplishments of certain wrestlers. Judō, on the other hand, as distinguished from the earlier *jujitsu* (more properly *jujutsu*), fell definitely into the category of martial arts, and had strongly nationalist connotations. Its origins lie in mid-Meiji, in a temple of the Low City. The two words, *judō* and *jujitsu,* are almost synonymous, *judō* being a development of *jujitsu* in the direction of "the way," the Chinese Tao, with emphasis upon spiritual training and upon utter concentration and dedication. Perhaps more remarkable than *judō* itself were the organizing skills of the founder, Kanō Jigorō. The huge following which *judō* came to have meant a return to tradition, which in Japan often means nationalism. Yet the growing popularity of baseball, also in the last decades of Meiji, informs us that the nationalism of those years was not the sort of revivalism that wished to return to the old isolation and reject importations.

With engaging openness and a regard for reality, the guide published by the city in 1907 includes the licensed quarters in its pleasure section, along with the theater and other places to see things, and with graves and cemeteries as well.

The licensed quarters had a rather bad time of it in Meiji. They had been important cultural centers, and, though prostitution continued to flourish, they declined badly as places of culture. Nowhere was the decay of the decadent more in evidence than here.

The playwright Osanai Kaoru stated the matter well.

One has no trouble seeing why playwrights of Edo so often set their plays in the Yoshiwara. It was the fashion center and the musical center of Edo. In the dress of the courtesans and in the dress of their customers as well were the wanton colors and designs for all the latest rages. The brightness of the samisen when the ladies were on display, the quiet sadness of the old schools of music, Katō and Sonohachi: one no longer has them at the Yoshiwara. The courtesan has degenerated into a taste-less chalk drawing, the stylish clientele has given way to work-men's jackets and flat-top haircuts and rubber boots, and men-dicant musicians [*enkashi*] who play "Katyusha's Song" on the violin. The Yoshiwara of old was the veritable center of Edo society. The daimyo with his millions, the braves of whom everyone was talking, robbers in the grand style who aimed at aristocratic houses, all of them gathered in the Yoshiwara. When an accidental meeting was required, therefore, the Yoshiwara was the obvious place to have it occur. No play-wright would be silly enough to put the Yoshiwara of our day to such use. A chance encounter under the lights of the beer hall at the main gate would most likely involve a person with a north-country accent and a home-made cap, and his uncle, in the city with a petition to the Ministry of Commerce and Agri-culture. The customer sweetening his coffee with sugar cubes in a Western-style salon, given a farewell pat on his new muslin undershirt, would most likely be a numbers man in a visor cap, or a wandering singer of Osaka balladry who does the outskirts of town. No one could think of the Yoshiwara as in the slightest degree a romantic setting.

This passage is quoted by Kubota Mantarō, who remarks that the decay was still more pronounced after the earthquake. "Katyusha's Song," commonly held to be among the earliest examples of popular music, had first been sung by Matsui Sumako, most celebrated of Taishō actresses (see below, page 274), in a stage version of Tolstoy's *Resurrection.* After the earthquake, says Kubota, it gave way to "Ara-bian Love Song."

The demimonde did not disappear or even decline, but it changed. The best of music and the dance, not inferior to that of the Kabuki, with which it shared a great deal, had indeed been found in the quar-ters, and especially the oldest and largest of them, the Yoshiwara. It was what the big spender wanted and got. There were both male and female geisha, but the performing arts of the quarters were largely the province of women, as those of the Kabuki were exclusively the province of men.

The elegant word for the bright centers of the demimonde has long been *karyūkai,* which an earlier edition of the principal Japanese-English dictionary defines as "a frivolous community," and the most recent edition, with less flourish, "the gay quarters." The expression means literally "streets of flower and willow." It comes from Li Po, the great T'ang poet, who made the flower and willow similes for the ladies of the demimonde. For the purist there was a distinction between the two which has largely been forgotten, the flower being the courtesan and the willow the geisha.

The distinction was never widely respected, and even when it was accepted in theory it quickly ran into trouble in practice. *Geisha* is one of the most difficult words in the Japanese language to grasp and define. Literally it is "accomplished person." Nagai Kafū lamented the degeneration of the word and the concept, especially in the "geisha" quarters of the Meiji High City. Some geisha doubtless had a nunlike dedication to their artistic accomplishments, but many would have had trouble naming any that they possessed. They were for sale if the price and the asker were right. The grander of Edo courtesans, on the other hand, were sometimes very accomplished indeed, as little designs and billets-doux which survive from their hands demonstrate most clearly.

For all these imprecisions, the geisha and the courtesan had different places in the elaborate organization of the Edo Yoshiwara. To the former was entrusted the early part of a big evening, music and dance often of a very high quality, and to the other the more carnal business of the smaller hours.

As Meiji moved on towards Taishō, the geisha languished in the licensed quarters even as she thrived elsewhere. The licensed quarters became places of prostitution and little else, and for a more elegant sort of evening the affluent pleasure-seeker went rather to one of the geisha quarters. The change is seen most clearly in the fate of the *hikitejaya,* literally "teahouses that take one by the hand." Central to the organization of the old quarters, the "teahouses" were guides to and intermediaries for the bordellos proper. Houses of high grade did not receive customers directly, nor did the wealthy merchant, as he set forth upon an evening of pleasure, think of going immediately to a brothel. Preparations were made by a teahouse, to which the customer went first, there to be taken by the hand; and so ties between teahouse and geisha, male and female, were close. The teahouses were in large measure guardians of the old forms, and as they declined prostitution became almost the exclusive business of the quarters.

The number of licensed prostitutes declined through Meiji, unlicensed prostitution flourished, and, as Nagai Kafū did not tire of telling us, certain geisha quarters, especially in the High Town, were little better than centers of prostitution. More to the point than this decline in the rolls of the professionals is the sharp decline in the number of teahouses. A successor institution, the *machiai*, prospered as the teahouses declined. Originally antechambers to tea cottages, *machiai* became places of assignation and presently restaurants to which geisha were summoned. "Streets of flower and willow" came presently to mean geisha quarters, as the old teahouses, the *hikitejaya*, and also the boathouses that had seen people so elegantly and comfortably to the Yoshiwara, merged with or gave way to the new *machiai*. It is not to be thought that the geisha quite disappeared from the

A brothel in the Yoshiwara, as rebuilt after the Great Fire of 1911

Yoshiwara, where, indeed, some of the most talented and accomplished geisha of the Taishō period plied their trade. Geisha from all over town came to them for lessons.

The first thing that Civilization and Enlightenment did to the Yoshiwara and the other licensed quarters was to "liberate" their courtesans. An order of liberation was handed down by the Council of State, the high executive of the new government, late in 1872. It seems to have been a direct result of the *Maria Luz* affair, which gave international prominence to the licensed quarters. The captain of the *Maria Luz*, a Peruvian ship, was in 1872 convicted by a Yokohama court of running slaves, specifically Chinese coolies. In the course of the recriminations the Japanese were accused by the Peruvians of being slave traffickers themselves, their chief commodity being the ladies of the Yoshiwara and the other licensed quarters.

So the ladies of the quarters were liberated legally whether or not they wished to be, or had other means of subsistence. Stern measures were taken for the repression of "private," which is to say unlicensed, prostitution. The aging aunt in Kafū's *The River Sumida* had gone to the uncle for help when she was liberated, and was among the fortunate ones, for he married her.

There were other marks of enlightenment in the quarters. An 1874 newspaper reported that the young men who traditionally patrolled the night with wooden clappers, urging vigilance against fires, had taken to using trumpets. Not well received, the practice was soon abandoned. A fad for Western dress coincided with the Rokumeikan period. An enterprising bawdy house had Western beds in some of its rooms. The same house had a somewhat cosmopolitan staff, which included the first Okinawan courtesans active in Tokyo.

With liberation, the old brothels became *karizashiki*, literally "rooms for rent," and the crisis passed. The old trade was permitted under a new jargon, the ladies now in theory being free agents. They were permitted to do business in the rented rooms, so long as they were licensed. Six centers in and around the city had rooms for rent: the four "post-stations," Shinagawa, Shinjuku, Itabashi, and Senjū, which were the points of entry into the old city; and the Yoshiwara and Nezu (just north of Ueno). Prosperity returned as the new system proved as functional as the old. "A thousand houses, four thousand women, seven districts," went a saying of mid-Meiji, declaring the proportions of the trade. (Senjū had traditionally been counted as two post-stations, because roads from the north converged there as they entered the city; hence "seven districts.")

The Yoshiwara, the largest district, dwindled alarmingly in early Meiji, and after a decade or so began to revive. The number of houses on the eve of the Sino-Japanese War was still smaller than in the last years of Edo, though some of them were larger and more ornate houses by far than Edo had ever seen, grand edifices, indeed, of four and five storeys, with chandeliers, stained glass, and the like.

The quality of the several districts may be gauged from the importance to each of its teahouses. It was considerably higher at the Yoshiwara than at Nezu, the next largest district. Of the old post-stations, Shinagawa maintained the highest ratio of teahouses to brothels, though it was lower than at the Yoshiwara and about the same as that at Nezu. Shinagawa had been the most particular of the Edo post-stations, because it commanded the most important point of access to the city, from the south and west, and the most demanding clientele, from the Kansai. What these facts tell us is that the old forms were more perdurable at the Yoshiwara than elsewhere. While there were teahouses there was at least a possibility that an evening at the Yoshiwara would not be given over entirely to fleshly things.

By the end of Meiji there were no teahouses at all in Itabashi, where the inland road from the Kansai entered the city. It was the smallest of the districts, notably unsuccessful at coming to terms with the new age. At Shinjuku, the most triumphantly successful of the old post-stations in this regard, there were only nine teahouses serving fifty-eight establishments with "rooms for rent." At the Yoshiwara the number was a dozen times as large. The Yoshiwara was, after all, in its fashion, a guardian of tradition.

It had its own cycle of festivals, closely tied to the seasons. Observances were less punctilious and elaborate in Meiji than during the last years of Edo, and less still so as Meiji progressed. In late Edo there had been grand processions of courtesans, so laden with robes and ornaments and elevated upon pattens to such heights that they had to be supported. These processions honored the flowers of the seasons, and especially the cherry blossoms of the third day of the Third Month under the lunar calendar, the iris of the fifth day of the Fifth Month, and the chrysanthemums of the ninth day of the Ninth Month. A curious custom known as "heaped bedding," *tsumi yagu,* was still to be seen in Meiji, though less frequently and less elaborately than in Edo. The great courtesans demonstrated their popularity and the wealth of their patrons by public displays of bedding. It was a curious custom, and it must have been very erotic as well. The bedding, especially commissioned for display, was in gold and silver brocades and colored silks of extreme gaiety.

At least three Yoshiwara events still attracted whole families, men, women, and children. The main business of the quarter prospered, of course, but could hardly account for the throngs. More innocent amusements included the "night cherry blossoms," which the whole quarter turned out to view, and much of the city, and especially the Low City, as well. In late summer and early autumn the quarter set out lanterns in memory of an eighteenth-century courtesan of great popularity and sensitivity and high attainments, while dances known as Niwaka were performed on wheeled stages that moved up and down the main central street. They were sometimes humorous and sometimes solemnly dramatic, and the performers were the geisha, male and female, of the quarter. For obscure reasons, the observance declined sadly in late Meiji. Then on the two or three "bird days" of November came the Bird Fair, observed throughout the city but with an especial crowding at the Eagle Shrine just outside the quarter. On the days and nights of the fair the back gates of the quarter were opened to roisterers and the curious in general—on other days the main north gate was the only point of egress and ingress. The press and the stir were wondersome. Higuchi Ichiyō thus described them in her novella "Growing Up."

Not given to letting such chances pass, young men poured into the quarter from the back gates. The main gate was quiet, and so it was as if the directions had suddenly reversed themselves. One trembled lest the pillars of heaven and the sinews of the earth give way in the roar. Gangs pushed arm in arm across the drawbridges and into the Five Streets, plowing the crowd like boats plowing their way up the river. Music and dancing, shrill cries from the little houses along the moat, and samisen in the more dignified heights, a delirious confusion of sounds that the crowds would not soon forget.

The Yoshiwara Main Gate as it was in late Meiji and early Taishō

In the spring of 1881, when the cherry blossoms were in their greatest glory, a new main gate of wrought iron was dedicated. The inscription was a Chinese poem by Fukuchi Genichirō, president of the Tokyo prefectural council. He was paid the equivalent of fifty thousand dollars, thought by some excessive. No one in the quarter, male or female, failed to attend the dedication. The poem, two lines of eight Chinese characters each, may be rendered thus:

The deepening of a springtide dream. A teeming street overcast
　　by cherry blossoms.
First tidings of autumn. Twin rows of lanterns down the street.

It refers, of course, to the first two of the three great annual Yoshiwara observances.

So the old pleasure quarter, greeting the visitor with Chinese poetry from an eminent hand, was still in mid-Meiji a place of some culture; but it was declining. The great fire of 1911, the last full year of Meiji, dealt a grievous blow. On April 9, just one day short of three decades after the dedication of the iron gate, the Yoshiwara was almost completely destroyed. Two hundred brothels and teahouses were lost, within a few score of the total number. The quarter was rebuilt, but in a manner that appeared to demonstrate what may be expected in such cases, or to illustrate the proposition that the worst thing the West did was to make things easy and inexpensive. Old methods were discarded. They were too dear and too troublesome. The results of the rebuilding had a certain charm when they were in the whimsically ornamental style of Taishō, but when simple and utilitarian, tended to be merely dull. With what remained of the old they formed a rather motley stylistic triad. The loss of the teahouses left a permanent scar. Very little of high culture remained. The Yoshiwara became what it was to be until the outlawing of prostitution on April Fool's Day, 1958, a place of just that and nothing more. Kafū exaggerated when he said that the Low City of Edo died in the flood of 1910 and the Yoshiwara fire of 1911, but the old Yoshiwara never really recovered its earlier, if decadent, glory.

None of the Five Mouths, as the post-stations fringing the city were called, lay within the fifteen wards of the Meiji city. A part of Shinjuku was incorporated into Yotsuya Ward just before the earthquake, and Shinagawa lay just beyond the southern tip of Shiba, the southernmost ward. The other two were more remote. (As has been noted, there were actually only four "mouths," Senjū at the north being counted twice.) Though not central to the culture of Edo as the Yoshiwara was, they provided essentially the same pleasures and services. Each made its way through the Meiji era in a different fashion, and so they offer interesting variations upon the theme of change.

Shinagawa was the busiest of the four (or five), and second in size only to the Yoshiwara among the quarters of greater Edo. Very conservative, the Shinagawa station and quarter sought to remain apart from the new day. In this endeavor it was perhaps too successful. It was left alone, and dwindled to insignificance.

There was strong opposition in Shinagawa to the Shimbashi-Yokohama railroad. It ran along the coast, partly on fills, to the present Shinagawa Station, in Shiba Ward. Had it continued on the coast it would have passed very near the quarter. Instead it passed some distance inland. The quarter itself doubtless had less influence than the army on these arrangements, but a result was that the district around the new railway station prospered, and the old post-station, the "mouth," was isolated. It survived as a pleasure quarter, but a certain determination was required to get to it. This was true also of the Yoshiwara, and doubtless had something to do with the decline of that place as a cultural center. The rashness of choosing to stand apart from new traffic patterns was apparent earlier, however, in the case of Shinagawa. Where the Yoshiwara had always had its own very special attractions, Shinagawa had flourished only because it was beside the main Tōkaidō highway. The Shinagawa district lost population in late Meiji. It grew again in Taishō, but pleasure centers for the new city were by then emerging elsewhere. A private railway put through the district in the early years of this century was not enough to relieve the isolation, because there was no transfer to and from the main government line. This did not come until after the earthquake. The automobile age brought traffic back to Shinagawa, for the highway to Yokohama followed the old Tōkaidō, but by then it was too late. There were other places to go. In late Meiji and early Taishō the old Shinagawa station presented the curious picture of a bawdy district, with a few geisha to give it tone, cut off from the world by an encirclement of temples.

The case of Shinjuku was quite the opposite. It had been a relatively unimportant way station in the Tokugawa period, and even in mid-Meiji, when Shinagawa was being left behind, it was the smaller of the two quarters. It lay on the road to the province of Kai, the present Yamanashi Prefecture. The principal inland route to the Kansai now passes through Yamanashi, but did not then. The number of customers who might be expected to wander in from the highway or pass one last night on the road before venturing into the city was small. Shinjuku, meaning "New Station," was the parvenu among the Five Mouths, put together when the older Takaido station came to seem a bit too far out to serve as a first stop on the way to Kai.

Shinjuku was a lonely place under the Tokugawa. It did not immediately spring into prosperity with the beginning of the new day. Like Shinagawa, it was circumvented by the new transportation system. The railway that ran north and south along the western fringes of the city passed slightly to the west of it, even as the Tōkaidō line passed west of the Shinagawa quarter. There were two important differences, however: the old station, the "mouth," lay between the new station and the city, and within easy walking distance, and so the stroller need not have such a strong sense of purpose to get there as to reach Shinagawa; and the new station was to become an extremely important transfer point for commuters, the most important, indeed, in all the land. A private railway line, later bought by the government railways, was opened from Shinjuku westwards to Tachikawa in 1889.

The growth of Shinjuku as a residential district proceeded so briskly that it was the only significant annexation to the city through the Meiji and Taishō Periods. Its prosperity brought the decline of such geisha districts, nearer the city, as Yotsuya and Kagurazaka. The old pleasures of the way-station also got lost in the prosperity. The bawdy houses, very conspicuous on the main highway westwards from the city, embarrassed the bright new Shinjuku. There were plans, very long in the formulation, to put them out of sight on back streets. With the assistance of fires, the plans were well on the way to fruition when the earthquake came, making relocation easier. The old quarter gradually dwindled, though it survived long enough to be outlawed on that memorable April Fool's Day of 1958.

Itabashi was the earliest of the Five Mouths to fall into a decline. By the middle years of Meiji it had fewer houses and ladies than Shinjuku, and no teahouses at all. The old highway on which it stood, the inland route to the Kansai, had been important; especially in the years after Perry, it accommodated grand processions fearful of the exposed seashore route, among them that of the royal princess who traveled east to become the wife of the fourteenth shogun. Itabashi fell in the revolution that put everyone on wheels. There are still traces of the old post-station, but one has to hunt for them. Most of the old quarter was destroyed by fire in 1884. Though it was partly rebuilt, the old business continued to decline. After the earthquake Itabashi began to attract commuters and developers, not customers for the old quarter. It does not, like Shinagawa, seem to have striven to be left behind by the new day, but somehow it was.

Senjū provided two of the Five Mouths. There were two clusters for pleasure and lodging, known as the Upper Station and the Lower, on either bank of the Arakawa River (as the upper reaches of the Sumida are called) and Senjū did more than double duty as a way station. Three important roads converged upon it: from Mito, seat of one of the "three Tokugawa houses"; from the far north; and from Nikkō, mortuary shrine of the first and third shoguns. Of all of them, it best gives a sense today of what an old way-station was like. Senjū never languished like Itabashi nor throve like Shinjuku, and it did not, like Shinagawa, seek to reject the swift new wheels. In between, it has kept more of its past than any of the others.

The traveler from Edo usually proceeded northwards on foot, having arrived at Senjū on foot or by boat, as the great poet Bashō did in the seventeenth century. The modern road to the north does not follow the old road, which, therefore, escaped widening. There was another road, farther to the west, for grand official processions to Nikkō, and so Senjū did not get exceedingly important people, as Itabashi and Shinagawa did. Probably nothing made by man is old enough to have been seen by Bashō as he set out on his narrow road to the north, but there are yet patches of richly brown latticework and heavily tiled roofs, to suggest the sort of road it was. To reach Asakusa and Shitaya, the first considerable areas of dense population, the traveler still had to pass extensive farmlands. Senjū was thus fairly safe from the fires that so frequently afflicted the city.

The last of the districts, Nezu, on the fringes of Hongō, was an inconvenience in early Meiji, for it lay just down the hill from the old estate of the Maeda, lords of Kanazawa, which became the campus of the Imperial University. The proximity was not thought appropriate, since the young men of the university were the future of the nation. They must be kept from temptation, at least within walking distance. The Nezu quarter could simply have been closed, but that posed another problem: Such facilities were necessary to a city absorbing great floods of unattached young men from the country. Edo always contained more men than women, and Tokyo continues the pattern. So in 1888 the Nezu quarter was moved bodily to Susaki, which means something like "sandbar," filled land in Fukagawa near the mouths of the Sumida. Great celebrations on the occasion of the removal let everyone know where the quarter had gone. Through the remainder of Meiji and indeed down to the outlawing of prostitution, the transplanted quarter was the chief rival of the Yoshiwara as a "nightless city." After the fires of early Meiji, it may have looked more like the Yoshiwara of Edo than did the Yoshiwara itself. Photographs and prints show low buildings in good traditional taste, comparing well with the Yoshiwara and its tendency towards the flamboyant. The old customs seem to have survived better at Susaki than at the post-stations.

As Meiji came to an end and Taishō began, the flower and willow of the old system were drifting apart. The flower was the more carnal of the two, the willow or geisha the more artistic and spiritual. The flower came to dominate the licensed quarters, while the willow was preeminent in the geisha quarters. *Machiaijaya,* literally "rendezvous teahouse," is what is usually referred to by the English term "geisha house." A Japanese word exists that may be literally rendered "geisha house," but it is not commonly used, and is more likely to be found in bilingual dictionaries than in the purely Japanese sort. The inference is strong that it is a translation from English for the convenience of foreign persons. The rendezvous teahouse, in any event, developed into an elegant restaurant to which geisha were summoned. Lest it seem that the music and dance of Edo declined absolutely as they declined in the six licensed quarters, the geisha districts ask to be looked at.

Edo had its "geisha of the town," distinguished from the geisha of the licensed quarters. Some of the "town" districts still present through Meiji were very old, going all the way back to the seventeenth century. Some of the most flourishing quarters, on the other hand, had their beginnings only in Meiji. A census of geisha, both those attached to the licensed quarters and those of the town variety, shows that they were concentrated, not surprisingly, in the Low City. Three-quarters were in four of the fifteen wards: Nihombashi, Kyōbashi, Shiba, and Asakusa.

Geisha quarters were scattered over the flatlands, and in the hilly regions at least one, Kagurazaka, commenced operations at about the time Commodore Perry arrived. Other districts grew up in the High City of Meiji. They were neither as expensive nor as elegant, on the whole, as the best of the Low City districts.

The two great geisha districts of Meiji were Yanagibashi and Shimbashi. The Yanagibashi district, on the right bank of the Sumida south of Asakusa, was the Meiji quarter most esteemed by the connoisseur of old ways, and much reviled, as well, by those who thought that it was squandering its legacy. Narushima Ryūhoku's *New Chronicle of Yanagibashi (Ryūkyo Shinshi)* is a classic among satirical writings of the new age, as Ryūhoku himself was a classic son of Edo, one of the professionals. Ryūhoku, an "elegant sobriquet," suggests affinities with Yanagibashi. Literally, "North of the Willows," it derives from Yanagiwara or "Willowfield," the banks of the Kanda River near its confluence with the Sumida. Born in Asakusa in 1837, of a family of minor bureaucrats, Ryūhoku lived for some years to the north of Yanagiwara, and a slight distance to the west of Yanagibashi, "Willowbridge." Yanagibashi is thought, though without complete certainty, to have taken its name, as Ryūhoku took his sobriquet, from Yanagiwara.

He was in attendance upon two shoguns. Though he was for a time under house arrest because of critical remarks about persons in high places, he was given important assignments, such as seeking to keep the blue-eyed peril at bay. He served in a capacity roughly equivalent to that of Foreign Minister. With the collapse of the shogunate he was of course out of work and, like so many other men of the losing side, he went into journalism.

The first part of *New Chronicle of Yanagibashi* was written in 1859 and expanded in 1860. The Yanagibashi district had been in existence since the late eighteenth century, but its best age was in the last decades of Edo. The first section of the chronicle, starting with the premise (which must have had great immediacy in those years after the arrival of Perry) that we cannot be certain of the morrow, chronicles the standards and practices of the quarter in great detail. It is of a genre common and popular in late Edo, a display of connoisseurship that may have been helpful to the adolescent son of Edo embarking upon a career as a spendthrift, but may seem a touch self-satisfied and even pretentious to the outsider.

The work would probably be forgotten, save among specialists and bibliographers, had it not been for the advent of Meiji, a development not pleasing to experts on pleasure among the sons of Edo. Ryūhoku wrote a second installment in 1871. Both installments were published in 1874. A third installment, written in 1876, was banned, and Ryūhoku spent a time in jail because of it. The acerbity of the satire apparently passed limits. Only the introduction survives. Ryūhoku continued his journalistic career after his release, and died in 1884, securely established among the Edokko.

The chief interest of the *Chronicle* is in its account of what Meiji did to Yanagibashi. The first section tells us what it was like in the days of good taste and deportment. Then came the depredations of the new establishment. There are accounts of the violent and boorish ways of the new men, of parties at which people talk politics and ignore the geisha and her accomplishments, of speakers of English, of liberators and improvers. The geisha of the old school has no place in the new world, and the new variety is more interested in money than in art, and not easy to distinguish from the prostitute. She buys copies of the official gazette to determine how much her clients make, and has trouble identifying the father of her child. Thus has the corruption advanced, the decay of the decadent, even so early in Meiji. The son of Edo can only lament, and remember.

Ryūhoku's chronicle was extremely popular, although it is written in a highly sinified and ornate prose, remote from the tastes of our day. It is one of several works which were said to have forced up the price of paper. However valid his strictures may have been, Yanagibashi boasted famous and accomplished geisha through Meiji and beyond. Among the prosperous quarters of Meiji, it continued to be the one that had the closest ties with the old mercantile elite. Shimbashi and later Akasaka were the haunt of the new bureaucrat and businessman, while it was to Yanagibashi that the *danna* went, the Low City shopkeeper or wholesaler. (If he was really successful he probably no longer lived in the Low City, but that was another matter.) Yanagibashi was still the nearest of the quarters to Edo. It was favored by its situation, on the Sumida, just above Ryōgoku Bridge, where that finest of summertime observances, the opening of the river, took place. Fukagawa, most storied of the quarters of late Edo, lay on the opposite bank. Only at Yanagibashi could a singer of amorous balladry be expected to come rowing his way up to a *machiai,* or a geisha and her customers to go boating among lanterns and samisen. The Sumida was in those days still fairly odorless.

Yanagibashi was the principal geisha quarter of very late Edo and early Meiji. With the rebuilding of Ginza, Shimbashi came to rival it. The new people, bureaucratic and entrepreneurial, formed the Shimbashi clientele. A concentration of government buildings lay just to the west, and the big companies had their offices to the north. Shimbashi was among the places where the modern league of business and government, admired by some and reviled by others, took shape. It served the new establishment.

There had been "town geisha" in Shimbashi and Ginza from about the time of the Perry visit, and that watery region was a center for the *funayado* (see page 53). Shimbashi had its tradition then, but its great day began some twenty years after the Restoration. In late Meiji it was the quarter most favored by persons of money and power. The Shimbashi archetype was the country girl with energy and ambition, and a certain ruthlessness as well, in contrast to the Yanagibashi geisha, who inherited, or so it was said, the self-sacrificing pluck and verve of the Fukagawa geisha.

There were other geisha quarters, and they suffered vicissitudes. Old ones went, new ones came. The count of such quarters (as distinguished from the licensed quarters that deteriorated so grievously through Meiji) ran to almost thirty from Meiji into Taishō. Osanai Kaoru, in his novel about the banks of the big river, caught the last days of the big spenders from the Low City. There were still big spenders, but they were far less likely to be from regions near at hand. In what happened to the quarters, licensed and otherwise, is a measure of what was happening to the old mercantile culture in general. It was being scattered, dissipated.

The two disasters at the end of Meiji, the flood of 1910 and the fire of 1911, certainly worked great damage on the Low City. If one is intent upon finding a date for the death of Edo, one could do worse than follow Kafū and set it in the last years of Meiji.

It may be, however, that we are too easily disposed to see the death of a much-honored head of state as the end of an era. Events at the end of his reign or early in the next are taken as watersheds and given a prominence in cultural history that they might not otherwise have had. Kafū himself went on finding remnants of Edo to almost the end of his life, usually near the banks of the Sumida. His native High City interested him much less. There remained a difference between the two divisions of the city, for all the dilution and dispersal of Edo culture. He may have been wiser when he sought evidences of life than when he professed to know exactly the date of the demise of Edo.

The weakening of its old pleasures has been more pronounced in

the last half of the Tokyo century than it was in the first. The son of
Tokyo who had money to spend continued to do it as the son of Edo
had, on the theater and closely allied pursuits. The Imperial Theater
opened late in Meiji, of course, and then there were the movies, and
Pavlova, but the pastimes that took his money continued to be largely
traditional. If the Yoshiwara offered fewer of them on the eve of the
fire than on the eve of the Restoration, and fewer after the fire than
before, they were still to be had in places like Yanagibashi. Even today
it is an insensitive person who, wandering the Low City of a long
spring evening, does not come upon intimations of Edo.

It may be objected that the life of Edo and Meiji was not all pleasure. If a son of Edo spent himself into bankruptcy at the theater and
in the pleasure quarters, his family did not really think that he had
done the city and the family honor. The proper merchant had a severe
code, and disinheritance was likely to come before bankruptcy. To
insist upon pleasure as central to the culture of the city, and upon the
decay of the way of pleasure as symptomatic of wider decay, may therefore be a distortion.

Yet a sense of evanescence hung over Edo in its finest day even as
it hung over the Heian capital of a millennium before. The best things
did not last. They were put together of an evening and vanished in the
morning sunlight. The difference was that the Heian aristocrat had
things his way. If he wished to fuss over perfumes and tints, there was
no one to gainsay him. The merchant risked rebuke and even seizure,
neither of them happy eventualities. His pleasures had to be more
clandestine. He had his way only when he patronized actors and went
to the pleasure quarters. This did not mean that he was a person
whose taste was inferior to that of the Heian noble.

Meiji had its two sides. One cannot believe that Hasegawa Shigure
dissembled when she described her father's exultation at the removal
of the Edo stigma. Boundless new energies were liberated. To dwell
upon inequity and repression is to miss this very important fact. Perhaps, facing braver and broader worlds, the son of Edo was ashamed
that so much of his attention had gone into things so small. The big
new things were often coarser things, however. The pleasure quarters
presently lost their geisha, and the geisha presently lost their accomplishments. The world of the geisha may have been a cruel one, as the
world of the dedicated Kabuki actor was. No one should be sentenced

to involuntary service in such a world. Yet it is a pity that people ceased submitting, and that no one was left to appreciate the sacrifice. The son of Edo knew a good geisha and an accomplished actor when he saw one. Less art and discrimination go into the making and appreciating of a Ginza bar girl and a first baseman.

5

LOW CITY,
HIGH CITY

The old Tōkaidō highway from Kyoto and Osaka ran through Ginza and crossed one last bridge, Kyōbashi, "Capital Bridge," before it came to its terminus at the Nihombashi bridge. The boundary between the two wards, Nihombashi and Kyōbashi, crossed the old highway at a point halfway between the two bridges. They have since been combined to make Chūō Ward, which means Central Ward, and indeed they were central to the Low City, the only two wards that lay completely in the Low City by any definition.

Seen together they have an agreeably solid and stable shape, from the Hama Palace at the southwest to Ryōgoku bridge at the northeast. When they are separated into the two Meiji wards, a difference becomes apparent. Because it keeps reaching out into lands reclaimed from the bay, the southern half, the Kyōbashi half (with Ginza inside it), has the more expansive look today. In early Meiji and in Edo it was the constricted half.

Both districts were largely cut off from the Sumida and the bay by bureaucratic and aristocratic establishments. Yet it would have been possible at the beginning of Meiji to walk the mile or so northeastwards across Nihombashi from the outer moat of the palace to the river and see no aristocratic walls. Only two or three hundred yards eastwards, across the Ginza district in southern Kyōbashi, one would have bumped into the first of them. Whether so planned or not, the Tokugawa prison in the center of Nihombashi was as far removed on all sides from the aristocracy as any point in the city. On land-use maps of late Edo, Nihombashi seems the only district where the townsman had room to breathe. By the end of Meiji the upper classes, whether of the new plutocracy or the old aristocracy, had almost completely departed the Low City, and so Nihombashi, solidly plebeian from the outer moat to the river, looks yet more expansive. So does Kyōbashi, filled out by reclamation and largely relieved of the aristocracy.

A new distinction took the place of the old. Nihombashi was rich and powerful (though the shogunate in theory granted no power to merchants), the heart of commercial Edo. There the rich merchant lived and there the big stores were, Mitsui and Daimaru and the like. Kyōbashi was poorer and more dependent on the patronage of the aristocracy, a place of lesser shopkeepers and of artisans.

This was the historical difference. In Meiji the difference was between the new and the old, the modern and the traditional. After the opening of the Tokyo-Yokohama railroad and its own rebuilding, Ginza, in southern Kyōbashi, emerged as the part of the city most sensitive and hospitable to foreign influences. Nihombashi remained the center of the mercantile city, though toward the end of Meiji Marunouchi had begun its rise.

It is a simplification. The northern part of Kyōbashi, beyond the Kyōbashi Bridge, did not plunge into the new world as eagerly as Ginza to the south did, and Nihombashi was at once conservative and the site of the modern buildings most celebrated by Ukiyoe artists. The Hoterukan in Tsukiji, the southeastern part of Kyōbashi, was the earliest such building and certainly much celebrated, but it lasted a very short time. Blocks of brick, not individual buildings, were what the artists liked about Ginza. Nihombashi provided them with their best—and largest—instances of Civilization and Enlightenment.

So it is a simplification. Yet if one had wished a century ago to wander about in search of what it was that Meiji was departing from, one would have been wise to choose Nihombashi. If the quest was for the city of the future, Kyōbashi would have been the better choice. At a somewhat later date one could have gone to the Rokumeikan, in Kōjimachi to the west, but that was an elite sort of place, not for everyone every day. One needed an invitation, and social ambitions would have helped too.

The Mitsui Bank in Nihombashi

The Nihombashi Fish Market, about 1918

The First National Bank in Nihombashi

Much about the Meiji Ginza, and the Rokumeikan as well, is charming in retrospect. One would have loved being there, and one must lament that nothing at all survives, save those willow trees out by the Tama River. Much of the charm is in the fact that all is so utterly gone, and if to the person with antiquarian tendencies Ginza is today pleasanter than certain other centers of the advanced and the chic, that is because it is less advanced and chic than they. A century ago it would have been the most extremely chic of them all. Nihombashi on the contrary was the place with the coziest past, and, except for the parts nearest the palace and later the central railway station, the place most reluctant to part with that past. Today one must go farther to the north and east for suggestions of the old city that in Meiji were within a few minutes' walk of the foreign settlements.

At the proud forefront of Civilization and Enlightenment, the inner, affluent side of Nihombashi was later blessed with the new Bank of Japan, finished in 1896, and said to be the first genuinely foreign building of monumental proportions put up entirely by Japanese. Nihombashi was thus the financial center of the country, more modern, in a way, than Ginza even after Bricktown was built, because it was there and in government offices that the grand design for modernity was put together.

These modern structures, and the big department stores as well, were within a few paces of the Nihombashi bridge. Right there northeast of the bridge was also the fish market. It is striking in late Meiji how little of the modern and Western there is in a northeasterly direction from the bridge, off towards the Sumida. When, after the earthquake, Tanizaki rejected Tokyo and moved to the Kansai, he did it in a particularly pointed manner because he was rejecting his native Nihombashi, the very heart of the old city.

Nihombashi occupies the choice portion of the land earliest reclaimed from tidal marshes, the first Low City. It looks ample on Meiji maps, right there at the Otemon, the front gate of castle and palace. It is bounded on the north and east by water, and cut by the Nihombashi River, the busiest canal in the city. All this water suggests commerce. It is less watery than the wards east of the river, but the latter look, on maps of the Meiji city, as if they were still in process of reclamation, while Nihombashi looks as if reclamation had been accomplished long ago, and the canals left from the marshes for good, productive reasons.

Very little of Meiji remains in Nihombashi, and scarcely anything of Edo. Already in Meiji the wealthy, liberated from old class distinctions and what had in effect been a system of zoning, were moving to more elegant places. Already, too, Ginza and Marunouchi were rising to challenge its entrepreneurial supremacy. Yet there is something conservative about the air of the place. It has welcomed grand commercial and financial castles in the modern manner, but it has not welcomed glitter. It has never flashed as Ginza has, or been a playground like Asakusa.

In photographs looking eastwards from the Mitsukoshi Department Store, across the main north-south street, there is little on the eve of the earthquake that could not have survived (whether after all those fires it did or not) from Edo. There are modern buildings on the east side of the street, which was the great dividing line, and there is a financial cluster north of the Nihombashi River, where the Yasuda Bank, now the enormous Fuji, started growing; there too, at the juncture of the Nihombashi and the Sumida, the Bank of Japan had its first building, designed by Conder. For the most part, however, low roofs and wooden buildings in the grid pattern of the earliest years stretch on to the Sumida. It was among the parts of the Low City that had a smaller proportion of streets to buildings at the end of Meiji than at the beginning, and it looks that way. It is as if the snugness of Edo were still present, even though one knows that it could not have been. Vast numbers of country people had moved in and people like the Mitsuis had moved out, and the diaspora of the children of Edo (made so much of by people like Tanizaki) was well underway. Still the sense one has of conservatism is not mistaken.

The western part of Nihombashi did not begin going really modern until fairly late in Meiji. On the whole, Nihombashi was slower to change than Ginza or Marunouchi. The Nihombashi River was still at the end of Meiji lined by the godowns, some of them converted into dwellings, that had always been a symbol of the district and its mercantile prosperity. The Tanizaki family lived for a time in a godown. E. S. Morse wrote enthusiastically of converted godowns, which were doubtless ingenious, but other accounts inform us that they were as

A row of merchant houses in Nihombashi, about 1919

damp and badly aired as ever the Ginza bricktown was.

The aristocracy did not occupy much of old Nihombashi, and neither did the religions. There were shrines, though what was to become the most famous and popular of them, the Suitengū, Shrine of the Water God, was moved from another part of the city only in early Meiji. There were a few Buddhist temples, most of them founded in Meiji, half of them on the site of the old Tokugawa prison, dismantled in 1875. Initially they had a propitiatory function.

Nihombashi was not without pleasures, but moderate about them, perhaps in this regard nearer the Tokugawa ideal than Asakusa or Ginza. Not since the removal of the Yoshiwara to the northern paddies after the great fire of 1657 (the occasion also for moving most Nihombashi temples to the paddies) had Nihombashi provided the more elaborate and expensive of pastimes. Nevertheless, it was in the Hamachō geisha quarter, near the river in Nihombashi, that O-ume romantically murdered Minekichi. Hamachō was a modest quarter compared to Yanagibashi in Asakusa Ward to the north and Shimbashi to the south. Of the major theaters in the city today, the Meijiza in Nihombashi has the longest history. Probably at no time, except perhaps briefly when rivals were rebuilding from fires, could it have been described as the premier theater of the city. Yet it has survived, eminent but not supreme. This seems appropriate to conservative, steady Nihombashi.

The Mitsui Bank and the First National Bank of early Meiji were both torn down at about the time the new Bank of Japan was going up. Printmakers contrived to show the two buildings in isolation, or perhaps to imagine what they would have been like had it been possible to view them in isolation. Photographers could not or did not achieve the same effect. There can have been nothing like them in Edo, except perhaps, in a very vague way, the castle keep. Yet they do not look out of place. They are as if imagined by someone who had never actually seen a Western building (in fact the builder of both had studied in Yokohama), and whose idea of the Western was the traditional made bigger and showier.

There is nothing Japanese about the Bank of Japan. It is a pleasing enough building, but it is obviously the creation of someone who had studied Western architecture well and did not presume to have ideas of his own. Very much the same can be said of the Mitsui buildings that

The Mitsui Bank in Nihombashi, by Kiyochika

went up on or near the site of the early Meiji bank. Only the Bank of Japan and some bridges—one of them the main Nihombashi Bridge itself and one of them, the Tokiwa, the oldest stone bridge in the city—survive from Meiji. The brick Mitsui buildings and the new stone building of the First National Bank have long since gone the way of their more fanciful predecessors.

The early buildings would obviously not have lent themselves to the purposes of increasingly monstrous economic miracles. Yet both institutions, the Mitsui Bank and the Daiichi Kangyō Bank, as it is now, are so hugely rich that they could have set aside their first sallies into Western design as museums, and so enabled us to see for ourselves something that cannot be quite the same in photographs and prints— something confused, perhaps, but also lovable, like a child trying to look regal in clothes brought down from the attic. Of course, since most of Nihombashi was lost in 1923, it is likely that the two buildings would have vanished then even if the mercies of the banks had been more tender.

So Nihombashi did not stand apart from all the Meiji changes. There were changes that were still invisible. Nihombashi may to this day perhaps be called the financial center of the city and the land, for it has the Bank of Japan and the stock exchange; but big management has for the most part moved elsewhere. Neither of the two banks that so delighted the printmakers has its main offices in Nihombashi. The beginnings of the shift may be traced to late Meiji. Rival centers were growing, to the south and west; the big movements in the modern city have consistently been to the south and west.

The novelist Tayama Katai came to Tokyo in 1881 as a boy of ten, and was apprenticed to a publishing house in Nihombashi. More than half a century later he mused upon the contrast between the old Nihombashi and Ginza, and between the parts of Nihombashi, bustling commerce on the one hand and stagnation on the other.

> There was not a day when I did not cross the Nihombashi and Kyōbashi bridges. A dank, gloomy Nihombashi main street, lined mostly with earthen walls, as against the bricks of Ginza, across Kyōbashi. Entarō horse-drawn omnibuses sped past, splashing mud and sending forth trumpet calls. On the right side a short distance north of the Nihombashi Bridge . . . two or three doors from each other, were two large bookstores, the Suwaraya and the Yamashiroya, their large, rectangular shop signs dignified and venerable, of a sort that one sees in Edo illustrations. Yet what gloomy, deserted stores they were! Two or three clerks in Japanese dress would always be sitting there, in abject boredom, and I did not once see a customer come in to buy a book. The contrast with the house on the corner, the Echigoya, forerunner of the Mitsukoshi, could not have been more complete. One can still find the latter, I believe, in old pictures, a one-storey building with a long veranda, livening the district with an incessant shouting. It sounded rather like *"Owai, owai."* Customers were seated in rows, and the noise emerged from clerks ordering apprentices to get wares from the godown. Not only the Echigoya: on a corner towards the north and east was the yet larger Daimaru, and from it came that same *"Owai, owai."* . . .
>
> Ginza was then in the new style, with what were called its streets of brick, but from Kyōbashi to Nihombashi and on to Spectacle Bridge there was scarcely a building in the Western style. . . .

I was in Peking some years ago, and the crowding and confusion outside the Cheng-yang Gate—a pack of little shops and
stalls, bystanders munching happily away at this and that—
reminded me of early Meiji. It was indeed no different from the
stir and bustle, in those days, at the approaches to the Nihombashi Bridge.

All up and down the main Nihombashi street there were
shops with displays of polychrome woodcuts. . . .

Off towards Asakusa were shops with displays of something
approaching erotica. I was somewhat surprised—no, I should
say that I would stand on and on, fascinated, as if, in that day
when there no magazines worthy of the name, I were gazing at
life itself, and the secrets deep within it. But I doubt that the
approaches to the Nihombashi Bridge of Edo were in such disorder. In the confusion something still remained of very early
Meiji. I grow nostalgic for it, that air of the degenerate.

Nihombashi was wealthy, and it was poor and crowded. It had its
gloomy back streets, lined by windowless godowns, and it had its entertainment quarter, off towards the river, on land once occupied by the
aristocracy. Land in Nihombashi was, or so the popular image had it,
worth its volume in gold, but for a decent garden in any of the lands
reclaimed by the shogunate one had to import loam from the hills.
Great care and expense went into little gardens squeezed in among the
godowns. Besides gardeners, there were dealers in earth—not land but
earth—brought in to make mossy gardens. By late Meiji the very
wealthy had left, but it was still not uncommon for the middle ranks of
the mercantile class to have houses and gardens in Nihombashi even if
they owned land in the High City.

Tanizaki wrote about the dark back streets of eastern Nihombashi,
only a short walk from the entertainment districts. If he remarked
upon the contrast with Ginza on the south, Hasegawa Shigure contrasted it with Kanda, on the north. She had an aunt in Kanda, and it
was there that she had glimpses of the West not to be had in
Nihombashi.

She took me to see the Nikolai Cathedral, then under construction. It was when I stayed with her that I first heard the

sound of violin and piano and orchestra. In our part of the Low City such sounds and such instruments were quite unknown. So it was that I first caught the scent of the West. Kanda was where the students had their dens, where the intelligentsia, as we would call it today, assembled.

Katai thought the confusion of Nihombashi unlike Edo. The reminiscences of Shigure, who was born in Nihombashi in 1879, make it sound very much like Edo as it has remained in art and fiction.

On a late summer evening the breeze would come from the river as the tide rose. Hair washed and drying, bare feet, paper lanterns, platforms for taking the evening cool, salty cherry-blossom tea—all up and down the streets, under the stars, was the evening social, not to be savored by the rich ones and the aristocrats. It was easier and freer than the gathering in the bathhouse. The rows of houses were the background and the streets were the gathering place. If a policeman happened to be living in one of the row houses, he would become a human being once more, and join the assembly, hairy chest bare, kimono tucked up, a fan of tanned paper in his hand. He would not reprove the housewife if too much of her was exposed, and took it as a matter of course that the man next door should be out wearing nothing but a loincloth. . . .

Shinnai balladry would come, and *Gidayū,* and koto and samisen together. They were not badly done, for they had a knowledgeable audience. Strange, wonderful, distant strains would emerge from the gardens of the teahouses. . . . The samisen and the koto duos were mostly played by old women, most of them from the old Tokugawa bureaucratic class.

Just as in the lumberyards of Fukagawa no native was until the earthquake to be seen wearing a hat, so too it was in my part of Nihombashi. Down to the turn of the century a hat was a rare sight. The only hatted ones were men of affluence in party dress.

Photographs from late Meiji of eastern Nihombashi give an impression of changelessness, low-tiled roofs stretching on and on, but it

Nihombashi Bridge looking east, 1911

is perhaps somewhat misleading. Edo must have been even thus, one thinks, and one forgets that the low roofs stretched over a wider expanse at the end of Meiji than at the end of Edo. The abodes of the less affluent stretched now all across Nihombashi to the river, as they had not in Edo. Such places of pleasure as Nihombashi did have—the quarter where Minekichi got stabbed, the shrine that had the liveliest feast days—stood mostly on land once occupied by the aristocracy. The departure of the aristocracy was not in any case the loss that the departure of the wealthy merchant class was. Though the pleasure quarters had been heavily dependent on the furtive patronage of the aristocracy, it had not provided open patronage, and it had remained aloof from the city around it. So perhaps an irony emerges: the changes that occurred in eastern Nihombashi through Meiji may have been of a reactionary nature. The area may have been more like the Low City of Edo at the end of Meiji than at the beginning.

Nihombashi was proud of itself, in a quiet, dignified sort of way. The young Tanizaki was infatuated with the West and insisted upon rejection of the Japanese tradition, but he never let us forget that he was from Nihombashi. Perhaps more in Meiji than in Tokugawa it was the place to which all roads led—for a powerless court in Kyoto still then had powerful symbolic import.

Pride in self commonly brings (or perhaps it arises from) conservatism. In certain respects Nihombashi, especially its western reaches, was every bit as high-collar, as dedicated to Civilization and Enlightenment, as Ginza. Yet it was far from as ready to throw away everything in pursuit of the new and imported. If Nihombashi and Ginza represent the two sides of Meiji, conservative and madly innovative, Nihombashi by itself can be seen as representative of contradictions that were not after all contradictions. Now as in the seventh and eighth centuries, when China came flooding in, innovation *is* tradition.

It has continued to be thus, even down to our day. The last Meiji building in Ginza has just been demolished. The Bank of Japan yet stands. Nihombashi itself—which is to say, the corps of its residents—has probably had less to do with the preservation of the latter than the Ginza spirit has had to do with the destruction of the former. Yet there is fitness in this state of affairs. Nihombashi did not, like the Shinagawa licensed quarter, explicitly reject change; but perhaps it was the more genuinely conservative of the two.

On the eve of the earthquake there were probably more considerable expanses of Edo in Nihombashi than anywhere else in the city. Even today, when one has to hunt long for a low frame building of the old sort, Nihombashi looks far less like New York than do Ginza and Shinjuku. As a summer twilight gives way to darkness in eastern Nihombashi, one can still sense the sweet melancholy that Kafū so loved, and observe the communal cheerfulness that Shigure described so well.

Kyōbashi was a place of easier enthusiasms. On the north it merged with Nihombashi. To the south of the "Capital Bridge" from which it took its name, it was narrower and poorer, a district of artisans, for the most part, where it was a plebeian district at all. Considerably under half of the lands south of the bridge and the canal which it crossed belonged to the townsman.

In Meiji the Ginza district, in the southern part of Kyōbashi, changed abruptly. Some might have said that it ran to extremes as did no other part of the city. The original Ginza was the "Silver Seat" of the shogunate, one of its mints, moved from Shizuoka to the northern part of what is now Ginza early in the Tokugawa Period, and moved once more, to Nihombashi, in 1800. The name stayed behind, designating roughly the northern half of what is now Ginza. It may be used to refer to the lands lying between the Kyōbashi Bridge on the north and the Shimbashi Bridge on the south. (The ward extended yet further north.) In this sense it was the place where the West entered most tumultuously.

Kyōbashi was a very watery place, wateriest of the fifteen wards, save Fukagawa east of the river, where the transport, storage, and treatment of the city's lumber supply required a network of pools and canals. The Ginza district was entirely surrounded by water, and the abundance of canals to the east made the Kyōbashi coast the obvious place for storing unassimilable alien persons. They could be isolated from the populace, and vice versa, by water. Virtually all of the canals are now gone.

The Tōkaidō of the shoguns was the main north-south street in Meiji, and the main showplace of the new Bricktown. It still is the main Ginza street. In other respects Ginza has shifted.

Business and fun tended in a southerly direction when the railroad started bringing large numbers of people in from the south. If there was a main east-west street in this watery region it was the one the shogun took from the castle to his bayside villa, the Hama Palace of Meiji. It is now called Miyukidōri, "Street of the Royal Progress," because the emperor used it for visits to the naval college and the Hama Palace. Presently a street was put through directly eastwards from the southern arc of the inner palace moat, somewhat to the north of the Street of the Royal Progress. When Ginza commenced moving north again, with the extension of the railroad to the present central station, the crossing of the two, the old Tōkaidō and the street east from the inner moat, became the center of Ginza, and of the city. This was a gradual development, somewhat apparent in late Meiji, but not completely so, perhaps, until Taishō. Though the matter is clouded by the enormous growth of centers to the west, it might be said that the main Ginza crossing is still the center of the city. There was a span of decades, from late Meiji or from Taishō, when almost anyone, asked to identify the very center, would have said Ginza, and, more specifically, the main Ginza crossing.

Both the fire and the opening of the railroad occurred in 1872. The two of them provided the occasion for the great change, which was not as quick in coming as might have been expected. Bricktown, parts of it ready for occupancy by 1874, was too utterly new. It was the rage among sightseers, but not many wanted to stay on and run the risk of turning, as rumor had it, all blue and bloated, like a corpse from drowning. (There were other rumors, too, emphasizing, not unreasonably, the poor ventilation and the dampness.) In the early eighties, midway through the Meiji Period, the new Ginza really came to life. In 1882 horse-trolley service began on the main street, northwards through Nihombashi, with later extension to Asakusa. That same year there were arc lights, turning Ginza into an evening place. The age of Gimbura, a great Taishō institution, had begun. *Gimbura* is a contraction of *Ginza* and *burabura,* an adverb which indicates aimless wandering, or wandering which has as its only aim the chance pleasure that may lie along the way. It originally referred to the activities of the young Ginza vagrant, to be seen there at all hours. The emergence of the pursuit as something for all young people, whether good-for-nothing or not, came at about the time of the First World War.

Ginza began prospering by day as well. What was known as "the Kyōbashi mood" contrasted with the Nihombashi mood. One characterization of the contrast held Nihombashi to be for the child of Edo, Ginza for the child of Tokyo. In a later age it might have been said that Nihombashi still had something for the child of Meiji, while Ginza was for the child of Taishō, or Shōwa. Nihombashi contains relics of Meiji, and nothing at all remains, no brick upon another, of the Ginza Bricktown. The last bit of Meiji on the main Ginza street, completed as that reign was giving way to Taishō, has now been torn down.

The Ginza of Meiji is commonly called a place of the *narikin*. A *narikin* is a minor piece in Oriental chess that is suddenly converted into a piece of great power. It here refers to the *nouveau riche*. As pejorative in Japanese as it is in French, the expression contrasts the entrepreneurs of Ginza with such persons as the Mitsui of Nihombashi. The new people of Ginza were not such huge successes as the Mitsui, or the Iwasaki, with their Mitsubishi Meadow, but they were perhaps more interesting. Their stories have in them more of Meiji venturesomeness and bravery, and help to dispel the notion, propagated by Tanizaki Junichirō among others, that the children of Edo were lost in the bustle and enterprise of the new day.

All up and down Ginza were Horatio Algers, and possibly the most interesting of them was very much a son of Edo. Hattori Kintarō, founder of the Seiko Watch Company, was born to the east of the Ginza district proper, the son of a curio dealer, and apprenticed to a hardware store in the southern part of what is now Ginza. Across the street was a watch shop, in business before the Restoration, which he found more interesting than hardware. Refused apprenticeship there, he became apprenticed instead to a watch dealer in Nihombashi. He also frequented the foreign shops in Yokohama, and presently set up his own business, a very humble one, a street stall in fact. (Ginza had street stalls until after the Second World War.) The watch was among the symbols of Civilization and Enlightenment. An enormous watch is the mark of the Westernized dandy in satirical Meiji prints. Hattori had come upon a good thing, but only remarkable acumen and industry thrust him ahead of enterprises already well established. Within a few years he had accumulated enough capital to open a retailing and repair business of a more solidly sheltered sort, at the old family place east of Ginza. In 1885, when he was still in his twenties, he bought a building at what was to become the main Ginza crossing, the offices of a newspaper going out of business. The Hattori clock tower, in various incarnations, has been the accepted symbol of Ginza ever since. The same year he built the factory east of the river that was to grow into one of the largest watch manufacturers in the world.

It is not a story with its beginnings in rags, exactly, for he came from a respectable family of Low City shopkeepers. All the same, there is in it the essence of Ginza, spread out before the railway terminal that was the place of ingress and egress for all the new worlds of Meiji, and their products, such as watches, which no high-collar person of Meiji could be without. If the Rokumeikan, a few hundred yards west of Ginza, was the place where the upper class was seeking to make political profit from cosmopolitanism, the Hattori tower, there where the two trolley lines were to cross, marked the center of the world for mercantile adventuring.

Other instances of enterprise and novelty abounded. Shiseidō, the largest and most famous manufacturer of Western cosmetics, had its start in a Ginza pharmacy just after the great fire. The founder had been a naval pharmacist. He experimented with many novel things—soap, toothpaste, ice cream—before turning to the task, as his advertising had it, of taking the muddiness from the skin of the nation. His choice of a name for his innovative enterprise contained the Meiji spirit. It is a variant upon a phrase found in one of the oldest Chinese classics, signifying the innate essence of manifold phenomena. Today a person with such a line for sale would be more likely, if he wished a loan word, to choose a French or English one.

It was not only the great houses in Nihombashi that profited from an alliance with the bureaucracy. In early Meiji there were in Kyōbashi Ward two confectioneries with the name Fūgetsudō, one in what is now Ginza, the other north of the Kyōbashi Bridge. It was a model contest between the new and the old. The northern one sold traditional sweets, the southern one cookies and cakes of the Western kind. During the Sino-Japanese War the latter received a huge order for hardtack, upwards of sixty tons. The traditional Fūgetsudō admitted defeat, and the innovative Fūgetsudō, House of the Wind and the Moon, became the most famous confectioner in the city. The most successful of early bakeries, also a Ginza enterprise, had General Nogi among its patrons, and he helped bring it huge profits during *his* war, the Russo-Japanese War.

July 4, 1899, was a day to remember for several reasons, one of them being the end of the "unequal treaties," another the opening of the first beer hall in the land, near the Shimbashi end of Ginza. Very late in Meiji, Ginza pioneered in another institution, one that was to become a symbol of Taishō. This was the "café," forerunner of the expensive Ginza bar. Elegant and alluring female company came with the price of one's coffee, or whatever. The Plantain was the first of them, founded in 1911 not far from the Ebisu beer hall, at the south end of Ginza. The region had from early Meiji contained numerous "dubious houses" and small eating and drinking places, mixed in among more expensive geisha establishments. The Plantain was still there in 1945, when it was torn down in belated attempts to prepare firebreaks. Shortly after it opened it began to have competition. The still more famous Lion occupied a corner of the main Ginza crossing, and had among its regular customers Nagai Kafū, the most gifted chronicler of the enterprising if somewhat trying life of the café lady. One of them tried to blackmail him.

Ginza had the first gentlemen's social club, the Kōjunsha, founded in 1880. The name, a neologism compounded of elements suggesting

The lobby of the Kōjunsha

conviviality and sincere, open discussion, was coined by Fukuzawa Yukichi, a great coiner of new words and the most important publicist for Westernization. He was the founder of Keiō University and the builder of its elocution hall, towards that same end. Japanese must learn public speaking, argued Fukuzawa, and they must also become capable of casual, gentlemanly converse. The Kōjunsha was Fukuzawa's idea, and the money for it was provided by friends. It opened near Shimbashi in 1880 and is still there, just a hundred years old, in a building put up after the earthquake and already a period piece in the newness of Ginza.

The emperor himself was stumped by one enterprising Ginza merchant. On his way to Ueno in 1889 to open an industrial exposition, he saw in the northern part of Ginza a shop sign which he could not read. The name of the owner was clear enough, but the article purveyed was not, and the emperor was a man well educated in the classics. A courtier was sent to make inquiry. He came back with the information that the commodity in question was the briefcase. The shopkeeper had put together the characters for "leather" and "parcel," and assigned them a pronunciation recently borrowed from China and indicating a container. Awed by the royal inquiry, the shopkeeper inserted a phonetic guide. The shop sign became famous, and the word and the character entered the language and have stayed there. The sign was burned in 1923.

Some of the most famous modern educational institutions had their beginnings in the southern part of Kyōbashi Ward. The first naval college occupied a site near the foreign settlement. The commercial college that became Hitotsubashi University was founded in 1875 by Mori Arinori, most famous of Meiji education ministers, assassinated for his Westernizing ways on the day in 1889 when the Meiji constitution went into effect. Fukuzawa drafted the statement of purpose, a somewhat prophetic one: the coming test of strength would be mercantile, and victory could not be expected without a knowledge of the rules. His disciples learned the rules very well. Opened as Mori's private school in very modest quarters, the second floor of a purveyor of fish condiments, the college moved in 1876 to Kobikichō, east of Ginza proper. It was taken over by the city, and in 1885 by the Ministry of Education, which moved it to Kanda.

The middle school and girls' school that were the forerunners of Rikkyō or St. Paul's University had their origins in the Tsukiji foreign settlement, and by the end of Meiji had not moved far away. The origins of another famous missionary school, the Aoyama Gakuin, also lay in the foreign settlement of early Meiji, but by the end of Meiji it had moved into the southwestern suburbs.

Ginza did not, in this regard, stay for long at the forefront of Civilization and Enlightenment. The foreign settlement was gone as a legal entity by the end of Meiji, though foreigners continued to live and preach and teach there until the earthquake; but the missionary schools were moving elsewhere and all would soon be gone, leaving only the naval college as a place of higher education.

. . .

In another field of modern cultural endeavor Ginza quickly began to acquire a preeminence which it still in some measure maintains. Though not on the whole very popular, the Ginza brick buildings early caught the fancy of journalists. The newspaper is a modern institution, with a slight suggestion of ancestry in the "tile-print" broadsheets of Edo. The first daily newspaper in Japan was founded in 1870, moving from Yokohama to Ginza in 1879. Originally called the *Yokohama Mainichi* (the last half of the name meaning "daily"), it became the *Tokyo Mainichi* in 1906, after several changes of name between. It is not to be confused with the big *Mainichi* of today, which had a different name in Meiji, and was, with the *Asahi,* an intruder from Osaka.

The earliest Ginza newspaper—it occupied the site of the Hattori clock tower—seems to have been founded in the Tsukiji foreign settlement by an Englishman, J. R. Black. He was somewhat deceitfully treated by the government, which wished to purge Japanese-language journalism of foreigners. Offered a government job, he accepted it, and as soon as he was safely severed from his newspaper, the job was taken away. Late in Meiji an English performer in the variety halls had a certain vogue. He was the son of J. R. Black. The vogue did not last, and the son died in obscurity shortly after the earthquake.

In mid-Meiji, the Ginza contained as many as thirty newspaper offices. It was at this point that Osaka enterprise moved in, and, by its aggressive methods, reduced competition. At the end of Meiji, there were fewer papers in the city and in Ginza than there had been two or three decades before. Two of the big three had their origins in Osaka, and all three were, at the end of Meiji, in Ginza. The *Yomiuri,* the only native of Tokyo among the three, stayed longest in Ginza, and now it too is gone. Large numbers of regional newspapers still have Ginza offices, but middle and late Meiji was the great day for Ginza journalism.

Nihombashi may have had the most romantic of Meiji murders, but Ginza had an equally interesting one, of a curiously old-fashioned sort. What is believed to have been the last instance of the classical vendetta reached its dénouement just north of the old Shimbashi station in 1880. The assassin, who avenged the death of his parents, was of military origins, his family having owed fealty to a branch of the great

Kuroda family of Fukuoka. His parents were killed during the Restoration disturbances—victims, it seems, of clan politics. No attempt was made to punish their murderer; he was in fact treated well by his lord and then by the Meiji government, under which he made a successful career as a judge. After duty in the provinces he was assigned to the Tokyo Higher Court. The son of the murdered couple came up from Kyushu and spent his days stalking. On the chosen day, having failed to come upon his prey outside the court chambers, the vengeful son proceeded to the Kuroda house in what is now Ginza, and made polite inquiry as to the judge's whereabouts. The unhappy man chanced upon the scene and was stabbed to death. The son received a sentence of life imprisonment but was released in 1892, whereupon he went home to Kyushu to live out his days. Though vendettas had been frowned on by the old regime and were considered quite inappropriate to Civilization and Enlightenment, a certain admiration for this sturdy fidelity to old ways may account for the leniency shown in this instance. The Kuroda family moved away from Kyōbashi two years later and took up residence in the High City, not far from Keiō University. They would doubtless have left soon enough even if the incident had not sullied the old residence. It was the pattern. The area is today thrivingly commercial.

The prominence of the Ginza district in the theater was partly a result of things that happened in Meiji, when both the Shintomiza and the Kubukiza went up a few paces east of Ginza proper. It had an earlier theatrical tradition, from the very early years of the shogunate down to the Tempō edicts of the 1840s. It was the setting for a most delicious bit of theatrical impropriety: A lady in the service of the mother of the seventh shogun fell madly in love with an actor. Pretending to do her Confucian duty in visits to the Tokugawa tombs, she arranged assignations. When it all came out, the actor and the theater manager were exiled to a remote island, and the theater closed. The lady was sent off into the mountains of central Japan. One may still view the melodrama on the Kabuki stage.

Many are the delights in reading of Meiji Ginza. The ardor with which it pursued the West is infectious, and the mercantile adventuring of which it was the center has brought the land the affluence and the prestige that military adventuring failed to do. Both kinds of adventuring inform us persuasively that in modern Japan the realm of action has been more interesting than that of contemplation. Of the two the mercantile kind has certainly been the more effective and probably it has been the more interesting as well. Doubt and equivocation have characterized the realm of thought, whose obsessive themes are alienation and the quest for identity, not so very different from the sort of thing that exercises the modern intellectual the world over. It also dwells at great length on helplessness, the inability of tiny, isolated Japan to survive on its own resources and devices. Meanwhile the manufacturer and the salesman, by no means helpless, have been doing something genuinely extraordinary. The beginning of the way that has brought us to semiconductors and robots is in Meiji Ginza.

Gimbura beneath the neon lights of a spring or summer evening is still such a pleasure that one looks nostalgically back to the day when Ginza was the undisputed center of the city and of the land. Yet Ginza and Gimbura have taken on a patina. There are noisier and more generously amplified entertainment and shopping centers to the south and west, and it is to them that the young are inclined to swarm. Gimbura has the look of a slightly earlier time. When it was all the rage, the person who now feels nostalgia for the Ginza of old might well have been drawn more strongly to conservative Nihombashi, where it was still possible to wander in the Edo twilight.

Had one gone about asking townsmen at the beginning of Meiji to define the northern limits of the Low City, there would probably have been a difference of opinion. Some would have said that it ended at the Kanda River or slightly beyond, and so included only Nihombashi, the flat part of Kanda, and perhaps a bit more. Others might have been more generous, and extended it to include the merchant quarters around the Asakusa Kannon Temple and below the Tokugawa tombs at Ueno. These last were essentially islands, however, cut off from the main Low City by aristocratic and bureaucratic lands.

At the end of Meiji everyone would have included Asakusa and Shitaya wards, the latter incorporating Ueno. These wards had filled up and the upper classes had almost vanished, along with many of the temples and cemeteries. Except for a few remaining paddy lands, the Low City reached to the city limits, and in some places spilled beyond.

"The temple of Kuanon at Asakǔsa is to Tōkiō what St. Paul's is to

London, or Nôtre Dame to Paris," said W. E. Griffis. It was a place that fascinated most foreigners, even Isabella Bird, who did not for the most part waver in her determination to find unbeaten tracks. Griffis was right, though Asakusa was more than a religious center—or rather it was a Japanese sort of religious center, one which welcomed pleasure to the sacred precincts.

Griffis's description was perhaps more telling than he realized. "At the north end are ranged the archery galleries, also presided over by pretty black-eyed Dianas, in paint, powder, and shining coiffure. They bring you tea, smile, talk nonsense, and giggle; smoke their long pipes with tiny bowls full of mild, fine-cut tobacco; puff out the long white whiffs from their flat-bridged noses; wipe the brass mouth-piece, and offer it to you; and then ask you leading and very personal questions without blushing. . . . Full grown, able-bodied men are the chief patrons of these places of pleasure, and many can find amusement for hours at such play."

The description suggests "places of pleasure" in a more specific sense, and indeed that is what they were. The back rooms were for prostitution—right there in the yard (the back yard, but still the yard) of the great temple. More than one early foreign visitor remarked, with a certain not unpleasant confusion, upon a very large painting of a courtesan which hung in the main hall, but no one seems to have noted the true nature of the archery stalls.

Griffis's description extends over more than a chapter of his memoirs. It is lively and it is sad. Today some tiny outbuildings and a stone bridge survive from Edo, and nothing else, save a few perdurable trees. The melancholy derives not only from physical change; if most of the buildings are gone, so too is most of the life. The main buildings, which had survived the earthquake, were lost in 1945. Asakusa continued even so to be a pleasure center. Then, gradually, people stopped coming. Troops of rustic pilgrims still visit the temple, but the urban crowds, and especially the young, go elsewhere. Asakusa was too confident. With its Kannon and its Yoshiwara, it had, so it thought, no need of railroads, and it was wrong.

Asakusa and Shitaya, from what is now Ueno Park to the Sumida, were a part of the zone of temples and cemeteries extending in a great sweep around the Tokugawa city. One could have walked from where the northernmost platforms of Ueno Station now stand nearly to the

river, passing scarcely anything but temples. Plebeian houses, waiting
to be flooded every two or three years, lined the river bank itself. (The
riverside park of our own day was laid out after the earthquake.) Edo
was a zoned city, and among the zones was one for the dead. Not
wanting them too near at hand, the shogunate established a ring of
necropoles at the city limits. Many temples remained at the end of
Meiji and a scattering remains today, making Asakusa and Shitaya the
most rewarding part of the city for the fancier of tombstones and epi-
taphs. A late-Meiji guide to the city lists 132 temples in Asakusa Ward
and 86 in Shitaya. Temple lands shrank greatly, however, as the region
became a part of the main Low City, and the pressure on lands near
the center of the city led to the closing and removal of cemeteries.

Along towards mid-Meiji the metropolitan government embarked
upon the creation of an early version of the public mall or shopping
center. On land that had been occupied chiefly by chapels in attendance upon the Kannon, the city built two rows of brick shops, forming
a lane from the horse trolley to the south or main front of the grand
hall. The city retained ownership and rented the shops. The original
buildings were casualties of the earthquake, but the prospect today is
similar to that of 1885, when construction was finished. It is not dis-
pleasing. Though no longer Meiji it rather looks it, and is perhaps
somewhat reminiscent as well of the Ginza Bricktown.

From late Meiji into Taishō there had grown up what sons of Edo
called the new Asakusa, generally to the south and west of the
Kannon. Then came the earthquake, to destroy almost everything save
the Kannon itself, and afterwards, those same sons inform us, the new
quite took over.

"The word 'Asakusa,'" said Akutagawa, who grew up in Honjo,
across the river, "first calls to mind the vermilion hall of the temple—
or the complex centered upon the hall, with the flanking pagoda and
gate. We may be thankful that they came through the recent earthquake and fire. Now, as always at this season, droves of pigeons will be
describing a great circle around the bright gold of the gingko, with that
great screen of vermilion spread out behind it. Then there comes to
mind the lake and the little pleasure stalls, all of them reduced to
cinders after the earthquake. The third Asakusa is a modest part of the
old Low City. Hanakawado, Sanya, Komagata, Kuramae—and several
other districts would do as well. Tiled roofs after a rain, unlighted

Ladies of the Kadoebi, a leading house of the Yoshiwara. Note the stained-glass windows.

The Meiji emperor and his empress pass the government buildings at Kasumigaseki, 1902.

Cherry-blossom time at Ueno Park, with the statue of Saigō Takamori, leader of the Satsuma Rebellion of 1877. From a lithograph dated 1915.

Two woodcuts by Yasuji, after Kiyochika. *Top:* A nighttime view showing the Mitsukoshi Department Store at left, and a shadowy Mitsui Bank (compare daylight scene on p. 192). *Bottom:* View from a pavilion on Atago Hill, looking eastward toward Tokyo Bay.

The Meiji emperor's funeral procession, 1912.

Hashiba, a favorite rural excursion site north of the Yoshiwara. Woodcut by Kiyochika.

Shops at Asakusa. Woodcut by Kiyochika.

Early spring in front of
Tokyo Station—a lithograph by
Kakiuchi Seiyō that epitomizes
the Taishō Look.

Another Taishō scene, in Hibiya Park. A lithograph by Itō Shinsui.

Right: A portion of the Taishō Exposition in Ueno Park, imaginatively tinted.

Below: Nihombashi Fish Market in 1898. From a lithograph that was originally printed reversed.

votive lanterns, pots of morning glories, now withered. This too, all of it, was left a charred waste."

The pleasure stalls, said Kubota Mantarō, "are the heart of the new Asakusa, Asakusa as it now will be":

> This Asakusa took the recent disaster in its stride. . . .
> But the other, the old Asakusa.
> Let the reader come with me—it will not take long—to the top of Matsuchi Hill. . . . We will look northwards through the trees, towards the Sanya Canal. The color of the stagnant water, now as long ago, is like blackened teeth; but how are we to describe the emptiness that stretches on beyond the canal and the cemetery just to the north, and on through mists to the fuel tanks of Senjū, under a gray sky? The little bell tower of the Keiyōji Temple, a curious survivor, and the glowing branches of the gingkos, and the Sanya Elementary School, hastily rebuilt, and nothing else, all the way north, to catch the eye.
> Let us go down the hill and cross Imado Bridge. . . . No suggestion remains of the old air, the old fragrance, not the earthen godown remembered from long ago, not the darkly spiked wooden fence, not the willow at the corner of the restaurant. In front of the new shacks . . . a wanton profusion of hollyhocks and cosmos and black-eyed susans, in a dreariness quite unchanged since the earthquake.

It is the common view, and in the years just after the earthquake, when these melancholy impressions were set down, almost anyone would have thought that the old Asakusa was gone forever, and that "the new Asakusa," represented by the flashiness of the park and its entertainments, had emerged dominant. In recent years there has been a reversal. The life of the park has been drained away by the new entertainment centers elsewhere, and to the north and east of the temple are still to be found little pockets answering well to Akutagawa's description of the old Asakusa. Not having flourished, certain back streets had no very striking eminence to descend from.

The novelist Kawabata Yasunari used to say that, though he found abundant sadness in the culture of the Orient, he had never come upon the bleakness that he sensed in the West. Doubtless he spoke the truth. Tanizaki remarked upon the diaspora to the suburbs and beyond of the children of the Low City. He too spoke the truth. Not many residents of Asakusa were born there, and still fewer can claim grandparents who were born there. One may be sad that life has departed the place, but one does not reject Asakusa. There is still something down-to-earth and carpe-diem about it that is not to be found in the humming centers of the High City, or in the stylish, affluent suburbs.

Shitaya and Kanda wards, to the west of Asakusa, were partly flat and partly hilly—partly of the Low City and partly of the High. The Shitaya Ward of Meiji contained both the old Shitaya, "the valley below," and Ueno, "the upland stretches." Lowland Shitaya, generally south and east of "the mountain," Ueno Park, was almost completely destroyed in the fires of 1923. The hilly regions of the park and beyond were spared. At the end of Edo the merchant and artisan classes possessed very little of even the flat portion of Shitaya—a cluster south of the great Kaneiji Temple, now the park, a corridor leading south along the main street to Kanda and Nihombashi, and little more. Almost everything else belonged to the aristocracy and the bureaucracy. Like the busiest part of Asakusa, the busiest part of Shitaya—the "broad alley" south of the mountain and its temple—was a plebeian island largely cut off from the main Low City.

By the end of Meiji the upper classes had for the most part moved west, and their gardens had been taken over by small shops and dwellings, a solid expanse of them from the Hongō and Kanda hills to the river. A brief account in the 1907 guide put out by the city suggests the sort of thing that happened.

> *Shitaya Park.* Situated in the eastern part of the ward. To the east it borders on Samisen Pond and Asakusa Ward, and to the north on Nishimachi, Shitaya Ward. It was designated a park in April, 1890, and has an area of 16,432 *tsubo*. Once an estate of Lord Satake, it returned to nature with the dismemberment of the buildings, and came to be known popularly as Satake Meadow. It presently became a center for theaters, variety halls, sideshows, and the like, and, as they were gradually

moved elsewhere, was assimilated into the city. It may no longer be said to have the attributes of a park.

There is no trace of a park in the district today. The expression rendered as "assimilated" says more literally that the Satake estate "is entirely *machiya*," meaning something like the establishments of tradesmen and artisans. Most of the aristocratic lands of Shitaya became *machiya* without passing through the transitional stages.

Northern Shitaya, near the city limits, was a region of temples and cemeteries, a part of the band streching all along the northern fringes of Edo. A part of Yanaka, north of Ueno, where the last shogun is buried and where also the last poem of Takahashi O-den may be read upon her tombstone, became the largest public cemetery of Meiji. The city has sprawled vastly to the south and west, and today almost anyone from southerly and westerly regions, glancing at a map, forms an immediate and unshakable opinion that anything so far to the north and the east must be of the Low City. In fact it was the new High City of Meiji. As temple lands dwindled it became an intellectual sort of place, much favored by professors, writers, and artists. There is cause all the same, aside from its place on the map, for thinking that it gradually slid into the Low City. Professional keeners for dead Edo would have us believe that what was not lost in 1923 went in 1945, and that most things were lost on both occasions. In fact the Yanaka district came through the two disasters well. Its most conspicuous monument, the pagoda of the Tennōji Temple, was lost more recently. An arsonist set fire to it one summer evening in 1957. The heart of the old Low City contained few temples and Yanaka still contains many. With its latticed fronts, its tiled roofs, and its tiny expanses of greenery, it is the most extensive part of the present city in which something like the mood of the old Low City is still to be sensed.

The Negishi district, east of Yanaka, gave its name to a major school of Meiji poetry. It had long been recommended for the *wabizumai*, the life of solitude and contemplation, especially for the aged and affluent, and had had its artistic and literary day as well. A famous group of roisterers known as "the Shitaya gang" had its best parties in Negishi and included some of the most famous painters and writers of the early nineteenth century. Like Yanaka in the hills and over beyond the railway tracks, Negishi still has lanes and alleys that answer well to descriptions of the old Low City, but it has rather lost class. No artistic or intellectual person, unless perhaps a teacher of traditional music, would think of living there. It is not a good address.

From Yanaka and Negishi one looked across paddy lands to the Yoshiwara. In late Edo and Meiji the owners of the great Yoshiwara houses had villas there, to which the more privileged of courtesans could withdraw when weary or ill. Nagai Kafū loved Negishi, and especially the houses in which the courtesans had languished.

Always, looking through the fence and the shrubbery at the house next door, he would stand entranced, brought to his senses only by the stinging of the mosquitoes, at how much the scene before him was like an illustration for an old love story: the gate of woven twigs, the pine branches trailing down over the pond, the house itself. Long unoccupied, it had once been a sort of villa or resthouse for one of the Yoshiwara establishments. . . . He remembered how, when he was still a child on his mother's knee, he had heard and felt very sad to hear that one snowy night a courtesan, long in ill health, had died in the house next door, which had accommodated Yoshiwara women since before the Restoration. The old pine, trailing its branches from beside the lake almost to the veranda, made it impossible for him to believe, however many years passed, that the songs about sad Yoshiwara beauties, Urasato and Michitose and the rest, were idle fancies, yarns dreamed up by songwriters. Manners and ways of feeling might become Westernized, but as long as the sound of the temple bell in the short summer night remained, and the Milky Way in the clear autumn sky, and the trees and grasses peculiar to the land—as long as these remained, he thought, then somewhere, deep in emotions and ethical systems, there must even today be something of that ancient sadness.

Shitaya Ward, now amalgamated with Asakusa Ward to the east, was shaped like an arrowhead, or, as the Japanese preference for natural imagery would make it, a sagittate leaf. It pointed southwards towards the heart of the Low City, of which it fell slightly short. The character of the ward changed as one moved north to south, becoming little different from the flatlands of Kanda and Asakusa, between which the point of the arrow thrust itself. The erstwhile estates of the aristocracy had been "assimilated," as the 1907 guide informs us.

Kanda was almost entirely secular. There were Shinto plots, and the only Confucian temple in the city. There were no Buddhist temples at all. The shogunate did not want the smell of them and their funerals so near at hand. The Akihabara district that is now the biggest purveyor of electronic devices in the city took its name from a shrine, the Akiba—"Autumn Leaf." The extensive shrine grounds, cleared as a firebreak after one of the many great Kanda fires, were Akibagahara, "field of the Akiba." Then the government railways moved in and made them a freight depot, and the name elided into what it is today. This is the sort of thing that infuriates sons of Edo, and certainly the old name does have about it the feel of the land, and the new one, as Kafū did not tire of saying, has about it the tone of the railway operator. Names are among the things in Tokyo that are not left alone.

The purest of Edo Low City types, popular lore had it, was produced not in the heartland, Nihombashi, but on the fringes. Quarrelsome in rather a more noisy than violent way, cheerful, open, spendthrift, he was born in Shiba on the south and reared in Kanda. It was of course in the Kanda flatlands that he was reared, with the Kanda Shrine (see page 134) to watch over him. (Like Shitaya, Kanda was part hilly and part flat.) Kanda had once been a raucous sort of place, famous for its dashing gangsters and the "hot-water women" of its bathhouses, but in Meiji it was more sober and industrious than the flatlands of Shitaya and Asakusa, nearer the river.

The liveliest spot in Kanda was probably its fruit-and-vegetable market, the largest in the city, official provisioner to Lord Tokugawa himself. Though not directly threatened by the forces of Civilization and Enlightenment, as the fish market was, the produce market of Kanda yet lived through Meiji with a certain insecurity. In the end a tidying-up was deemed adequate, and the produce market escaped being uprooted like the fish market. The big markets were where the less affluent merchant of the Low City was seen at his most garrulous and energetic. The produce market, less striking to the senses than the fish market but no less robust, is a good symbol of flatland Kanda and its Edo types.

The western or hilly part of Kanda was the epitome of the high-collar. There it was that Hasegawa Shigure, child of Nihombashi, had her first taste of the new enlightenment (see page 194). Hilly Kanda had by the end of Meiji acquired the Russian cathedral, one of the city's grandest foreign edifices, and it had universities, bookstores, and intellectuals. The Kanda used-book district that is among the wonders of the world was beginning to form in late Meiji, on the main east-west Kanda street, then so narrow that rickshaws could barely pass. Losses in 1923 ran into tens of thousands of volumes.

Kanda had the greatest concentration of private higher education in the city, and indeed in the nation. Three important private universities, Meiji, Chūō, and Nihon, had their campuses in the western part of Kanda Ward—three of five such universities that were situated in Tokyo and might at the end of Meiji have been called important. All three were founded in early and middle Meiji as law schools and had by the end of Meiji diversified themselves to some extent. Law was among the chief intellectual concerns of Meiji. If Western law could be made Japanese and the foreign powers could be shown that extraterritoriality no longer served a purpose, then it might be done away with. The liberal arts did not, at the end of Meiji, have an important place in private education. Meiji University had a school of literature, one among four. Nihon had several foreign-language departments, while Chūō had only two branches, law and economics. The liberal arts and the physical sciences were for the most part left to public universities. In Kanda professional and commercial subjects prevailed. This seems appropriate, up here in the hills above the hustlers of the produce market, and perhaps it better represents the new day than does public education. It defines the fields in which the Japanese have genuinely excelled.

The regions east of the river were the saddest victims of Civilization and Enlightenment. This is not to say that they changed most during Meiji—the Marunouchi district east of the palace probably changed more—but that they suffered a drearier change. Someone has to be a victim of an ever grosser national product, and the authorities chose Honjo and Fukagawa wards, along with the southern shores of the bay, after a time of uncertainty in which small factories were put up over most of the city.

Lumberyards in Kanda, late Meiji

It would be easy to say that the poor are always the victims, but the fact is that the wards east of the river, and especially Honjo, the northern one, do not look especially poor on maps of late Edo. Had there been a policy of putting the burden on the lower classes, then Nihombashi and Kyōbashi would have been the obvious targets. The eastern wards were chosen not because they were already sullied and impoverished but because they were so watery, and therefore lent themselves so well to cheap transport. They were also relatively open. Many people and houses would have had to be displaced were Nihombashi to turn industrial.

Though more regularly plotted, the Honjo of late Edo resembles the western parts of the High City, plebeian enclaves among aristocratic lands. Wateriest of all, Fukagawa was rather different, especially in its southern reaches. It contained the lumberyards of the city. The lumberyards were of course mercantile, though some of the merchants were wealthy, if not as wealthy as the great ones of Nihombashi.

By the end of Meiji the wards east of the river were industrial and far-from-wealthy makers of things that others consumed. Nagai Kafū wrote evocatively of the change. The hero of *The River Sumida*, returning to Asakusa from a disappointing interview with his uncle, wanders past rank Honjo gardens and moldering Honjo houses, and recognizes among them the settings for the fiction of late Edo, to which he is strongly drawn. In certain essays the laments are for the changes which, in the years of Kafū's exile overseas, have come upon "Fukagawa of the waters."

Heavily populated as the city spilled over into the eastern suburbs, Honjo and the northern parts of Fukagawa were but sparsely populated at the beginning of Meiji. Akutagawa Ryūnosuke, who was born in 1892 and spent his boyhood in Honjo, described the loneliness in an essay written after the earthquake and shortly before his suicide.

In the last years of the nineteenth century and the first years of the twentieth, Honjo was not the region of factories that it is today. It was full of stragglers, worn out by two centuries of Edo. There was nothing resembling the great rows of mercantile establishments one sees in Nihombashi and Kyōbashi. In search of an even moderately busy district, one went to the far south of the ward, the approaches to Ryōgoku Bridge. . . .

Corpses made the strongest impression on me in stories I heard of old Honjo, corpses of those who had fallen by the wayside, or hanged themselves, or otherwise disposed of themselves. A corpse would be discovered and put in a cask, and the cask wrapped in straw matting, and set out upon the moors with a white lantern to watch over it. The thought of the white lantern out there among the grasses has in it a certain weird, ominous beauty. In the middle of the night, it was said, the cask would roll over, quite of its own accord. The Honjo of Meiji may have been short on grassy moors, but it still had about it something of the "regions beyond the red line." And how is it now? A mass of utility poles and shacks, all jammed in together. . . .

My father still thinks he saw an apparition, that night in Fukagawa. It looked like a young warrior, but he insists that it was in fact a fox spirit. Presently it ran off, frightened by the glint of his sword. I do not care whether it was fox or warrior. Each time I hear the story I think what a lonely place the old Fukagawa was.

The "moderately busy" part of Honjo was the vicinity of the Ekōin Temple, at the eastern approaches to Ryōgoku Bridge, one of five put across the Sumida during the Tokugawa Period. The Ekōin was founded to console the victims of the great "fluttering-sleeve" fire of 1657, so called from a belief that it was spread by a burning kimono. It was among the great temples of Edo, though Basil Hall Chamberlain and W. B. Morse thought it less than elevating. They said of it, in the 1903 edition of their guide to Japan, that it "might well be taken as a text by those who denounce 'heathen temples.' Dirty, gaudy . . . the place lacks even the semblance of sanctity."

The Ekōin attracted places of refreshment and entertainment, solace to the living as well as the departed, less varied and on the whole shabbier than those of Asakusa. The "broad alley" of Ryōgoku fared badly in Meiji and after. At the end of Edo it was one of the three famous "broad alleys" of the Low City. Ryōgoku continued until the Second World War to be the Sumō center of the land. There it was that the big tournaments were held from late Edo down to the Second World War, but they moved away. The gymnasium was requisitioned by the American Occupation and then sold to a university, and the Sumō center of the city and the nation has for three decades now been on the right bank of the river.

Not much remains at Ryōgoku. It became a commuter point when a railway station was finished in 1903, but a minor one, serving some of the poorest parts of the city and only the Chiba Peninsula beyond. So it may be said that Honjo, once unpeopled, is now crowded and subdued. No part of the city is without its pockets of pleasure and entertainment, but Honjo has none that would take the pleasure-seeker out of his way.

On a single evening every year, something of the old joy and din came back. It was the night of the "river opening," already described, admired by U. S. and Julia Grant, E. S. Morse, and Clara Whitney, among others. The crowds were so dense at the 1897 opening that the south rail of the bridge gave way, and people drowned.

Still in late Meiji the district from northern Honjo into the northern and eastern suburbs was much recommended for excursions. It enjoyed such excursions in perhaps the greatest variety in all the city, though they were becoming victims of material progress. The 1907 guide put out by the metropolitan government thus describes the state of affairs: "Under the old regime the district was occupied by townsmen and the lower ranks of the aristocracy. It was also the site of the official bamboo and lumberyards. Today it is mostly industrial. To the

north, however, is Mukōjima, a most scenic district, and in the suburbs to the east are such attractions as the Sleeping Dragon Plum and
the Hagi Temple, for especially pleasant excursions." The temple survives, but the *hagi* (*Lespedeza bicolor*) of autumn does not. Neither do
the plum blossoms of spring. Kafū's description, in *The River Sumida*,
is of joyous springtide, out beyond the blight; but the blight was advancing.

"They who make the count of the famous places of Tokyo," says
the guide a few pages later, "cannot but put a pair of scenic spots,
Ueno and Mukōjima, at the head of their lists."

Cherries had from the seventeenth century lined the left bank of
the Sumida, from a point generally opposite Asakusa northwards into
the suburbs. Though gnawed at by industrial fumes from late Meiji,
they still attracted throngs during their brief period of flowering that
were second only to those of Ueno. The Sumida was still clean enough
for bathing—or at any rate no one had yet made the discovery that it
was not.

Grassy banks led down to the river on the Honjo side, and small
houses lined the Asakusa bank, waiting resignedly for the next flood.
The river was open, no bridges in sight north from Asakusa, with at
least four ferry landings well within sight on either bank. As the city
took to wheels, bridges came into demand, but the ferry must have
been the pleasanter way to cross, especially in cherry-blossom time.
The last of the Sumida ferries, much farther downstream, did not
disappear until after the Second World War.

Tokyo is today, and it must have been in late Meiji, a city where
one learns to gaze only at the immediate prospect, blotting out what
lies beyond. Crossing Azuma Bridge at Asakusa, one would have had to
do this, unless a background of chimneys and smoke and utility wires
could be regarded as pleasing. Yet the foreground must have been very
pleasing indeed.

The view across the Sumida from Honjo to Asakusa was quiet
urban harmony, and that in the other direction was pastoral calm,
broken by those noisy vernal rites when the cherries were in bloom. In
the one direction was the "old Asakusa" of Kubota Mantarō, low
wooden buildings at the water's edge with the sweeping roofs and the
pagoda of the Asakusa Kannon beyond, and Matsuchi Hill, the only
considerable rise in the Low City, slightly upstream. In the other

direction was the Sumida embankment, surmounted by cherry trees that blocked off all but the top portions of the industrially productive regions beyond, still suggesting that over there somewhere a few old gentlemen of taste and leisure might be pursuing one or several of the ways of the brush.

Beyond the city limits on the left bank, in what was to become Mukōjima Ward, was a pleasant little cove much heard of in amorous fiction of late Edo and Meiji. It was watched over by the Shrine of the River God, tutelary to the Sumida, and it was a good place, remote and serene, to take a geisha. No trace of it remains. The Sumida has been rationalized and brought within plain, sensible limits, with a view to flood control.

A victim of pollution, Honjo was also subject to natural disasters. It suffered most grievously among all the wards, perhaps, not in terms of property losses but in terms of wounds that did not heal, from the Great Flood of 1910. Most of the wealthy who had maintained villas beside the river withdrew, hastening the end of the northeastern suburbs as a place of tasteful retirement. The flood-control devices of

Honjo in the Great Flood of 1910

Another view of Honjo during the Great Flood

Taishō and since have been very successful, but they have also been somewhat unsightly. It may be that not many in our day would wish to view the sights and smell the smells of the Sumida (and only stuntsters venture to swim in it). Even if the wish were present, it would be frustrated by cement walls.

On maps of Edo, northern Fukagawa, the southern of the two wards east of the river, looks very much like Honjo, but the watery south is different, solidly plebeian, as no part of Honjo is. Across the river from Nihombashi, Fukagawa was nearer the heart of the Low City. Though not among the flourishing geisha quarters of Meiji, Fukagawa did in the course of Meiji get something that was just as good business, the Susaki licensed quarter (see pages 178–179). Fukagawa was among the better heirs to the great tradition of Edo profligacy.

The Susaki quarter did not, like the Yoshiwara, have a round of seasonal observances, but it was at times a place for the whole family to visit. Shown on certain maps from late Edo as tidal marshes, the strand before the Susaki Benten Shrine was rich in shellfish, and clam raking was among the rites of summer. This very ancient shrine had stood on an island long before Fukagawa was reclaimed. All through the Edo centuries it was presided over by the only feminine member of the Seven Deities of Good Luck. So the quarter had an appropriate patroness, well established. In certain respects Susaki was more pleasing to the professional son of Edo than the Yoshiwara. Not so frequently a victim of fire, there in its watery isolation, it was not as quick to become a place of fanciful turrets and polychrome fronts. Indeed it looks rather prim in photographs, easily mistaken, at a slight remove, for the Tsukiji foreign settlement.

The Fukagawa of late Meiji had more bridges than any other ward in the city, a hundred forty of them, including those shared with Honjo and Nihombashi. Only two were of iron, and a hundred twenty-eight were of wood, suggesting that the waterways of Fukagawa still had an antique look about them.

The beginnings of industrialization, as it concerned Tokyo, were at the mouth of the Sumida and along the Shiba coast. The Ishikawajima Shipyards, on the Fukagawa side of the Sumida, may be traced back to public dismay over the Perry landing. A shipbuilding enterprise was established there by the Mito branch of the Tokugawa clan shortly after that event. It followed a common Meiji course from public enterprise to private, making the transition in 1876.

Over large expanses of the ward, however, Kafū's "Fukagawa of the waters" yet survived, canals smelling of new wood and lined by white godowns. Kafū was not entirely consistent, or perhaps Fukagawa itself was inconsistent, a place of contrasts. On the one hand he deplored the changed Fukagawa which he found on his return from America and France, and on the other he still found refuge there from the cluttered new city (see pages 45–46). His best friend, some years later, fled family and career, and took up residence with a lady not his wife in a Fukagawa tenement row. There he composed haiku. In Fukagawa, said Kafū approvingly, people still honored what the new day called superstitions, and did not read newspapers.

The grounds of the Tomioka Hachiman were in theory a park, one of the original five. Much the smallest, it had a career similar to that of Asakusa. It dwindled and presently lost all resemblance to what is commonly held to be a public park. The Iwasaki estate in Fukagawa, now Kiyosumi Park, is far more parklike today than this earlier park. The history of the two is thus similar to the history of Ueno and

Asakusa. It was best, in these early years, to keep the public at some distance from a park. Deeded to the city after the earthquake, Kiyosumi Park was the site of the Taishō emperor's funeral pavilion.

The beauties of the Fukagawa bayshore are described thus in the official guide of 1907:

> One stands by the shrine and looks out to sea, and a contrast of blue and white, waves and sails, rises and falls, far into the distance. To the south and east the mountains of the Chiba Peninsula float upon the water, raven and jade. To the west are the white snows of Fuji. In one grand sweep are all the beauties of mountain and sea, in all the seasons. At low tide in the spring, there is the pleasure of 'hunting in the tidelands,' as it is called. Young and old, man and woman, they all come out to test their skills at the taking of clams and seaweed.

One senses overstatement, for the guide had its evangelical purposes. Yet it is true that open land and the flowers and grasses and insects and clams of the seasons were to be found at no great distance beyond the river. When, in the Taishō Period, the Arakawa Drainage Channel was dug, much of its course was through farmland.

Among the places for excursions, only the Kameido Tenjin Shrine and its wisteria survive. Waves of blue, mountains of raven and jade, are rarely to be seen, and the Sumida has been walled in. Yet the more remarkable fact may be that something still survives.

There is the mood of the district, more sweetly melancholy, perhaps, for awareness of all the changes, and there are specific, material things as well, such as memorial stones and steles. Some of the temple grounds are forests of stone. Kafū's maternal grandfather and Narushima Ryūhoku are among those whose accomplishments will not be completely forgotten, for they are recorded upon the stones of Honjo and Mukōjima. The great Bashō had one of his "banana huts" in Fukagawa. It too is memorialized, though finding it takes some perseverance.

The other industrial zone was along the bayshore in the southernmost ward, Shiba, which was also the ward of the railroad, the only ward so favored in early Meiji. The Tokyo–Yokohama railroad entered the city

A mikoshi (god-seat) at the Fukagawa Hachiman Shrine Festival

at the southern tip of Shiba, hugged the shore and passed over fills, veered somewhat inland, and came to its terminus just short of the border with Kyōbashi. Closely following the old Tōkaidō, it blocked the plebeian view of the bay (or, it might be said, since Meiji so delighted in locomotives, provided new and exciting perspectives). It may or may not be significant that the line turned inland to leave such aristocratic expanses as the Hama Palace with their bayshore frontage.

Shiba at the south and Kanda at the north of the Low City were honored in popular lore as makers of the true child of Edo. The fringes were not as wealthy as the Nihombashi center, and so their sons, less inhibited, had the racy qualities of Edo in greater measure. Most of Shiba is hilly and not much of it was plebeian at the end of Edo. Edo land maps show *machiya,* "houses of townsmen," like knots along a string. There was a cluster at the north, around Shimbashi, where the first railway terminus was built, a string southwards to another knot, between the bay and the southern cemetery of the Tokugawa family, and another string southwards to the old Shinagawa post-station, just beyond the Meiji city limits.

It was through Shiba that the foreigner and his goods entered

Tokyo. Had it not been for the Ginza fire, its northern extremes might have become preeminent among places for the purveying of imported goods. The region did in fact prosper. The southern cluster, by the Tokugawa tombs, did not do as well. It came to harbor one of the quarters commonly called slums, though it may be doubted that Tokyo knows what a real slum is—in that regard, it has never quite caught up with the rest of the world. Since Kanda, the partner of Shiba in producing the true son of Edo, contained no "slums," its flatlands were probably more prosperous in Meiji than those of Shiba.

Shiba was the earliest legation quarter. When Sir Rutherford Alcock, the first British minister, went to call upon the shogun, his way lay almost entirely through what was presently to become Shiba Ward. It seems to have taken him around the western or hilly side of the Tokugawa cemetery, where also there was a plebeian fringe. He makes it sound like a lesser Asakusa.

> After a mile of the Tocado, our road turns off into a side street, narrower and more crowded. A Daimio's residence extends the greater part of its length on one side, with a large and imposing-looking gateway in the centre, from which stretches a long line of barred windows. . . . A small, narrow, and very muddy moat, little more than a gutter, keeps all intruders from too close prying. But these outbuildings are only the quarters of the numerous retainers. . . . In many cases these extend for a quarter of a mile on each side of the main entrance, and form in effect the best defence for their lord's apartments. . . .
>
> We soon emerge into an open space in front of the Tycoon's Cemetery, and through it a small river runs, fringed with fresh green banks, and a row of trees. . . . Here, in open space above, forming a sort of boulevard, Matsuri, or public fairs, are often held, and, in their absence, storytellers collect a little audience. A few noisy beggars generally take up their position by the wayside. . . . Here a party of jugglers may often be seen too, collecting a crowd from the passers-by. Blondin and the Wizard of the North might both find formidable rivals here;— for the Japanese performers not only swallow portentously long swords, and poise themselves on bottles;—but out of their mouths come the most unimaginable things . . . flying horses,

swarms of flies, ribbons by the mile, and paper shavings without end.

On crossing the bridge, we traverse one of the most densely populated of the commercial quarters, through which, indeed, we can only ride slowly, and in single file, amidst pedestrians and porters with their loads. Bullock-cars, Norimons, and Kangos are all here, jostling each other in contending currents. Over a gentle hill, then sharp round to the right, through a barrier gate, we approach the official quarter, in the center of which, within three moats of regal dimensions, the Tycoon himself resides. But we are not yet near to it. We pursue our way down some rather steep steps—a Daimio's residence on one side, and the wall and trees of the Tycoon's Cemetery, which we are skirting, on the other. As we emerge from this defile, we pass through a long line of booths, where a sort of daily bazaar is held for the sale of gaudily-coloured prints, maps (many of them copies of European charts), story books, swords, tobacco pouches, and pipes, for the humbler classes; and in the midst of which a fortune-teller may habitually be seen. . . . Something very like the gambling table of our own fairs may also be seen in the same spot; but, judging by the stock-in-trade and the juvenile customers, the gambling, I suspect, is only for sweetmeats. Their serious gambling is reserved for teahouses, and more private haunts, where the law may be better defied. On festive occasions, a row of dingy booths divided by curtains into small compartments is often seen, provided for the lowest class. The Social Evil is here a legalized institution, and nowhere takes a more revolting form.

In later years a place along the other side of the tombs, the east side, was known to Clara Whitney and her friends as "the thieves' market." It also contained one of the lesser geisha districts of the time. So the old pattern may be seen once more, places of pleasure and commerce accumulating around places of worship, in this case the great Zōjōji Temple, the southern equivalent of the Kan-eiji at Ueno.

The circle of temples and cemeteries that started at the Sumida and fringed the old city came through Shiba and ended at the bay. The

Zōjōji was the grandest of Shiba temples, though today the most famous is probably that which contains the ashes of the Forty-seven Loyal Retainers (see page 48). The grounds of the Zōjōji were one of the five original parks. There it was, on a moonlit night, that a moping Kafū, back from France and hating everything Japanese, had his first mystical experience of traditional beauty.

Virtually nothing remains of the old Zōjōji. As for the park, it is enough to say that the remains of the shoguns and their ladies, including the sad princess who became the bride of the fourteenth shogun, have been squeezed into a narrow walled enclosure, so that commerce may thrive. Hibiya Park, newer and some slight distance to the north, is today more open.

The hilly sections of Shiba Park were so heavily wooded, we are told, that there was darkness at noon. Today they are dominated by Tokyo Tower, of Eiffel-like proportions, while the graves of the shoguns lie naked under the midday sun. In 1873 arsonists destroyed the main hall of the Zōjōji, around which the graves were once disposed. The culprits, self-righteous young men of the military class, resented the temple's failure to separate itself from Shinto, which must be pure, uncontaminated by foreign creeds. Rebuilt, the hall was destroyed again on April Fool's Day, 1909, this time by accident. A beggar built a fire under it to warm himself in that chilly season.

To accommodate the electric trolleys of late Meiji, a street was put through almost directly south from the castle to the old Tōkaidō highway, which it joins some distance north of Shinagawa. It bisected the Zōjōji grounds. The portions east of the new street were those earliest given over to development, which has today quite engulfed them, leaving scarcely a trace of park. Yet farther east was what might be called the southernmost extremity of the old Low City, and along the bayshore was an early center of heavy industry.

Tokyo Shibaura has been a leading manufacturer of machinery ever since its founding in 1875 by a man from Kyushu. Shibaura means "Shiba coast." Its main factories on land reclaimed by the shogunate, the company was an early manufacturer of telegraphic equipment. In spite of all these industrial endeavors, Shibaura remained the most popular of watering places. The young Tanizaki went there gathering clams.

Shibaura had clams in spring and cooling breezes in the summer, and a view up the Sumida to Ryōgoku Bridge for the "opening of the river." Meiji graphic art tends, except in certain erotica, to emphasize the clams. It was only at the end of the period that the youth of the land turned with enthusiasm to sea bathing. Advertisements from middle to late Meiji recommend it as something which, since foreigners find it pleasant and healthful, Japanese might try too. The places where pretty clam-diggers posed for photographers, skirts tucked up to reveal sturdy legs, now lie beneath a freeway, and already at the end of Meiji reclaimed lands were creeping eastwards.

Just north of the Tokyo Shibaura plant was, at the end of Meiji, the Number One Gashouse of the Tokyo Gas Company; and just north of that, to remind us that it was not only the lower classes who had factories for neighbors, the Shiba Detached Palace, a salubrious retreat for royalty.

"Twenty years ago," wrote the novelist and playwright Osanai Kaoru, some years after the earthquake, "Shibaura was a place with flair. There the geisha came, the genuine sort, for delicious assignations.

"I went the other day for a look at it, the first in I do not know how many years. I was shocked, at the wide expanses of reclaimed land, at the big new docks along the shallow bay, where there once had been beaches, at the warehouses, at the utter disappearance of the old restaurants and inns.

"Only the black pines of the Hama Palace, across the canal, remained from other years."

In its shady western hills, Shiba Park had perhaps the most famous Japanese restaurant of Meiji. Called the Kōyōkan, House of the Autumn Colors, it does not survive. It was built in 1881 as a sort of club for the elite, who in the Rokumeikan period saw the need for a good Japanese restaurant not associated, as most of them then were, with the demimonde. The improving spirit of the day is here again to be noted. No one under the old regime, except perhaps for a few of the more unbendingly puritanical bureaucrats, would have seen a need for the separation. Some of the most prominent names in the land were on the list of stockholders. Radically innovative in one sense, the Kōyōkan sought to be traditional in another. Kyoto food was served, and the waitresses were asked to have Kyoto accents, whether they came naturally or not. Much frequented by bureaucrats, politicians, and intellectuals, the Kōyōkan figures more prominently in Meiji literature than does the Rokumeikan.

Shiba was the most hapless of the three large early parks. We have seen how Saitō Ryokuu contrasted Ueno and Asakusa, the latter noisy and down-to-earth, the former sternly edifying. Shiba was neither the one nor the other, and since the most recent destruction of its temple, in 1945, it has seemed almost unpeopled, as that word may be understood in Tokyo. Already in Meiji it was being left behind. From a short distance south of the Tokugawa tombs a branch of the Tōkaidō led northwards into the High City—it is the route Sir Rutherford Alcock seems to have taken—while the main road led to Nihombashi. The tombs lay between the two, and on either side was a flourishing district of the sort described by Sir Rutherford. The railroad passed them by. As they declined, it was the far north of Shiba, by Shimbashi Station, that thrived.

Shimbashi, always called Shibaguchi, "the Shiba Mouth," by such cognoscenti as Kafū, did not get modernized after the great Ginza fire. It is where the old merchant and artisan city narrowed from the spread of Nihombashi and Kyōbashi to a constricted corridor leading southwards towards the city limits and Shinagawa. Before the Meiji ward boundaries were drawn, separating Ginza and Shimbashi, it could be distinguished from its northern neighbor by little save its greater remoteness from the center of things—a remoteness and a lack of affluence which made it the proper breeding ground for children of Edo.

If Shimbashi had become a part of the new Ginza Bricktown it might also have become, like Ginza, the sluice through which the delightful new things of the West came flooding. It was immediately in front of the station, while Ginza was a bit removed. After the trauma of the rebuilding, Ginza did eventually retrieve its standing as a place of revelry, of tiny drinking and lechering establishments, but through most of Meiji that function was assumed by Shimbashi. It was as if, having had their look at Ginza, which of course everyone wished to see, people turned back and relaxed in Shimbashi, where they felt at home. One is reminded of the typical estate of a Meiji plutocrat, consisting of a grand Western building (by Conder, perhaps) for garden parties and foreign dignitaries, and a Japanese wing somewhere in the background for everyday use. Ginza had its broad streets and colonnades, and Shimbashi was a warren, where one felt snug and secure.

A part of Shimbashi was known as Hikagechō, "Shadyville," which seems just right.

The Shimbashi geisha district, with Yanagibashi the greatest of them through most of Meiji, has been the most peripatetic. It was named from its proximity to Shimbashi, the New Bridge on the Tōkaidō, and moved northwards and then eastwards. Today, though still called Shimbashi, it is largely in the Tsukiji district, where the foreign settlement was and the fish market is. In the decades since Meiji it has done better than Yanagibashi, but it may be that the geisha profession is a dying one. Elegance and ritual survive, if perhaps the old standards in song and dance have fallen.

The original Shimbashi Station, northern terminus of the railway from Yokohama and later from Kobe, is said by experts on Meiji architecture to be something of a mystery, though it was endlessly photographed and made into woodcut prints. The original plans, by an American, have been lost, and no detailed description survives. So it was observed by millions of eyes (some three million passengers got on

Shimbashi Station, 1881

and off in 1907 alone), and drawn and photographed countless numbers of times—and yet we cannot know exactly what was seen by all those eyes. Among stations in the West, it seems to have resembled the Gare de l'Est in Paris most closely.

Some places have a way of coming back from hard blows, others do not. Yanagibashi is being destroyed by the ugly wall that cuts it off from its river. Shimbashi lost its station, and did not seem to notice. After 1914, when Tokyo Central Station was completed, Shimbashi was no longer the terminus and the old station was no longer used for passengers. A new and less important station was built some slight distance to the west, right on top of Shadyville. Shimbashi might have languished. Because the Low City was made to feel rejected by the new central station, however, people from Kyōbashi and Nihombashi preferred to board their trains at the new Shimbashi Station. So in the warrens of Shiba Mouth there was revelry as never before. Ginza moved northwards and Shimbashi went on doing the old thing, more intensely.

At the end of Meiji, Nihombashi was no longer a center holding the Low City together. The genuine child of Edo may have been born in Shiba and reared in Kanda, but from both places, while Edo was still Edo, he looked towards Nihombashi as a height or a hub. Wonders of power and progress were achieved in Meiji, but these things do not happen without cost. The Low City was no longer what it had been through the last century or so of Edo, the cultural capital of the land, and Nihombashi, still the geographic center of the Low City, looked about it at a scattering rather than a system.

There was no reason for modern ward lines to follow the ridge line that separated the hilly half of the city from the flat half; and they did not. Each of the wards along the western fringe of the flatlands reached into the hills, and the eastern portion of Hongō, largely in the hills, lay beyond the ridge and in the flats. The boundary is somewhat imaginary in any case. The two halves were and continue to be different from each other, but the ridge line is no more than a convenience for dividing them.

The line entered the Meiji city north of Ueno and left it near the present Shinagawa Station, where the hills came almost down to the bayshore. Had one walked through Edo generally following the ridge line, there would have been only one stretch of the route where the division between High City and Low City seemed quite clear, and even so one would have had to stray eastward from the precise topographical line. There was a cultural chasm along the outer ramparts of the castle. In Meiji it became the line separating Kōjimachi Ward and especially the Marunouchi business district, within the circle, from the several wards, notably Kyōbashi and Nihombashi, that lay outside it. Before the fall of the shogunate, the highest of the bureaucracy and the military aristocracy dwelt within the circle, to the west of the moat. To the east lay the heart of the Low City, Nihombashi and Kyōbashi.

The outer moat survived through Meiji and down to the recent past, but it was early decided that His Majesty's abode did not require such defensive works as Lord Tokugawa's had claimed. So the outer gates were quickly dismantled, and the district between the outer and inner moats put to several uses.

Great changes have come over Nihombashi and Ginza, to the east of the chasm, and Marunouchi, to the west; but on a holiday in particular the old difference is still to be observed. The outer edge of the circle teems with shoppers and pleasure seekers, the inside is dead. The former continues to be the land of the merchant and his customer, the latter is the land of the office worker, who withdraws to the suburbs on holidays, or perhaps steps across the line into Ginza for something self-indulgent.

Mention has been made of the late-Meiji photographs taken by Ogawa Isshin from the roof of the City Hall. They are striking for the unfinished look of the Marunouchi district, but among specific objects the most remarkable is perhaps the great wall that is being put up to the east, as if to keep off barbarian hordes, or to keep a restless populace at home. It is the elevated railroad to the new central station, and it did have the effect of emphasizing divisions, even though no guard was present to enforce them. As of old, the lines of commerce and passage went north and south, from the Nihombashi bridge to the Kyōbashi bridge and the Shimbashi bridge, and the station was rather for the accommodation of the executive and the office worker. The division still survives.

The mansions and government buildings near the palace, on what was to become Mitsubishi Meadow, did not all disappear at once. Some did disappear but some were for a time put to the uses of the new bureaucracy; but by the end of Meiji all were gone. The lands immediately east of the palace became public park (though not a part of the municipal park system), and Mitsubishi presently took over and began to develop its Londontown when the bureaucracy withdrew from lands farther east. In search of relics by which to remember the old castle complex, one would at the end of Meiji have come upon stones and trees, a scattering of gates and bridges, and no more. Parts of Kanda or Nihombashi repeatedly destroyed by fire would have been more redolent of Edo than Marunouchi.

To the west of what in late Meiji became Hibiya Park, still in the Kōjimachi flatlands, was the main bureaucratic complex. It was chiefly brick by a variety of foreign architects in a variety of styles, on the whole more up-to-date, from the foreign point of view, than the Classical Revival styles that were to prevail among Japanese architects. A single building, the Ministry of Justice, remains from the bureaucratic center of late Meiji. Though several German architects are usually given credit for the design, the original one seems to have been revised in the direction of simplicity. The Germans seem to have been fond of traditional frills, and it was these that were disposed of.

The first Diet building rose south of Hibiya Park, not far from the Rokumeikan. It promptly burned down, a victim of electric leakage, and was rebuilt in 1891, in a half-timbered Renaissance style, far less imposing than, for instance, the highly Italianate General Staff Headquarters, which occupied a much more imposing site somewhat to the west, perhaps the finest in all the city. In front of it was the palace moat, and beyond that the grassy embankment and the venerable pine trees beyond which a new residence had been built for the emperor. Although the symbolism cannot have been intentional, it seems to put Meiji democracy in its place.

Kōjimachi was also the diplomatic ward. At the end of Meiji it contained most of the legations and embassies, although the American embassy stood on the land it still occupies, in the northeast corner of Akasaka Ward, and two legations still remained in the old Tsukiji foreign quarter, near which there was a lesser bureaucratic center. The German embassy and the British embassy stood grandly on the inner moat. The former was the grander, and the most frequently photographed of all the embassies, part of an impressive row with the War Ministry and General Staff Headquarters. The embassies have followed the movement of the city to the south and west, and only the British, among the old ones, remains in what was Kōjimachi Ward. When in late Meiji land was chosen for the American legation and embassy, it was eccentrically far south, but the flow of the city has left it nearer the pulsing bureaucratic heart than any of the others.

Though the foreign settlement still contained hotel accommodations at the end of Meiji, the big hotel in the Western style was the Imperial. A Tokyo Hotel had been put up some years earlier in the same part of Kōjimachi, but foreign relations were proceeding briskly and treaty negotiations arriving at a hopeful stage. Something more elaborate was thought to be needed. With government encouragement and a grant of land (and some of the most successful entrepreneurs of the day among the investors), the Imperial opened for business in 1890. Almost immediately the Diet burned down, and the Imperial became temporary accommodations for the House of Representatives.

It was a three-storey wooden building with verandas and arches not at all out of keeping with the Rokumeikan, its neighbor. Sources vary on the number of guest rooms, but there were not above a hundred. So perhaps two or three hundred guests would have filled all the exotic hostelries in the city. One senses what a pleasantly remote and isolated place Tokyo continued to be, despite its emergence into the great world, and its prospect of brilliant successes in the art of war.

Prince Itō, the prime minister of the "dancing cabinet," he who was host to the masquerade ball at the climax of the Rokumeikan period, regularly took meals at the Imperial. The hotel replaced the Rokumeikan as the gathering place of the international set. Over the years it has moved back and forth across its ample public domains, a new one being put up on one half and itself becoming "the old Imperial" when yet another new one is put up on the other half. The first Imperial was destroyed by fire while the second one, by Frank Lloyd Wright, was under construction.

The southern and eastern parts of Kōjimachi had yet more monumental piles in the Western manner. The Imperial Theater was finished at the very end of Meiji, across from the palace plaza. Beside the outer moat of the palace as it crossed the ridge line and entered the

The first Imperial Hotel, with one of the old castle moats in foreground

A lounge inside the Imperial Hotel

High City was the Akasaka Detached Palace, finished in 1908. It was built on the site, expanded by gifts and purchases, of the main Edo mansion of the Wakayama Tokugawa family. There it was that the Meiji emperor, left homeless by the palace fire of 1873, spent roughly the first half of his reign. The mansion became the crown prince's residence upon completion of a new main palace. The new Akasaka palace was put up for the crown prince, who, whether he wished it or not, had a far grander residence than his father. Now serving as the guesthouse for visiting queens, popes, and the like, the Akasaka Palace consists of three floors of brick and granite in the Versailles manner.

The Imperial Theater and the Akasaka Palace were designed by Japanese architects. It is an indication of the distance come. After the first hybrid curiosities, built by Japanese "master carpenters," came the foreign period dominated by such people as Josiah Conder. Beginning with the Bank of Japan, Japanese architects commenced doing the big foreign thing for themselves. Although Wright was summoned to build the second Imperial, foreign architects would never again be so important. No one would say—as it was said in early Meiji—that Japanese foreign architecture was foreign to any known style. It could not, on the other hand, be said that there was anything very original about the Gallic exercises of late Meiji (although the Imperial Theater did, until the earthquake, bear atop its dome a large statue of a Kabuki actor). Amateur exuberance gradually gave way to a professional discipline that was perhaps too tightly controlled.

The flat parts of Kōjimachi Ward, within the outer moat and to the east and south of castle and palace, may have had no geographic features to distinguish them from the flatlands beyond the outer moat, but no son of Edo would have thought them a part of the Low City— his city. Today they are the most national part of the city, where financial and productive endeavors are regulated, and from which the land is governed. As one crosses the ridge line, following the inner moat or the avenue where the outer moat once was, one is clearly in the High City. The British embassy has perhaps the best address in the whole city, but it is more isolated than the American embassy, because the system of rapid transport has until recently been reticent about intruding upon affluent residential neighborhoods.

. . .

The High City was sparsely populated in Edo and largely emptied by the Restoration. The high ranks of the military aristocracy went away, presently to come back with titles and new mansions. The lower ranks provided some of the most successful Meiji bureaucrats, politicians, and entrepreneurs, and ample stories of tragedy and desperation as well, including those of O-den, O-kinu, and O-ume, the eminent murderesses.

Then they all went away, and the High City was turned over to tea and mulberries. The Meiji government, after initial hesitation, began a policy of confiscating unused lands and encouraging their return to agriculture. There were for a time more than a hundred acres of tea and mulberries in what was to become Akasaka Ward. The avenue that leads southwest from the Akasaka geisha quarter seems to have passed through mulberries and little else. Shibuya, beyond the Meiji city limits and one of the thriving entertainment and shopping centers of Taishō and since, was known for the excellence of its tea. The "tea-and-mulberry policy" was a brief expediency which left no lasting mark upon the High City. The tea bushes and the mulberry trees soon withered, and development came, to make the High City the half (or somewhat more than half) of Tokyo that has grown hugely in this century.

From mid-Meiji, the repopulation of the High City progressed furiously, accounting for well over half the total population growth through the Meiji years. When the population reached a million, approximately the highest Edo figure, Yotsuya Ward in the High City still had the smallest population of the fifteen, and Akasaka, immediately to the south, was the least densely populated. Their opposites were of course in the Low City, Kanda with the largest population and Nihombashi with the highest population density. The population of the city reached two million by the end of Meiji, but growth in the central wards, the Low City plus Kōjimachi, was slow, and in some places population was actually declining.

A line north and south from the center of the palace grounds would have divided the Meiji city into two almost equal parts, and on its way to the city limits at either extremity it would have passed almost entirely through hilly regions. Today the portion of the twenty-three wards that lies west of the line is larger than the eastern portion, and much more populous. A line north and south from the westernmost point of the Meiji city would divide the present city—the twenty-three wards—into approximately equally populated parts. It is a change indeed, when one remembers that the Low City had more than half the population of late Edo. The city has moved westward and goes on doing so, and the old Low City figures much less than it once did.

Though growing rapidly, the High City did not really begin splitting its seams until after the earthquake. When the novelist Tokutomi Roka, among the most popular in his day of all Meiji writers, fell under the spell of Tolstoi and wished to live the Tolstoian life, he only had to go five or six miles west of Shinjuku and the Meiji city limits to be among the peasants. This was shortly after the Russo-Japanese War—and Shinjuku was the most rapidly growing of the new transportation centers. In 1920 a part of it became the first considerable annexation to the fifteen Meiji wards.

For all these frantic changes, the High City changed less in some respects than the Low City. Class distinctions, once very clear if measured by money, tended to disappear from the Low City. They remained valid in the High City. So also, to a remarkable extent, did the pattern of land usage, the distribution of land between the affluent and the more straitened. In both parts of the city the street pattern, despite revolution and disaster, has continued to resemble that of Edo. It is sometimes said that the Japanese succeeded in putting together a rational city, by which seems to be meant one of gridwork, only when building themselves a capital in the Chinese style. In fact Edo was rather like Kyoto, the longest-lived of the Chinese-style capitals. The commercial center was laid out with reasonable consistency and thoroughness in a series of grids. The grids tended not to join one another very well, but that is another matter. Over considerable expanses the right angle and the straight line prevailed.

A map of the High City, on the other hand, puts one in mind of a vast, ancient country village, with the streets following animal tracks and the boundaries of fields. So too it is with Kyoto, a grid where the old city was laid out, but something quite different in outlying districts. It is as if, having paid homage to the Chinese model, the Japanese settled back into something familiar and comfortable.

Finding an address in the High City is a matter of navigating in more or less the right direction, and asking aid and comfort upon approaching the bourne. It must have been worse in Edo, when there were no house numbers, and the person of the Low City rarely ventured into that cold, alien land, the High City. There is a charming Kafū story about a young girl from a Shimbashi geisha establishment who is sent on a bill-collecting expedition into the High City, and the dreadful time she has finding the delinquent customer of whom she is in pursuit, and her resolve, upon returning safely to Shimbashi, never again to accept so hazardous an assignment.

The High City is not merely a jumble of hills. It is a pattern of ridges and valleys. The main roads out from the city followed ridge lines and valleys, so that the premodern city had, and the modern city has preserved, a resemblance to the cobweb plan admired by planners. Lesser routes climbed up and down the slopes to join the greater ones. The residences of the upper classes were on the heights, and there were farmlands and plebeian clusters in the valleys and along the main roads. A map from late Meiji therefore shows, typically, a tract of undivided land, perhaps private, perhaps a parade ground or a religious or educational establishment, with a somewhat orderly arrangement of small blocks beside it, or on more than one side of it. The main streets are arteries radiating from the heart, with innumerable capillaries between them. From a combination of orderliness and confusion the modern pattern of the uplands grew, remarkably like Edo both in the configuration of the streets and the pattern of land use, except for the fact that farmlands were soon eliminated.

There were other respects as well in which the streets and roads did not change greatly. A very few of the main avenues had been widened to accommodate trolleys, but for the most part they were pitted, narrow, and badly drained. Kafū's little bill collector made her way westwards towards the city limits through a sea of mud. The novelist Tokuda Shūsei recalled that in mid-Meiji the main street past the university in Hongō was as rough and narrow as a rustic lane—and this street was the beginning of a principal Tokugawa highway, running out past the Itabashi Mouth and on through the mountains to the Kansai.

The hilly part of Kōjimachi Ward, to the west of the palace, where the British legation and embassy has stood for upwards of a century, is the Kōjimachi of Edo. Some think that it was the site of a yeast works, and therefore that the name means something like Yeastville. Others hold it to be a pun on *daimyō kōji*, "daimyo alley," and yet others combine the two and make it "daimyo ferment." The second and third are nicely descriptive, for the ward was given over to the residences of the lesser military orders, the *hatamoto*, the humblest who could still claim access to the shogun's presence. It was bisected by a narrow mercantile strip along the Kōshū highway, leading westwards to the Shinjuku Mouth and the province of Kai. The *hatamoto* departed. Many of their houses remained, to be taken over by the bourgeois of the new day, the bureaucrat, the merchant, the journalist. The Nagai family lived there for a time in Kafū's childhood.

Yet if the displacement of the old inhabitants was virtually complete, the district was the least changed physically of any in the immediate environs of the palace. At the end of Meiji *hatamoto* houses still survived in large numbers. The Arishima family, from which sprang Takeo the novelist and Ikuma the painter, as well as another novelist who used the pseudonym Satomi Ton, possessed one of them.

Still living in it after the earthquake, Ikuma wrote:

I do not know whether it is a hundred years old or two hundred years old. I know from old maps that it once belonged to a lesser *hatamoto* called governor of something or other, but I do not know who might have built it or lived in it over the years. I have no notion of the joys and sorrows that came and went. Nor have I had any urge to learn. They who come after me will probably not know about me, or have an urge to learn. It does not seem likely that there will be one among future dealers in culture who love this house for the reason that I love it, one reason only, that it is old. In the not distant future it will probably suffer the common fate and be torn down. The proverb has it that the head of a sardine can be deified if one is of a mind to do it. So we may account for my inability to think of giving up this shabby old house and its grounds. Not many are left of the *hatamoto* houses that lined the Banchō district. The fires that followed the earthquake reduced half of it to ashes.

Banchō, "the numbered blocks," Block One through Block Six, was another designation for the Kōjimachi district proper, the part of Kōjimachi Ward immediately west of the palace. Through a rearranging of numbers the British embassy was presently to acquire its fine address, Number One Block One. Arishima's reminiscences inform us that Banchō came through Meiji fairly well, and was grievously damaged in 1923. Though under new ownership in Meiji and early Taishō, it wore an aged aspect that was different from surviving parts of the Edo Low City, a graver, more sedate look. Because of massive gates and high garden walls, there was little here of the street life that prevailed in the Low City. Tiny garden plots lined the streets of the Low City, but the walled garden was virtually gone there by the end of Meiji.

Banchō had not contained the great estates of the daimyo, but the moderately ample places of the lesser aristocracy. The former became detached palaces and parade grounds and the like, while the latter were nicely proportioned to the needs of the upper middle class of the new day. In search of the look of the Edo High Town, therefore—an austere, walled-in, perhaps somewhat forbidding look—one might best, at the end of Meiji, have gone for a walk through Banchō.

The northern and southern parts of the High City have, in the Tokyo century, gone different ways. The beginnings of that difference were already apparent in Meiji. The two southern wards, Akasaka and Azabu, became the home of the highly affluent, and of the international and diplomatic set. There were such people in the north too. The Iwasaki family of the Mitsubishi enterprises had the most lavish of their several estates in Hongō. For those who wished to be near the rich and fashionable, however, and participate in their doings, the northern wards of the High City, Hongō and Koishikawa, were on the wrong side of the palace, and ever more so as the decades went by. The Low City, of course, was even farther removed from Society. The wards to the west, Yotsuya and Ushigome, tended to be rather more like the north than the south.

Insofar as they remained within the city limits at all, the good addresses came to be concentrated in the two southern wards. It says something, perhaps, that these two wards seem the least interesting of all the Meiji fifteen. They contained interesting people, no doubt, but, save for a few enclaves like the Akasaka geisha quarter, they were not interesting neighborhoods. Indeed the word "neighborhood" scarcely seems to apply. They encouraged the exclusiveness of the Tokugawa military classes.

Less wealthy, the northern wards—and to an extent the western wards too—had an artistic and intellectual tone. Sometimes the lack of wealth was extreme. Yotsuya Ward, west of Kōjimachi, contained one of the "slums" of which historians of the city seem so proud. There it was that Hanai O-ume, the murderess, died in 1916. It was almost next door to the Akasaka Palace, where the Meiji emperor spent a good part of his reign. The High City has always accommodated, side by side, the extremely well placed and the extremely poorly placed. The Yotsuya slum seems not to have been industrial, but a gathering of uprooted farmers.

It would probably be a simplification to say that the divergence north and south began with the disposition made of the grand estates. Yet that does seem to point the directions taken. Of the estates scattered around the castle, four stand out on Edo maps as rivals of the castle itself. They chanced to fall into four Meiji wards, all in the High City. The mansion and park of the Wakayama Tokugawa family, in Akasaka, became the Akasaka Detached Palace; the Nagoya Tokugawa estate in Ushigome became the military academy; the Mito Tokugawa estate in Koishikawa became an arsenal and later an amusement park, with a fragment of the Mito garden tucked somewhat sootily into a corner. And finally there was the one among the four that was not Tokugawa, the Maeda estate in Hongō, which became the Imperial University, and so Hongō, with the hilly parts of Kanda, became the student quarter of the city, and one of its intellectual and literary centers as well.

The origins of the university are complicated. It did not settle completely on the Maeda estate until mid-Meiji. Its earliest beginnings may be traced to certain institutions established by the shogunate for the study of the Western barbarian, and for more genteel Chinese studies as well. A South School and an East School each lay in a southerly direction from the Maeda estate. The Occidental and traditional branches feuded chronically and bitterly, but by the time of the move to Hongō in the eighties the former was ascendant.

Until the earthquake the Maeda family still occupied a generous—though by old standards restricted—expanse at the southwest corner of their old estate. Before it became the university campus the

Maeda estate had provided housing for Western persons who taught here and there and were otherwise of service to the government. E. S. Morse lived on the Maeda estate or Kaga Yashiki, as he called it, from the name of the province that was the Maeda fief.

His description suggests what was happening to many of the old aristocratic tracts: "Kaga Yashiki is now a wilderness of trees, bushes, and tangled masses of shrubbery; hundreds of crows are cawing about; here and there are abandoned wells, some of them not covered, and treacherous pits they are. The crows are as tame as our pigeons and act as scavengers. They . . . wake you in the morning by cawing outside the window."

Immediately to the north of the university stood that most haughty institution, the First Higher School. It was founded late in 1874 as the Tokyo School of English and did not move to its Hongō grounds until 1889. The Hongō site is now occupied by the agricultural college of the university, which in Meiji was in the southwestern suburbs. The First Higher School was perhaps even haughtier than the university, which was certainly haughty enough. All gifted and ambitious lads wanted to attend both, and the higher school had the fewer students. Most of its graduates who lived long enough became eminent in one way or another. More than half the graduates of both institutions went routinely into the bureaucracy or the academic life.

A short distance from the university on the other side was the most elite of schools for women, the Women's Higher Normal School. When, as soon happened, other institutions that called themselves universities came into existence, they congregated in the regions to the north of the palace. There were some famous boarding houses in Hongō, which, with Kanda, had more of them than any other part of the city. The most famous produced approximately one doctor of philosophy per year during the quarter of a century after its establishment. At least one such house survives from late Meiji, a three-storey wooden building of a kind that fire regulations would not permit today. It was considered so exciting an addition to the university quarter that there were lantern processions for three nights to honor its opening.

We have seen that the Nezu licensed quarter, down the hill in the flat part of Hongō, was moved lest it cause students to lay waste their treasures. Upland Hongō seems on the whole to have been a sober district, its students aware of their elite status and their responsibilities. The higher school was relatively the rowdier, but the university seems to have set the tone. There was and has been very little in its vicinity to suggest a Latin Quarter. It is commonly thought today that the quiet was brought by the Second World War—this despite the fact that much of the district escaped the fires. It seems, however, to have been rather quiet all along.

The most famous novel about the student life of late Meiji is Natsume Sōseki's *Sanshirō*, whose title is the name of its hero. The campus pond, a survival from the Maeda days, is known as Sanshirō's Pond. Sanshirō lives in Hongō, and does not have a very exciting time of it. He sees a performance of *Hamlet,* which strikes him as full of odd remarks, but the pleasurable event described at greatest length is a viewing of the chrysanthemum dolls at Dangozaka, just north of the university. The novelist Tokuda Shūsei remarked upon how students had to go to Kanda for almost everything, from school supplies to Kabuki. Hongō was very much a part of the High City, he said, informing us, probably, that the students of the private universities may have set the tone in Kanda, but Hongō was dominated by more austere sorts, professors and intellectuals and the young men of the future.

Along its eastern border with Shitaya, Hongō extended a short distance into the flatlands. There was situated the soon-to-depart Nezu licensed quarter. At the top of the ridge a short distance south lay an older and unlicensed pleasure quarter, that of Yushima. In Meiji it was patronized chiefly by Nihombashi merchants, but the clientele also included the more affluent sort of student. There does not seem to have been any thought of doing to it what was done to Nezu.

The Yushima quarter had come into being because the huge Ueno temple complex, ministering to the Tokugawa tombs, was so near at hand. It was not proper for priests to frequent the usual sort of teahouse, and so they took their pleasure at establishments called *kagemajaya,* in which Yushima specialized. Written in a fashion that invites translation as "shady teahouses," the *kagemajaya* offered male geisha and prostitutes. Such places did not go out of business immediately upon the Restoration and the destruction of the temple. Towards the end of the nineteenth century Yushima shook off its past and became a more conventional geisha quarter.

Many professors dwelt in the vicinity of the university, and many literary persons as well, including Natsume Sōseki and Mori Ogai, the two of them the most revered of all Meiji novelists. Nagai Kafū has a memorable description of a visit to Ogai's "Tower of the Tidal Vista," not as fanciful a name as it may seem. Ogai lived north of the university, and the Hongō and Ueno rises were still much acclaimed for the views they offered over the Low City, low then in skyline as in elevation, towards the Sumida and the bay.

There was a *gakusha-machi,* a "professorial neighborhood," which has since disappeared. The Abe family, lords of Fukuyama in what is now Hiroshima Prefecture, had an estate very near the main gate of the university. Late in the Meiji Period they undertook to sell parcels at very low rates to professors, and to lend half the money needed for building houses upon them. Because the Abe had surrendered title, and the current holders could dispose of it as they wished, this admirable endeavor was defeated. In the years after the earthquake addresses to the west of the old city became fashionable among intellectuals. The professors moved there, and the Abe lands went to others. It is another episode in the westward movement of the city. Intellectuals may have had antibourgeois tendencies in some respects of intellectual import, but a good address for the businessman has been a good address for the professor too.

In Koishikawa, the ward to the west, the Iwasaki family attempted a similar endeavor in the years after the earthquake. Their main estate straddled the boundary between Hongō and Shitaya, and so graced both High City and Low. The Western house had been placed by Conder upon the ridge, and the main gate down at the Shitaya end. The house survives. The Iwasaki estate is probably the best place in the whole country for acquiring a sense of how the Meiji plutocracy lived. A few of the Japanese rooms that once stretched all along the west verge of the garden survive. The Western mansion was of course for show, and the lawn, more like an English park than a traditional Japanese garden, must have provided a grand setting for parties; the Japanese rooms were where the family chose to live.

The story of the survival is interesting. The holocaust of 1923 destroyed another Iwasaki mansion by Conder in Fukagawa, but spared the Hongō one, as did the holocaust of 1945. The tract and the buildings on it passed to the government as a result of American efforts to disperse the assets of rich families. Most of it was presently en-

The Iwasaki mansion in Hongō, designed by Conder. A survivor from Meiji

trusted to the Supreme Court, which decided to clear the site for a
legal institute and housing for judges. Destruction was proceeding
briskly and had overtaken most of the Japanese wing when the Cultural Properties Commission intervened and declared the remainder,
and the Western mansion, an Important Cultural Property under the
protection of the state. The Supreme Court acceded; had it wished to
have the designation revoked, it would have had to go to court like
anyone else.

Life has at times been difficult for the very rich of modern Japan.
The head of the Yasuda enterprises, now Fuji, was assassinated in
1921. There are subterranean passages on the Iwasaki property. Many
sinister things are said to have occurred in them, while the house was

used by Americans for counterintelligence operations. Earlier occupants had in fact dug the passages, because they could never be sure when they might have to flee. From such details one may sense what life was like for the Rokumeikan set.

It would seem that even before the earthquake professorial and intellectual sorts were beginning to move westwards. A 1918 work, one of large numbers describing the "prosperity" of the city, offers brief characterizations of each of the fifteen wards. Those for the Low City are rather obvious. It may be that, compared to the High City, the Low City was static and simple to classify, not the place of the future. Kyōbashi is "high-collar," Nihombashi "Japanese." The several directions in which the High City seems to be moving are apparent, as is the divergence between the north and the south. Akasaka is the place of the aristocracy, Azabu that of "the voices of insects," suggesting wide gardens and tracts still awaiting development, there at the southern edge of the city. Hongō is the place of the student (as is Kanda, but of the sort of student who must work for his board), and Koishikawa, in the northwest corner of the Meiji city, is the place of the *gakusha,* the professor or scholar.

Koishikawa produced Nagai Kafū, the most sensitive and diligent chronicler of the city, but on the whole it was the less distinguished of the two wards on the northern tier of the High City. It had very little, in the days before a baseball stadium and an amusement park came to occupy the site of the old Mito estate, that people would wish to go out of their way for. The circle of temples along the outskirts of Edo extended westwards and southwards through Koishikawa and Ushigome. Koishikawa contained two very solemn temples, both close to the Tokugawa family, and having none of the popular appeal of the Asakusa Kannon. There were also gardens of some note, including the university botanical garden, founded in the seventeenth century as the shogun's own medicinal gardens. The oldest educational building in the city, once the university medical school, is in the botanical garden.

Koishikawa contained pockets of industry, one of them dear to chroniclers of the proletariat. The valley behind the Denzūin, one of the two grand temples in the district, was a printing center. Being somewhat better educated than most members of the proletariat, printers early acquired class consciousness, and so provided Japanese counterparts of Joe Hill. On the whole, however, Koishikawa was a region of solid if not high bourgeoisie. For some reason this northwesterly direction was not the one in which people who could go anywhere chose to go; nor was it a quarter of the city that was being pushed under in the rush to the suburbs. The outer boundary of Koishikawa was still not far from the real limits of the city.

Ushigome and Yotsuya, the wards to the west of Kōjimachi and the palace, had that same air of the modestly bourgeois. They did, from time to time, show more distinguished things to the world. Kagura-zaka, in Ushigome, was for a time the only High City district of flowers and willows that rivaled Akasaka. Kafū thought it had High City sleaziness in uncommon measure, but he was difficult to please. The best time for Kagurazaka was immediately after the earthquake. Ushigome was the only ward among the fifteen that suffered no fire damage. So it drew people who, in a happier day, would have preferred the older and more conservative quarters of the Low City. Presently Kagurazaka was left behind in the great rush to the western suburbs.

Still in mid-Meiji the least populous of the fifteen wards, Yotsuya was on the most frequented of the migratory routes westwards. Just before the earthquake it was enlarged to include a part of the Shinjuku district, the most rapidly growing of the western suburbs, presently to excel Ginza as a place for shopping and pursuing pleasure.

The Arishima family bought a *hatamoto* house in Kōjimachi, and Ikuma was still living in it after the earthquake. Nagai Kafū's father bought two *hatamoto* places in Koishikawa, and tore them down to have a house and garden more suited to the new day. Only traces of the old gardens, dread places inhabited by foxes, remained in Kafū's boyhood. It would seem to have been typical. The rows of *hatamoto* houses in Kōjimachi supported one another and gave the place its tone, and so they remained. In the wards farther north and west the larger estates were broken up or put to public use, and the *hatamoto* lands in among them attracted people who were not of an antiquarian bent. So the outer wards must, at the end of Meiji, have looked much less like Edo than did Banchō.

The southern wards were lacking in places one might wish to show a country cousin. Azabu was the ward of the singing insects, but of course he had quite enough insect voices at home. Akasaka had its detached palace, through whose iron gates it was possible, at the end of Meiji, to gaze upon the Gallic pile where dwelt the crown prince.

There were extensive barracks in the southern wards, and from them the Roppongi section of Azabu got its start as a pleasure center, the only major one in the present city that is not also a transportation center. The military origins of Roppongi are not commonly remembered in our day. It is a place where pleasure-seeking pacifists assemble.

The other place for military revelry in late Meiji was Shibuya, beyond the city limits to the southwest, one of the directions in which the city was pressing most urgently. Famous for its tea in early Meiji, Shibuya was by late Meiji becoming richly suburban, the chief rival of Shinjuku in its power to draw people and money from the center of the old city.

On Meiji maps, Akasaka "of the aristocracy" looks as if it might have had noisier insect voices than Azabu. It was not the principal abode of the highest aristocracy, the court stratum. Of fourteen houses recognized as princely in late Meiji, seven were in Kōjimachi, between the inner and outer moats of the old castle, and five were scattered through the southern wards of the city, only one of them in Akasaka. One remained in the old capital, Kyoto, and one was still in the Low City, beside the Sumida above Asakusa. None were in the northern wards of the High City, which were distinctly less titled and moneyed.

Yet Akasaka had great tracts of public and royal land, and the princeliest personage among them all, the next emperor. Had one been good at scaling walls and evading guards, one could have walked the whole of the way across the ward, from the city limits to the outer moat, without setting foot on private, nonroyal land. Across certain wide expanses singing insects may have been hard pressed to survive. The new Akasaka parade grounds, to be the site of the Meiji emperor's funeral and then to become public gardens in his memory, were as dusty as the old Hibiya grounds. A scorched-earth policy thought to be good for instilling a soldierly mood prevailed in both places.

Though it did not have the smallest population, Azabu must in late Meiji have seemed the most rustic of the fifteen wards. Indeed we have the testimony of rickshaw runners that they preferred to stay away from it, and had no great difficulty doing so, for it had little need of their services. Its streets and lanes wandered their own way with little regard for the ways of their fellows, and the runner was likely to suffer the professional humiliation of getting lost.

The main thrust of the city, as it spilled over its limits in late Meiji, was directly to the west, past Yotsuya to Shinjuku. The next most powerful was to the southwest, past Akasaka towards Shibuya. So the pattern at the end of Meiji was as it had been at the beginning, energetic commerce along the radial strands of the cobweb, and residential districts of varying density and greatly varying affluence scattered among them.

The great shift of Meiji and since has been more than a matter of population. The High City was accumulating the money, the power, and the imagination. Culture tends to go where money goes, and so the Low City was ceasing to be original in this important regard. It may seem strange to say that power was leaving the Low City, since under the old regime absolute power had been concentrated in the shogun's castle. Yet, as we have seen, the aristocracy was scattered all over the Low City (especially in places with water frontage and pleasant prospects), and the wealthy of the merchant class, such as the Mitsui family, had much more power than Tokugawa theory permitted.

Today there is an illuminating confusion in defining the boundaries of the Low City. The affluent of the southern and western wards tend to think that all of the poorer northern and eastern wards are Low City. In fact, however, they straddle the ridge line that originally divided the two, and the Hongō and Yanaka districts were significant artistic and intellectual centers in Meiji, most definitely a part of the High City. The confusion is illuminating because it informs us that the great division today, especially in the minds of the high bourgeoisie, is between the richer and poorer halves of the city. It was not so in Edo and early Meiji. Then, if any generalization held, it was that the High City was the more patrician of the two, and the Low City the more plebeian.

Today, poring over rosters of literary societies, one may come upon an occasional address in the northern wards, but scarcely any in the flatlands east of the Ueno rise—in the classical Low City. Writers and artists were moving out all through the Meiji Period, as were the old military aristocracy and the mercantile elite. Few stayed behind after the great flood, and by the time of the earthquake the withdrawal was almost complete. Nagai Kafū loved the Low City, but it would not do for everyday. He lived in Tsukiji, near the foreign settlement and even nearer the Shimbashi geisha district, for a time in mid-Taishō, but several years before the earthquake he built himself a house in wealthy, hilly Azabu. His diary for the Tsukiji time is a grouchy document. The Low City was noisy and dusty.

The Low City was the home of the literature and drama of late Edo, insofar as those pursuits had to do with the new and not the traditional and academic. The drama changed gradually, because of the improvers and because of inevitable influences from abroad, and its base in the Low City was dissipated. The literature of Edo continued to be popular until about midway through Meiji, when the modern began to take over.

Of the difference between the traditional and the modern in literature, many things can be said. The popular literature of Edo had not been very intellectual. The literature known as modern, with its beginnings in the Rokumeikan decade, the 1880s, is obsessively, gnawingly intellectual. If a single theme runs through it, that theme is the quest for identity, an insistence upon what it is that establishes the individual as individual. The importance of Christianity in Meiji thought and writing, an importance which it has not had since; the rebellion against the family and the casting of the authoritarian father into nether regions; the strong autobiographic strain in modern fiction: all of these have in common the identification of modernism with individualism.

They were concerns of the High City. The Low City went on for a time reading and producing the woodcut books beloved of the Edo townsman. The leaders of modernity had utter contempt for these, and as the afterglow of Edo faded, the Low City offered no serious competition with modernity. Nor was it remarkably steadfast in its devotion to the old forms. Not many people of Taishō could, and almost no one today can, make out their antiquated, ornate language and quirkish calligraphy.

A strong sense of locale was present in the literature of Edo. One can with no great exaggeration say that Edo had its literature and Tokyo does not. Modern literature is altogether more national and cosmopolitan than Edo literature, which is not to be understood and appreciated without reference to very specific places—from Shiba on the south to Kanda, Shitaya, and the Asakusa-Yoshiwara complex on the north, and eastwards beyond the Sumida. Though people like Kafū and Kubota Mantarō made the changing city their chief subject, they were exceptions. Modern literature calls to mind not specific places like Shiba and Kanda but that great abstraction "suburbia."

To say that the Low City was the cultural center of Japan in late Edo and Meiji is to say that it created the most interesting culture. This is different from being a cultural capital, the products of which are purveyed all through the land. The boundaries of the Low City as we see them on a late-Edo map defined a cultural region. The boundaries of the High City today do not. It is bigger than it looks. The story of modern literature is, like the story of prime ministers, philosophers, and the like, a national one, something that has happened in Tokyo but is not of it.

All these several stories are interesting, certainly. Giving them a few lines and then moving on, I may seem to be dismissing the grander story, that of the transformation of a small and isolated country at a far corner of the earth into a modern technological giant, and of the intellectual and emotional processes that accompanied the transformation and made it possible. Yet it may after all be less a story of change than one of survival. The modern novelist and thinker have been dedicated evangelists for individualism, and yet the great strength of modern Japan may be in the willingness of most Japanese, even in the absence of authoritarian precepts, to suppress their individuality.

The growth of the High City in size and influence has made Tokyo more of an abstraction and less of a community. Beginning in Meiji and continuing all through the century since Meiji began, the change is a profound one. The baseball-and-television culture of the Low City of our day is an altogether lesser entity than was the culture of the Low City a century ago; and the culture of the High City is much more considerable. The High City still has poor people enough, but it has all of the exceedingly rich people. The other elements, literary and artistic and philosophical and the rest, have followed money, even when they have thought of themselves as constituting a resistance.

The High City gets higher and higher. The Low City is still the warmer and more approachable of the two, but the days of its cultural eminence are gone. They are for elegists and threnodists.

6

THE TAISHŌ LOOK

July 20, 1912, was the day scheduled for the *kawabiraki*, the opening of the Sumida (see pages 136–138), most delightfully crowded of Low City observances. It was called off, for on that day came the announcement that the Meiji emperor was grievously ill. He had been ill for a week, and had fallen into a coma from uremic poisoning.

The rest of the summer was hushed. The street festivals for "taking in coolness," which made the oppressive heat of August a happy thing, were subdued, as was the mood of the pleasure quarters. Geisha who found it necessary to go about their business did so in ordinary dress, lest they attract attention. Even the stock market reacted, pessimistically, for there was an instinctive feeling that the end of an age had come, and no one could be certain about the one that was to follow.

Notices of the state of the royal health were sent out from the palace by pony express and put up before police boxes. There were silent crowds in the palace plaza. Public-minded persons (not, it seems, the city) provided water. There were crowds as well at shrines near the palace—Kanda to the north, Sannō to the south, the Hibiya Shrine near the Imperial Hotel. From temples poured great clouds of smoke, day and night, the burning of sesame seeds being an ancient form of exorcism, and ancient beliefs about malign spirits yet widespread. Vehicular traffic made every attempt to move silently when it

Outside the palace as the Meiji emperor lay dying

had to move past the palace. Rags muffled the sound of wheels along the trolley track that followed the palace moat from Hibiya towards Yotsuya and approached fairly close to the royal apartments on its southwest arc. From the plaza, the cannon that since 1871 had fired the *don* at noon each day was moved to a remoter spot.

The emperor died late on the night of July 29. The announcement came early on July 30, and so the forty-fifth year of Meiji became the first year of Taishō. Rain began falling a few minutes past midnight and fell as the announcement was made, but crowds, standing or kneeling, remained in the plaza all through the night.

Demonstrations of grief and affection continued through the weeks before the funeral. Theaters called off all performances upon the announcement of the death, and some remained closed until the funeral. The variety theaters seem to have been the quickest to go back into business. Many shops closed, especially in commercial districts near the palace. Sales throughout the city fell by perhaps a fifth, perhaps as much as a third, during the early days of mourning. The grief had a streak of anger in it; the house of the emperor's chief physician was stoned.

There was a movement to have the interment in Tokyo, but Fushimi, on the southern outskirts of Kyoto, had already been selected. The funeral took place on September 13. Newspaper descriptions emphasize the stillness of places usually noisy, save only the railway stations, and especially Ueno, accommodating travelers from the poor and conservative northeast. The Nihombashi fish market, usually closed only at the New Year, was silent on the day of the funeral. Shops remained closed all over the city. Asakusa was described as quieter than in the aftermath of the great flood two years before. The ladies of pleasure beneath the Twelve Storeys in Asakusa observed the day solemnly.

The weather was good. The funeral was a combination of the old and the new, richly symbolic of the era that had ended. Night had always been the time for the most sacred of Shinto ceremonials, and the funeral was at night. The guards regiment fired a salute at eight in the evening. Naval vessels off Shinagawa answered, and temple bells all through the city started tolling. The cortege left the southeast gate of the palace to a bugle call and funeral marches played by the guards band. The way to Babasaki, on the other side of the plaza, was lighted by gas torches in iron baskets, while attendants in the immediate cortege carried pine torches. The funeral pavilion, at the Akasaka parade grounds, was also lighted by gas, in that latter day of gaslight. Five oxen in single file drew the hearse. Some attendants wore ancient court dress, others modern uniforms.

The cortege made its way southwards from Babasaki past Hibiya Park, westwards along the outer moat, and then south to the parade grounds, which it reached at about eleven. At Babasaki the crush was so great that there were injuries. All windows and utility poles along the way were draped in black and white, all lights were put out, and all shop signs were either draped or removed. The body was taken to Kyoto by train on the fourteenth, and that night interred at Fushimi.

With the energetic Shibusawa Eiichi in charge, planning for a memorial shrine began immediately. Land belonging to the royal household in the western suburbs, beyond Akasaka Ward, was chosen for the site of the shrine proper, and the parade grounds, site of the funeral, for the "outer gardens." The iris gardens that are the most famous part of the shrine grounds are said to have been designed by the Meiji emperor himself for the pleasure of his empress, to whom the shrine was also presently dedicated. It was begun in 1915 and dedicated in 1920, although construction was not finally completed until late the following year. The outer gardens were not finished until 1926, the year in which another reign began, the Shōwa, which yet continues. On the day of the dedication a bridge collapsed, leading to a construction scandal already remarked upon (see page 31). It coincided with a scandal over gas rates. The double scandal led to the resignation of the mayor.

The most remarkable happening attendant upon the funeral was the suicide of General Nogi and his wife. It seems to have occurred as the temple bells began tolling at the start of the obsequies. The Nogi house, a modest one which yet stands, is very close to the parade grounds. In that day when the southern wards were so little developed, it may have been visible from the funeral pavilion.

No shrine would be dedicated to the Taishō emperor, successor to the Meiji emperor, nor can his passing have seemed so clearly the passing of an age. Meiji is remote as a person, but as a symbol he

Funeral procession for the Meiji emperor

remains important. Of Taishō this cannot be said. His last years were spent in shadows deep even for an emperor. A regency was proclaimed in 1921, with the crown prince, the present emperor, then a youth of twenty, as regent. Gingerly, we are told in biographical notes that the emperor had fallen ill. That the illness was mental is one of those facts which no one speaks of but everyone knows.

The Taishō reign was a short one, only a third as long as Meiji. The emperor had ceased to exist as a public figure, and his death, coming so soon after the earthquake, must have seemed an event of no great moment for the populace of the city, where manifestations of grief for his father had been conspicuous. One wonders whether, if he had died before his father and the present emperor had succeeded as a boy of ten or eleven, the period from 1912 to 1926 would be thought by historians to constitute a unit at all.

In any case, it might be described as unexciting, compared with the preceding and following reigns. The former brought huge successes, the latter brought a catastrophe of its own making and now brings successes of a quite different order. Taishō had its war, a comfortable one for the Japanese, in which the principal action was far away in Europe and certain fruits of victory lay near at hand. The expressions with which "Taishō" is most commonly associated are "the great Taishō earthquake" and "Taishō democracy," the latter a pale flower that bloomed briefly after the First World War and left nothing behind save its name. Taishō history contains little to be either very proud of or deeply ashamed of.

We are accustomed to thinking of modern Japanese history in terms of reigns, however, and so there are Taishō literature, the Taishō theater, and the like. The fact remains that the things of Taishō do have their own look.

Wandering through the more crowded parts of the Low City, one comes upon pockets that survived the conflagration of 1945, and there it is, the Taishō look. Very rarely is the Meiji look to be come upon, and almost never the genuine Edo object. One recognizes Taishō in the pressed-metal fronts of little shops, in irrelevant turrets, in oriel windows and shutters that fold rather than slide. Nagai Kafū rejoiced in the obliviousness of the regions east of the river to the call of Civilization and Enlightenment, but Taishō may be seen as the time when they started paying attention at least to its decorative elements.

In 1914 the city sponsored a great fair called the Taishō Hakurankai, the Taishō Exposition. The purpose was to honor the new reign and, in the Meiji spirit, to promote industry. It got off to a bad start. The contractors did not seem very intent upon promoting industry. Construction was incomplete on opening day, and the emperor had to make his way to the site through a sea of mud. Letters to editors objected to the inclusion of a mummy among exhibits felicitating the new era, but the exposition was on the whole a success. More than seven million people purchased tickets. Whatever it may have done for industry, it did succeed in giving the Taishō reign a certain independence from its predecessor, an identity of its own.

There were other expositions, one of which celebrated the semicentennial of the establishment of Tokyo as capital; another honored the conclusion of the war to end wars, and itself ended just a year and a half before the earthquake. But no exposition was more important than the Taishō Exposition. It introduced and established the Taishō look, right there at the beginning of the reign.

Tokyo led the way into the new era, as it had into the old. By the end of Meiji, monumental architecture in the Western style had become soberly, somewhat academically Western. The earliest exercises in Western architecture, such as the Hoterukan, had been something different—different, indeed, from anything Western. Much the same may be said of the influence which the Taishō Exposition had upon shop and domestic architecture, nowhere more conspicuously than in the pleasure quarters. Extremes of fancifulness make them look like Disneylands before their time. E. Philip Terry, that writer of colorful if not wholly reliable guidebooks, thought the Yoshiwara "Pompeiian." Looking at pictures of what was lost in 1923, others might think that it was Venetian, rather, in the exuberance and liberality of its decoration. It had something of San Marco in it.

There was a Taishō look in people too, more noticeable in women than in men. The day of the flapper did not arrive until after the earthquake. Men had for the most part taken to Western dress before the earthquake, but Japanese dress prevailed among women. The Taishō woman in Japanese dress looks more Western, somehow, than

A Yumeji girl—with cat

does the Meiji woman in Western dress. The bustles and bonnets of the Meiji woodcut are all very gay, and, at the remove of a century (however they may have looked to a Parisian couturier of the time, and indeed did look to Pierre Loti), seem authentic enough, but the face is of an earlier day. A languorous beauty of Taishō, by contrast, speaks of a world-weariness that has been studied well and mastered, and it is not of domestic provenance.

Two years older than Tanizaki, the painter and illustrator Takehisa Yumeji was in his late twenties when Taishō began. Among all artists and craftsmen he is the most symbolic of Taishō. His creative years were mostly in Taishō, and his illustrations, while they may not be great art, speak more eloquently of Taishō than do those of any other artist. Wan, consumptive, with sloping shoulders and lips, the Yumeji girl would have felt at home in the Germany of a century before.

Edo artists in the woodcut admired slender beauty, certainly, but it is an abstract, fleshless sort of beauty, very far from this wasted flesh. The Yumeji girl may look ill, but she smiles sometimes, albeit wanly. The Edo beauty did not smile, and the Meiji beauty did but rarely. All manner of smiles flash across Taishō paintings and posters, and give a sense that Western things have been absorbed and become part of the organism as they had not earlier been. The enterprising cosmetologists of the Shiseidō may at length have succeeded in clearing the national skin of its murkiness.

The painter Kishida Ryūsei, who was born in Ginza in 1891, thought he found a Taishō look in men too, and especially actors. "There is a certain briskness about these handsome figures. There is something that suggests Valentino." He wrote of the quality after the earthquake, but it must have been there before. The Valentino look may be associated with the Taishō look—though "briskness" is the last word one would apply to the Yumeji girl. It is a pity that we have no Yumeji boys.

The population of the fifteen wards grew during Taishō, and the population of the prefecture grew yet more rapidly. By the time of the earthquake the former had risen to well over two million, and the population of the prefecture to almost four million.

The High City was reaching beyond the city limits in all directions, especially the south and west. At the beginning of Meiji the city did not fill the fifteen wards, and at the end of Taishō the fifteen wards no longer defined the city. The city proper was larger in area than Yokohama, Kobe, or Kyoto, but covered less than half the area of Osaka, and only a little more than half that of Nagoya. Not until almost a decade after the earthquake were the city limits expanded to encompass most of the population, and such burgeoning suburbs as Shibuya and Ikebukuro. The municipal government seems to have been reluctant to press for expansion. The city was vulnerable to incursions upon its autonomy, and any approach to the size of the prefecture meant risking a return to the old "special" status, with a governor and no mayor.

Yet it seems to have been thought inevitable that the city would expand. Aside from Tokyo itself, there was still at the end of Taishō only one incorporated city in the prefecture. Much more populous districts than that one city, Hachiōji, lay just beyond the fifteen wards. It seems to have been assumed that these would presently become wards themselves. In 1932, they did.

The governor continued to be a faceless bureaucrat from the Home Ministry, while the mayor was sometimes a man of considerable eminence. There were mayors of ministerial stature, such as Gotō Shimpei, he of the "big kerchief," who would have had the earthquake and its aftermath to preside over had he not resigned in the spring of 1923.

None of the eight mayors of Tokyo during the Taishō Period was born in the city. Gotō may have been the most famous of them, but probably the most popular was his predecessor, Tajiri Inajirō, so eminent an authority on administration that he lectured at the Imperial University. He had to resign because of the bridge that collapsed while the Meiji Shrine was being dedicated. An eccentric in a way that made people like him, he wore hand-me-down clothes and walked to his office from Koishikawa, his lunch tied up in a kerchief like that of any other worker. A tendency towards incontinence in moments of tension was taken as a mark of earnestness.

The nation enjoyed a war boom, and the city shared in it. Industrial production in 1919 was almost four times what it had been in 1910. As for finance and management, there was a rush to Marunouchi, the old Mitsubishi Meadow. In 1922 more than a third of companies with a capitalization of over five million yen had their headquarters in Kōjimachi Ward, chiefly Marunouchi. The number was about equal to the combined total for Nihombashi, the heart of the old merchant city, and Kyōbashi. The city was falling into its present shape by mid-Taishō.

Across from the central railway station, the Marunouchi Building, largest in the land, was finished on the eve of the earthquake. The Marine Insurance Building, finished in 1917, was the first to be called *biru,* short for "building." (Most office buildings are now so designated.) The two buildings represented another Taishō look, the box-like one. The small shopkeeper may have fancied oriels and turrets, but big builders were eschewing unprofitable decorations. Another lesson had been learned.

.   .   .

The First World War produced inflation, and at the end of it came riots over the high price of rice. They led to the formation of the first government based on political parties, an event generally held to mark the beginning of "Taishō democracy." The rioting reached Tokyo in mid-August of 1918, having begun on the coast of the Japan Sea ten days earlier.

Police dispersed a rally in Hibiya Park on the night of August 13, and marauding bands ranged through Kyōbashi and Nihombashi. There was more rioting on the evening of the fourteenth. One swath of violence began in Hibiya and extended from Shimbashi northwards through Ginza and Kyōbashi into Nihombashi. The other was more interesting. It began in Asakusa and advanced upon Ueno, where the crowd was estimated at twenty thousand, and upon the Yoshiwara, where sixty-nine houses were damaged. Arson and looting occurred.

On the fifteenth, riots struck the same parts of the Low City and for the first time moved west into the High City. On the sixteenth there was violence in Ginza once more, but in Ueno mounted troops scattered a band of eager rioters. No reporting on the riots had been allowed since the fourteenth. On the seventeenth it resumed, the papers having protested and the peak of the troubles having passed.

The riots led to the resignation of a prime minister who as a lad not yet twenty had served with the Restoration forces, they that overthrew the shogunate, and to the investiture of a new kind of prime minister, symbolic of Taishō democracy. Another important man of a new sort first came into prominence because of them. Shōriki Matsutarō was in command of the police who dispersed the initial Hibiya riot, and got into the newspapers because he suffered a gash on the forehead. He was so forceful and energetic a man that he was bound, sooner or later, to make his appearance in chronicles of the twentieth century. The riots were the occasion for his debut. Shōriki later became president of the *Yomiuri,* which, when he took charge, was fifth or sixth among the dozen or so newspapers in the city. He made it the largest of them all in terms of Tokyo circulation (and it is a native of the city, and not, like the *Asahi* and *Nichinichi* or *Mainichi,* Osakan). He may be called the father of professional baseball and commercial television; and so there are few Japanese lives upon which he has had no effect.

The provincial riots clearly originated in discontent over inflation. There is room for disagreement about the real meaning of the Tokyo riots. Probably the national government would not have been called upon to resign had the violence not reached the capital but been restricted to remote fishing villages. Yet there is always a suggestion in Tokyo rioting that participants gather for fun and excitement. In these events, a thousand were arrested. About a quarter received prison sentences, the highest fifteen years. Few of the accused seem to have been poverty-stricken.

Nagai Kafū thought that he detected certain leisurely, recreational tendencies in it all.

I turned into a side street and noted that the rows of geisha houses were silent, their shutters closed and their lights out. Back on the main street, I was passing time in a beer hall when a young man who seemed to be a student told me of attacks on Ginza shops and on geisha establishments in the Shimbashi district.

So I first learned of riots over the price of rice. From the next day there were no newspaper reports in the matter. I heard later that the rioting always occurred in the cool of evening. There was a good moon every evening during those days. Hearing that the rioters gathered menacingly before the houses of the wealthy when the evening had turned cool and the moon had come up, I could not put down a feeling that there was something easy and comfortable about it all. It went on for five or six days and then things returned to normal. On the night of the return to normal, it rained.

The city was becoming somewhat more fireproof, and the flowers of Edo were being stamped out. The biggest fire of Taishō, excluding the gigantic one of 1923, was another in the fine series of Kanda fires. It came in the first year of the reign, and destroyed more than twenty-five hundred buildings from Kanda eastwards into Nihombashi and Kyōbashi. Among Taishō fires of some note was the one that destroyed the first Imperial Hotel on the eve of the opening of the second. Improved firefighting methods may have had something to do with diminished losses, bur fireproofing no doubt played a larger part. In 1916 thatched roofs were banned for new buildings. The fire brigades of Edo, spirited and cheerful, remained on the job right up until the earthquake. The central fire department was reduced to ashes in 1923, along with most of its equipment. Such a disaster was needed to bring unified and centralized firefighting. The new system was not, of course, able to prevent the disaster of 1945, nor can it hope to be completely effective against similar disasters in the future.

The great flood of late Meiji was the last to devastate the center of the city. In 1917 the Kabukiza, east of Ginza, was knee-deep in water, but that was because a typhoon blew the bay inland. The Arakawa Drainage Channel was begun after the great flood and finished on the eve of the earthquake. Even before its completion it worked well, controlling torrential rains in the summer of 1918. The Tone River system still floods the farthest eastern wards from time to time, but the Arakawa Drainage Channel has contained the more mischievous Sumida.

The channel was the most ambitious engineering project the city had seen since the shogunate filled the marshy mouths of the Sumida to make the Low City. The money came from the national government, and the Home Ministry directly supervised operations, digging a wide new watercourse for upwards of fifty miles, from deep in Saitama Prefecture to the bay. In its upper reaches it generally followed the old Arakawa River. From approximately the point where the Arakawa changes names and becomes the Sumida, it swept eastwards, entering the bay at a point about halfway between the eastern boundary of Fukagawa Ward and the eastern limits of the present city. Sluices control the flow of water into the Sumida.

Nowhere did the new channel pass through any of the fifteen wards of the Meiji and Taishō city. The land was acquired at what was then thought to be a very great expense. Since the regions it crossed were then mostly suburbs and farm and fishing villages, the cost would have been several times as much a few years later. The endeavor showed great vision, and the results were splendid. The floors of a few houses may sometimes even now be under water from a cloudburst, but no major flood has been caused by the Sumida since 1910.

Perhaps inevitably (though one wonders why it must be so), fires and floods have been controlled at a cost of beauty. A somewhat fire-proof concrete box does not have the tones of aging wood, nor has a flat roof pasted over with tar paper the appeal of a massive, deep-eaved roof of thatch. One now looks across the river not at grassy embankments and expanses of reed and rush, but at walls of splotchy concrete.

.   .   .

Writing in 1920, E. Philip Terry warned the tourists whom he hoped to have as readers that they need not expect night life in Tokyo.

> After dark Tokyo is a big dusky village to all but the initiated, and to some an intolerably dull one. Unless one figures in the diplomatic swing, and officiates at the almost ceaseless round of entertainments enjoyed by that favored class, there is little for the average man to do outside the comfortable hotel. . . . On the other hand, the Japanese, who do not go in much for a fast life, and who are easily pleased, find the decorous allurements of Tokyo so potent that they are drawn to them, as by magnets, from all parts of the Empire. To hobnob perpetually with a tiny pot of insipid, sugarless tea and a tobacco-pipe with a bowl no bigger than a bullet, the while listening to the beating of a tom-tom and the doleful ditties of pantomimic *geisha,* fills them with rapture; and once installed in the capital they regard with positive pity all who are so unfortunate as to dwell outside it.

It is a lively account, and the tourist must have found truth in it. Had Terry known as much about Japan as did Chamberlain and Mason, those authors of a much superior guidebook, he would have known that there was more night life in Taishō than the city had known before. Edo had been black and silent after dark, its nocturnal pleasures reserved entirely for men, and not for many of them. The crowds that poured forth on Ginza with the coming of its bricks and bright lights were quite new. It was an innocent sort of night life, perhaps, but still it offered something for all the family, and especially for the younger adult members, who had rather been left out of the pleasures of the pleasure quarters. The great day of Gimbura, "killing time in Ginza," began in Taishō and lasted until the Second World War, though by then such western centers as Shinjuku were drawing away the youthful crowds.

Ginza and Gimbura were the heart of Taishō Tokyo. Nihombashi, the heart of mercantile Edo, was being challenged by Marunouchi as the place for big planners and managers, but it went on being the place for the big retail sell. Mitsukoshi and Shirokiya, the two department-store pioneers in the mercantile revolution of late Meiji, continued trying to outdo each other. Mitsukoshi, as has been noted, was the better of the two at advertising.

Losing crowds to Ginza, Nihombashi might have seemed to be losing its mercantile preeminence as well—for the purpose of advertising is to draw crowds. Yet one should remember that conservative, systematic Nihombashi had not been a place to draw huge crowds, and the Gimbura crowds, such a new phenomenon, were not of a sort to buy expensive merchandise. It would be decades before Nihombashi had rivals as the big shopping center of the city. Gimbura was merely a pleasant way for people about twenty years old to pass time, among people indistinguishable from themselves, the sort they liked best. It may have been the first time that the city had a place for them—and for the most part only them—to go. The expression Gimbura has fallen into disuse and the largest crowds have moved westwards; but the crowds go on being about twenty years of age.

The famous willows, symbol of Ginza in the years when Gimbura

The willows of Ginza, 1921

was coming into vogue, disappeared on the eve of the earthquake. They had been badly damaged by the typhoon which in 1917 brought the waters of the bay within a block or two of the center of the district. In 1921, when the main Ginza street was rearranged to give less room to pedestrians and more to vehicles, authorities replaced them with gingkos, which were more compact, and better served the convenience of motorists.

By then, of course, the day of the motorist had arrived, and his convenience had become the most important thing, as it has remained. The first automobile is said to have come from abroad (in those years all internal-combustion engines did) in late Meiji, and to have been the property of a man with a curious name, Isaac Satō. There were taxicabs from the beginning of Taishō. By the time of the earthquake there were several hundred motorcycles in the city. G. B. Sansom, the British historian, liked to say that he had the very first one in the land. He brought it in shortly before the First World War and used it to explore the countryside.

The opening of the new Ginza main street was not a complete success. The part of the street for vehicular traffic other than trolleys had been uncertainly surfaced, and as a result was often muddy or dusty. Now it was covered with wooden blocks, the interstices filled with asphalt, a technique assuring durability and thought appropriate to the anticipated weight of traffic. On the day of the opening, heavy rains caused a large number of blocks to float, and the splashing was extreme. There was similar trouble the following year, and trouble with melting asphalt in the torrid August sun. Finally, in 1923, the street caught fire and burned up. So in a way the story of Tokyo's first half-century is bracketed by Ginza fires.

For the masses, however things may have been with the managers, Taishō was the era of Ginza and Asakusa. Only on the eve of the earthquake was the name "Ginza" officially applied to the full length of the district as it is today. It had in the strictest sense designated only the northern blocks, where the old mint, the "Silver Seat," had been. Most people would have thought Ginza the center of the city, but it was not really "downtown." It did not possess really big things, except perhaps in journalism and the theater. It was a mood, rather, not easy to define or characterize. For all the accomplished world-weariness of the Yumeji girl, Taishō had a younger culture than Meiji. It was then that the *mobo* and *moga,* the "modern boy" and "modern girl," emerged and started having fun on next to nothing. Ginza was the main place where they had it.

Asakusa is where the masses went to do what the masses of Edo had been wont to do, find performances to view and thereby ruin themselves. It was the show center, and it had the best range of little roistering places and unlicensed lechering places as well. It was traditional in the sense that the most popular temple in the city, the Asakusa Kannon, had long been friendly to such places. At the end of Edo, Asakusa had a near-monopoly on the theater and served as the final station on the way to the most distinguished of the pleasure quarters, but its great day, between the two world wars, continued the old tradition and was very modern as well.

Asakusa had a flair for the new mass culture. It kept up with the times and may have been a little ahead of them, leading the masses its way. In the years after the Russo-Japanese War, it contained the most thriving cluster of movie palaces. Asakusa was preeminent in this respect through Taishō and on into Shōwa. Kafū would go there to look at the "motion picture" posters, and so keep up with the times. Asakusa still had Kabuki. The Miyatoza, behind the temple, was looked upon by connoisseurs as the last ground of Edo Kabuki.

Kabuki was not, however, the popular form it once had been in its own Low City, and cinema, though growing and favored with such talents as Tanizaki's (he wrote scripts), was still something of a curiosity. Between the two, popular Kabuki and monstrously popular movies, came the best day of the music halls, and Asakusa was where they throve. The Asakusa of Meiji may have been the noisiest pleasure center in Tokyo, but it had rivals in other cities. The Asakusa of the music halls, middle and late Taishō and into the present reign, was without rivals, the place where Tokyo outdid itself and the rest of the nation at the fine old art of viewing things.

"Asakusa opera" is the expression that covers musical endeavors in Asakusa during middle and late Taishō. It is a generous term, encompassing everything from pieces that would without challenge call themselves operas in the West, through various strains of light opera, domestic and foreign, all the way to the chorus-line revue.

Shopping "mall" in Asakusa

Opera in the narrow sense was a form which it was thought necessary to have if Japan was to be civilized and enlightened. Very shortly after the opening of the Imperial Theater in 1911, the entrepreneurs and dignitaries who were its backers set about this new task, the importation of opera. They found a willing Italian, G. V. Rossi, in England, where he was a choreographer and director of light opera. He undertook to manage what was to be a permanent repertory troupe at the Imperial. He was somewhat disappointed to learn, upon his arrival in 1912, that the Imperial was not, as the name had suggested, the state theater of Japan, but, having been given a very large sum of earnest money, he stayed.

His first production was *The Magic Flute* with a Japanese cast. This seems unrealistic, and indeed it was. Even today, with training and competence in Western music so vastly improved, *The Magic Flute* is among the operas the Japanese are not quite up to. The Imperial production must have had a makeshift look about it. The same soprano, with a stand-in at the point where the two encounter each other, did Pamina and the Queen of the Night. Rossi decided that lighter things would better suit the available talent. Though he continued to produce Italian opera in the narrow sense, he gambled also on operetta.

The gamble did not succeed. The permanent repertory theater lasted only three years. Rossi was dismissed in 1916. The venture had not been a financial success. He had another try, at Akasaka in the High City, where he bought a movie house. It became the Royal (in English), famous in the history of Western music in Japan, but no more successful than the Imperial. The Royal closed in 1918, and Rossi left Japan for America, a disappointed man.

He was an important teacher. Many of the people who were to become famous in Asakusa were among his Imperial and Royal singers. Insofar as Asakusa opera was genuine opera, it could not have existed without him. His troupe had started deserting him while the Royal still persevered, and upon its closing they all went off to Asakusa. One might have advised the hapless Rossi to go there himself when the Imperial fired him. Akasaka has its geisha and hosts of rich people, but it was not a place to attract crowds. It was on the southwestern edge of the city, to be reached by a trolley line along which few trolleys ran. Asakusa was where things were happening.

There was another strain, a more important one, in Asakusa opera. A skit called *The Women's Army Is Off for the Front* was such a huge success early in 1917 that the date of its opening is called the birthday of Asakusa opera. It was a frivolous war piece, about the First World War. There being a shortage of men on the Western Front, a women's army is dispatched. Mostly the piece is song and dance, including a hornpipe and a Highland fling (so we are told, though descriptions make it seem more Cossack). Because of it "Tipperary" became very popular, sung along all the coves and strands of the nation. The pack day after day was such that people had to be rescued by stagehands at closing time and hustled out through back doors.

This popular strain was the dominant one, though lists of performances at Asakusa show an occasional opera of the genuine sort, such as *Rigoletto* or *Lucia*. "La donna è mobile" from *Rigoletto* was among the big hits of the years before the earthquake. A memorable event occurred in relation to *Rigoletto*. No competent tenor being available, the duke was once sung by a soprano. Operetta and revue prevailed, however. Among Westerners, Suppé (of the "Light Cavalry" overture) seems to have been the most popular. Facing each other across an Asakusa lane were a theater that specialized in the Western and one that went in for the native. Domestic productions, tending towards the erotic, outnumbered Western.

That there should have been genuine opera at all and that it should have been popular is remarkable. Yet it must have gone on looking makeshift, and having a somewhat traditional sound to it. The two most famous Asakusa tenors had scarcely any formal musical training. They were both still to be heard in the years after the Second World War, and one of them survives in this year 1982, in his eighties, still belting away on television. His early career was with the Mitsukoshi boys' band. He said proudly, not long ago, that when the band performed at Hibiya he could be heard in the farthest corners of the park. How considerable an achievement this was is hard to judge. The farthest corner is some four hundred yards from the bandstand where the boys performed. There are many trees to be gone through along the way, and so it may indeed have been a feat, but the important point is that the singer seemed to prize volume above all else. Even today there is more volume than art in his singing. The crowds of Asakusa loved it.

Asakusa opera was astonishingly popular, especially among the young. That eroticism is what most attracted them is scarcely to be doubted. But a decade or two before, young men of Meiji had gone in great numbers to see (and hear) pretty girls perform traditional music (see page 163 for the popularity of *musumegidayū*). Their motives, too, are scarcely to be doubted. The Taishō look was different from the Meiji. In addition to the strong foreign influence, "Tipperary" in its own right and in many a native adaptation, the Asakusa opera was far more open. The sudden exposure of firm young flesh was the most obvious element in the new openness. Pretty legs went kicking in every direction. The performer of *musumegidayū* might as well not have had legs, for all the use she made of them. And the soprano duke and flailing legs were alike part of Asakusa opera.

There were intellectual and bourgeois types among its followers, as there could not fail to be, since it numbered an Italian and the Imperial among its forebears. The fanatical devotees known as *peragoro* were young and often penniless. There are two theories as to the origin of the word *peragoro*. Everyone agrees that the first two syllables are the last two of "opera." As for the last two, some say that they derive from "gigolo," others that they are from *gorotsuki,* an old word for "thug" or "vagrant." The latter signification, whether or not it was there from the start, came to predominate. The *peragoro* were the disorderly elements that hung around the park. They went to the theaters night after night, provided unpaid claques for favorite singers, and formed gangs, whose rivalries were not limited to vehement support for singers. There were violent incidents. A non-*peragoro* could not with impunity protest the excessive vehemence in the theaters. *Peragoro* gangs would gather in the park, each having plighted its allegiance to a popular singer, one gang under the statue of Danjūrō, another under the wisteria bower by the lake. Two marches upon the theaters would occur each night, one for the more affluent at opening time, one for the more straitened when the signals sounded that half-fare time had come.

They were there for the excitement, of course, as crowds of young people are at all times in all places, but devotion to the Asakusa opera was their primary motive. That is the mark of its popularity. Their lady friends, often from the dubious little houses below the Twelve Storeys, were sometimes called *peragorina,* though this expression had by no means the currency of *peragoro.*

When, in the diminished Asakusa of our latter day, old persons reminisce upon the good times, it is not the Asakusa described by Morse and Griffis that they are thinking of. It is the Asakusa of the opera. Nothing in the new entertainment districts, Shinjuku and the like, has quite taken its place. The Low City may be essentially conservative, but it changes, and good things are lost. Some of the best were lost when the crowds departed Asakusa. There is a Kafū story at the wistful ending of which the hero wearies of Asakusa and moves west. That is what the crowds did.

The division of literary history into reigns seems somewhat forced. What began happening at about the time of the Russo-Japanese War went on happening in the new reign, and if there is a Taishō look in literature it does not really become prominent until late in the reign, when it might as well be incorporated into the next one.

The theater, and especially the Kabuki, the art so central to the culture of the city, better accommodates the division into reigns. Generations of actors do correspond rather well to reigns. The most famous of Meiji actors all died in the last decade of the reign. It took a few years, during which there were many laments for the death of the form, before the generation of Taishō actors had established itself.

The Kabukiza, east of Ginza, has been the grand stage for Kabuki ever since it was opened, in 1889. It was the biggest and the best situated, immediately east of Ginza, and in 1912, the year of the change of reigns, it came to have energetic Osaka management, with which to bludgeon its rivals. Morita Kanya (the twelfth of that name, who was active during Meiji—the line has continued) died a few years after the opening of the Kabukiza, which quite overshadowed his Shintomiza.

For all the grandeur, and some may say arrogance, of the Kabukiza, it had rivals during the Taishō Period—more interesting, possibly, than it was. Among these were the "little theaters" scattered all over the city. The one most fondly remembered is the Miyatoza, that guardian of tradition in Asakusa. Of the three "big" theaters of late Edo, one was gone by the end of Meiji; the other two—the Shintomiza, formerly the Moritaza, and, in southern Shitaya, a few minutes' walk from the Yanagibashi geisha quarter, the Ichimuraza—both prospered. The sixth Kikugorō and the first Kichiemon, two fine actors who survived the Second World War and brought the great tradition down to our time, held forth there.

Then there was the Meijiza in Nihombashi, today the oldest Kabuki theater in the city. It may not have provided the best of Kabuki, but its chief actor, the second Sadanji, was a worthy successor to Kanya in the matter of innovating and improving. He was the first important Kabuki actor to study abroad, and the first to act in the new Western theater.

He joined Osanai Kaoru (see page 54), one of the leading entrepreneurs of the new theater, to form, in 1909, a troupe called the Jiyū Gekijō, the Free Theater. In the years that followed, the Free Theater presented in translation plays by such Westerners as Ibsen and Maeterlinck. This was very different from the sort of thing that the fifth Kikugorō had essayed in, for instance, his balloon ascent. A kind of realism and cosmopolitanism had been introduced in Meiji that was less a matter of style than of accessories. Little Western bibelots were introduced, and actors appeared in Western dress. All of this seems in retrospect amusing and not serious.

What Sadanji undertook was very serious. He was a Taishō man. As with the Yumeji girl, we may say that the pursuit of Western things had become more than exoticism. It had sunk deeper. Sadanji set the example. It has become common for Kabuki actors in these latter days to appear in Western or Westernized vehicles. In many a subtle way the influence of the West has insinuated itself into Kabuki. The Valentino look came to stay. Today it could be called the television look. All of this began with Sadanji.

Sadanji's Free Theater was not the only troupe that undertook performances in the Western style, in translation and by Japanese writers. From the first uncertain sproutings in the political drama of Meiji, the "new theater" increased and multiplied. There was a bewildering proliferation of troupes between the two wars, and from them emerged a most energetic movement in the experimental theater.

The most celebrated performer of early Taishō was an actress. That this should have been the case has, again, the Taishō look about it. The most celebrated female celebrities of Meiji had been murderesses. In this regard the women of Taishō were not up to their Meiji forebears. No Taishō murderer or murderess had the appeal of Takahashi O-den, though there were interesting murders, sometimes of a technically advanced kind. In 1913 a thief used power from a high-tension line to dispose of a policeman. (Taishō was not a happy time for policemen. In the wartime and postwar inflation, police wages rose only a third as much as average wages.)

The Taishō celebrity was of a different sort, positive in her attainments, and sufficiently prominent, as no Meiji woman had been, to be called a symbol of her day. Matsui Sumako was vibrantly symbolic, and she came to the kind of sad end best loved in Japan and best suited for immortality. A country girl born in 1886, she arrived in Tokyo at the turn of the century, worked as a seamstress, was married and divorced, and entered the Bungei Kyōkai or Literary Society, a dramatic group founded in 1905 by, among others, Tsubouchi Shōyō. Shōyō was a man of many parts, a pioneer in the new novel and drama. (It was probably a production of *Hamlet* by the Literary Society that so puzzled Natsume Sōseki's Sanshirō.) Sumako had her first great success in 1911, as Ibsen's Nora. The Literary Society was disbanded in 1913, largely because Shōyō disapproved of a flamboyant affair Sumako was having with Shimamura Hōgetsu, his favorite disciple and an eminent theorist in the new movement. Hōgetsu and Sumako organized their own troupe, the Geijutsuza (Art Theater) that same year. Her greatest success was in Tolstoy's *Resurrection*. "Katyusha's Song" from that production, her song, so to speak, is held by historians of the subject to mark the beginning of modern Japanese popular music. It was popular all through the Japanese empire, and, we are told, in North China as well.

Hōgetsu died a sudden and solitary death in the influenza epidemic of 1918. On January 15, 1919, after a performance in Hibiya, Sumako returned to the Ushigome theater which the two of them had struggled to build and where, in one of the back rooms, he had died, and there hanged herself.

She was a willful woman, who seems to have caused endless trouble in both troupes, and she was also passionate and courageous, representative of the new, liberated womanhood. Taishō had other representatives of the type. The soprano Miura Tamaki, for instance, was a member of Rossi's company at the Imperial Theater and the first Japanese to perform Madame Butterfly abroad; she came into prominence for a shocking practice, riding a bicycle to music lessons at Ueno. But Sumako was first among the new women. She could not have existed in Meiji. The old ways were still too strong in Meiji for women to be among the examples that defined it.

In the Taishō Period the popular entertainments went resolutely international. It may be that similar resolve would have come to nothing in Meiji, because only with the advent of movies were international celebrities placed in front of everyone. There could have been no Meiji equivalent of the Chaplin caramels that were vastly popular before the earthquake, and made huge amounts of money for the Meiji Confectionary Company. A song from just before the earthquake has the *shareotoko,* the dapper youth, accoutered in a blue shirt, a green tie, bell bottoms, a bowler hat, and *roido* spectacles. *Roido* seems to be a transliteration of "Lloyd," from the horn-rimmed spectacles worn by Harold Lloyd. A less pleasing theory derives it from the last syllable of "celluloid." Most probably it is both, for the Japanese have always loved a pun. Lloyd and Chaplin were as well known to the populace of

Taishō Tokyo as to the populace of any place on earth. Perhaps the nearest Meiji equivalent was Spencer the balloon man. Perhaps, again, it was General Grant.

With Chaplin and Lloyd in everyone's movie theater, visits of prominent foreigners may not have been quite the festivals they were in Meiji; or it may be that the city and the land, ever more modern, were more resistant to such excitement; or that the excitement was there, but in a less obvious form. In any case, eminent visitors in Taishō tended more towards the intellectual and the artistic than had General and Mrs. Grant.

Pavlova, Schumann-Heinck, and Prokofiev were at the head of the stream of performers who met with acclaim and good fees in Tokyo. Then there were Margaret Sanger and Einstein, whose visits were not affairs of state but caused great stirs all the same. After the visit of the former, which occurred in 1920, a local counterpart known as the "Margaret Sanger of Japan" appeared, handing out devices. Einstein's modest, somewhat comical warmth greatly affected the Japanese. He liked them too. He said that they were pleasanter people than Americans. He came to Japan the year before the earthquake and spent two months on a lecture tour. No one seems to have been called "the Einstein of Japan." Perhaps that was the greatest mark of respect the Japanese could have accorded him.

Frank Lloyd Wright was probably the most famous foreigner to come on business in the narrow sense of the term. His Imperial Hotel, the second one, under construction from 1915 to 1923, was formally opened in 1922 and finished just in time for the earthquake, which it survived so famously.

Wright had a wide variety of troubles in the building, and left Japan after the formal opening without staying to view the completed structure. There seems to have been resentment at the presence of a foreign architect, and in this one sees a contrast between Taishō and the golden Meiji days of Conder. There was labor trouble, one more new Taishō institution, and trouble with the underworld, which had strong roots in the building trades. The old Imperial was demolished by fire on the eve of the opening of the new. Wright's original backers found in the fire their pretext for withdrawing. Their real reason was financial: the enterprise was running several times over the original budget.

The result of all the trouble was worth it. The old Imperial (as it would be called in the last years before its destruction in 1968, for by then yet a third—and now likewise departed—Imperial Hotel had been put up) was a fine building. It gave repose in the noisy heart of the city. Its famous performance in the earthquake did not, however, demonstrate that Wright's principle of floating piles on mud was superior to that of driving them through to bedrock. The old Imperial settled badly, while more traditional buildings in the Low City, such as the Bank of Japan, did not. Some of the corridors came to have a wavy, rubbery look about them. Perhaps it had to go, but its departure, occasioned less by the unevenness of the floors and corridors than by the implacable urge to put valuable land to more intensive use, was the greatest loss that postwar Tokyo has had to endure. The façade may be viewed in Meiji Village near Nagoya (despite the fact that it is not Meiji but Taishō). For those who know what once lay beyond that façade, it is less comforting than saddening.

The Sanger and Einstein visits were events of national moment, even though they may not have touched off quite the surge of fervor that met the Grants. The visits of Charles Beard, the American historian, were more specifically Tokyo affairs. There was one before the earthquake and one after. Beard was received by the most eminent statesmen and financiers in the land, but Tokyo was the reason for the visits. Immediately upon assuming office, Gotō Shimpei, that famous mayor whose sweeping plans for the city were known as "the big kerchief," assigned his son-in-law, resident in New York, the task of luring Beard, who would surely contribute greatly to the contents of the kerchief. Beard studied the city for six months just before the earthquake and wrote a report on the city administration that is still widely read. Many of his recommendations could have been adopted in the aftermath of the earthquake, and few were.

He made practical suggestions and some that were not so practical. He urged the installation of electric meters, because the system of charging by the number of bulbs was wasteful. He also argued for simplified administration and local autonomy. He wanted a single government for greater Tokyo—for the prefecture—a system that was not adopted until 1943. Here he may be taxed with inconsistency, since the reason for the dual structure, a prefectural office and a city office, was that it permitted a measure of local autonomy.

He admired the metropolitan bureaucracy but lamented the ab-

sence of a popular base and of control over its own finances. Though
Beard is often credited with inventing the notion of Tokyo as a cluster
of villages, it seems to have been almost commonplace. We have seen
that John Russell Young, in attendance upon General Grant, regarded
the city in that light almost a half-century before. The center of Tokyo
enjoyed a certain preeminence, Beard said, because it was the place
from which the nation was governed, but the surrounding towns were
more considerable than in any other metropolitan complex of his ac-
quaintance. He concluded that this state of affairs should be remedied
by pumping capital into the central district. Today the vogue among
planners is all for decentralization.

The report continues to be admired, probably because it is Beard's;
but it is a chilly document, not as alive to the humanity and the variety
of the city as it might be.

The neologisms of Taishō often have a High City, bourgeois sound to
them, and so inform us that the Low City, which had slipped into a
secondary position by the end of Meiji, was slipping ever further. Some
of the new words are surprising. That English words should have
supplanted native ones for the most intimate and complex of personal
relationships seems strange indeed. It was in Taishō that "mama" and
"papa" came into currency among the bourgeois and intellectual types
of the High City. Now they are next to universal. The explanation may
be that they are easier to use than the native words, which introduce
delicate honorific problems, and because of their complexity had always been unstable. What the High City chose to do in such matters,
in any event, the Low City tended to follow. Cultural hegemony had
passed from the Low City.

On the eve of the earthquake the sexes may have been more clearly
differentiated from each other than on the eve of the Restoration. Most
of the men among the Ginza crowds wore Western dress and most of
the women Japanese. Even working women tended to favor Japanese
dress, although nurses were pioneers in dressing Western. Photographs of telephone exchanges look very quaint, with the operators in
kimono, their hair swept up in the traditional styles. (Why a telephone
operator in kimono should seem quainter than one in Western dress is
not easy to explain. The universal Japanese notion that Japanese dress

The switchboard, Tokyo Central Telephone Exchange

is impractical, difficult to maintain and given to falling to pieces, may be part of the explanation.) The middy blouse, to become universal for girl students, first appeared in Taishō. So did sewing schools. Girls had learned the simple old ways of sewing from their mothers. Bathing dress became big business in Taishō.

If the sexes were clearly differentiated by dress, their hair styles tended to merge. Women took more easily to Western coiffure than to Western dress. Long hair became the mark of the "modern boy" and short hair that of his female companion. Hairdressers in the traditional styles belonged to a dying trade. They had a place to go if they wished, however, because wigmakers prospered; there continued to be occasions of a ceremonial kind when the old styles were appropriate. Few women, in that day of short hair, had an adequate supply.

The "all-back" style for men, with the hair combed straight back from the forehead and not parted, became popular among the young because an American stunt pilot, Taishō successor to Spencer, affected it. For women there was something very new, the "ear-hiding" style. Ears and napes of necks had been left exposed by the old styles, and were thought erotic. Now, irony of the new day of liberation, they disappeared. The shampoo style of the Meiji geisha had sometimes obscured these points, but the "eaves" coiffure, in the Western style, had not (see page 93). Eye shadow and the hairnet also became stylish.

Fashion, in the chic sense of the term, was created in Taishō by the agency that always creates it, advertising. There had been fads and vogues in Edo, often induced by Kabuki actors, but styles of dress changed slowly until advertising took over. Advertising arranged that dress be increasingly loud and polychrome in the years before the earthquake.

Western sweets were in ever greater vogue, especially the Chaplin caramel. Chocolate was a luxury. The Taishō emperor bought some jelly beans at the Taishō Exposition. There was a soda fountain in Ginza just before the earthquake, though in this respect Tokyo seems to have been behind Yokohama. A measure of modernization has been the advance of dairy products upon this nonpastoral society. Meiji had ice cream and Taishō had "milk parlors." Butter and cheese were slower to take hold. The intelligentsia of Taishō, they who made Taishō democracy, gathered in milk parlors to engage in rarefied conversation and read the official gazette over milk toast and waffles.

From late Meiji into Taishō there was a great increase in university students, and in ideology. The Marx boy and Marx girl made their appearance in early Taishō, somewhat in advance of the words for (if not the fact of) "modern boy" and "modern girl." Students have always delighted in larding their speech with foreign expressions. Some of the Taishō neologisms have stayed with us, such as *rumpen,* from "lumpenproletariat," signifying a vagrant, and *saboru,* "sabotage" converted into a Japanese verb. The latter seems to have been invented during the Kawasaki Shipyards strike of 1919. It has come in more recent years to signify cutting class, or staying away from work for no good reason.

The Meiji Period had been all in favor of education, but Taishō was the time of *kyōyo,* a word which falls within the general meaning of education, but carries connotations of enrichment, self-fulfillment, and gracious living. It lends itself to such expressions (these are taken from dictionaries) as "enrich one's education" and "enhance the level of one's culture." The modern intelligentsia had arrived.

The Peace Exhibition held in Ueno Park in mid-Taishō.
Dignitaries included the Prince of Wales (right)

There were all manner of new schools besides universities: driving schools, beauty schools, English-language schools, typing schools. The day of the office girl (now known as the O.L., for "office lady") dawned in Meiji, with the telephone operator, the nurse, and the shop girl, and now its sun rose radiantly. There was a popular song which began "I'm a typist, I'm a typist," and whose refrain was "Typist, typist," this word in English. Girls first appeared as bus conductors in the years before the earthquake. Theirs was an almost exclusively feminine calling until, with the emergence of the "one-man" (in English) bus, in the last decade or so, it went into a precipitous decline.

Proletarian education and "liberal" education may be dated to the first "labor school," founded by Christians very early in the Taishō

Period. From late Meiji the city had several *himmin gakkō,* rendered by certain dictionaries as "pauper schools" and "ragged schools." They were first administered by the city, then transferred to the wards. Their chief purpose was to provide classes for the children of indigents and transient laborers. The distribution of such schools at the end of Taishō gives interesting evidence of where the ragged dwelt: five were in the two wards east of the river, and the remaining six, on the other side of the river, were evenly divided between the High City and the Low. There was one in Azabu, among the richest of the fifteen wards; the High City has always accommodated extremes of affluence and penury.

The tourist bus was of course a new Taishō institution. The standard route included old things and creations of Taishō as well—Tokyo Station, the Meiji Shrine, the house and graves of the Nogis. It may be that the last will make their way back to the list one day soon, for the suspicion of military immortals that prevailed after 1945 is fading. On the whole, the monuments of Taishō have been supplanted. The standard list today is made up largely of earlier and later wonders. Here too, Taishō has the look of a valley between two eminences.

As at the end of Meiji, one might have remarked at the end of Taishō upon the remarkable tenacity of tradition. Taishō lists of annual observances are strongly traditional, though with a sprinkling of triumphal and patriotic observances from Meiji and after, and a sprinkling as well of Western events and practices, such as April Fool's Day. The seasonal pattern of the flowers, grasses, birds, and insects is familiar.

Certain places for having these natural pleasures have disappeared by late Taishō, new ones have appeared. Among the lost places and things are the chrysanthemum dolls in Hongō, visited by Sōseki's Sanshirō, and the night cherries of the Yoshiwara, but there are still places for chrysanthemum dolls and an ample selection of places for cherries, Ueno and the Sumida embankment still first among them. Although with improved transportation and the spread of the city into open lands, spots for the appreciation of grasses and flowers are sometimes more distant on Taishō lists than on Meiji ones, most of them are still present. The Yanaka cemetery glows with fireflies on a warm, damp evening and the Sumida embankment is a chorus of singing autumn insects. It is striking, indeed, that so many natural pleasures of late Taishō lie near the heart of the city. The Sumida embankment appears with some frequency, though the favored spots of Edo have clearly fallen victim to blight. Insect voices, wasted moors, and the like are farther upstream.

Among fairs and festivals on Taishō lists are many old ones, closely joined to the grasses and flowers, such as those in May at which one bought bugs, bells, and goldfish in preparation for the summer. There are new ones too, such as the opening of the university baseball season in September. Baseball was ever more popular.

In those same years Sumō wrestling enjoyed a renaissance. Early Taishō was for Sumō, as for Kabuki, a quiet period, when many a voice lamented its demise. The great wrestlers of Meiji had withdrawn from active service. A half-dozen years into the new reign began the flowering. The Sumō stadium burned down in 1917, just as the bud was opening. Until a new stadium was finished in 1920, semiannual tournaments were held at the Yasukuni Shrine. There was another Sumō strike in 1923 (for an earlier one, see page 165). In 1926 professional wrestlers organized a Sumō Association, an incorporated foundation. This major event in Taishō democracy is held to mark the final emergence of the Sumō world from feudalism, but in the long history of the sport, it sounds rather like one of those new names that do little to change reality.

In late Meiji and Taishō the city seemed to be growing so rapidly that its weight might bring it down. Waste disposal was among the urgent and interesting problems. There were public collection points for garbage. Some was burned and some devoted to filling the bay or fertilizing paddies east of the bay. The burning was al fresco, and the unremitting smell of burning garbage is a detail commonly remarked upon in memoirs from east of the river.

Sewage was the real problem. The night-soil cart continued to be the chief agent of disposal. Because there was a distance beyond which cartage became impractical, the problem reached crisis proportions. From about the end of the First World War, houses near the center of the city could no longer sell their sewage, but had to pay someone to take it away. As the crisis mounted, tanks would be deliberately broken in order that the stuff might quietly slip away, or sewage was carried out and dumped during the night. Edo was no doubt a smelly city; but Tokyo as it passed its semicentennial must have been even worse.

In 1921 the city finally began to assume limited responsibility for sanitation. Still, by the end of the Taishō Period, three years after the earthquake, the city was disposing of no more than a fifth of the total mass. Tokyo was by then much larger than Edo had been, but in certain respects it had not much changed from the Edo pattern. The Low City was necessarily more advanced than the High City in this public service, because most of the High City lay nearer to farmlands than did the heart of the Low City. The crisis was less acute there.

In the lore of sewage disposal are numerous curious details. Farmers, in the days when they bought, were willing to pay more for sewage the higher the social level of the house. The upper-class product was richer in nutriment, apparently. So, apparently, was male excrement. In aristocratic mansions where the latrines were segregated by sex, male sewage was more highly valued than female. It seems that the female physique was more efficient.

Edo had a system of aqueducts bringing water from the west. It was expanded in Meiji and Taishō. Even so, estimates of the number of persons still dependent on wells within the city run as high as a third of the total. Wells were often noisome and brackish, and so water vendors still went the rounds of the Low City.

We hear more about the problem of traffic and transportation than that of garbage and sewage. Late in Meiji, Nagai Kafū used an overcrowded and badly organized trolley system for one of his most beautiful soliloquies (see page 45). Matters were even worse in the years just before the earthquake. Kafū's diary is quite splashed with mud. Tanizaki, having settled in the Kansai, looked sourly back on the Tokyo of "those years":

> I doubt that in those years, the years of prosperity during and immediately after the World War, there was anyone even among the most ardent supporters of Tokyo who thought it a grand metropolis. The newspapers were unanimous in denouncing the chaotic transportation and the inadequate roads of "our Tokyo." I believe it was the *Advertiser* which in an editorial inveighed against the gracelessness of the city. Our

politicians are always talking about big things, social policy and
labor problems and the like, it said, but these are not what
politics should be about. Politicians should be thinking rather
of mud, and of laying streets through which an automobile can
pass in safety on a rainy day. I remember the editorial because I
was so completely in agreement. Foreigners and Japanese alike
denounced our capital city as "not a city but a village, or a
collection of villages." . . . Twice on my way from Asakusa
Bridge to Kaminari Gate I was jolted so violently from the cush-
ion that my nose hit the roof of the cab. . . . And so, people
will say, it might have been better to take a streetcar. That too
could be a desperate struggle. . . . With brisk activity in the
financial world, all manner of enterprises sprang up, and there
was a rush from the provinces upon the big cities. Tokyo did
not have time to accommodate the frantic increase in numbers
and the swelling of the suburbs. . . . For the general populace
there was no means of transport but the streetcar. Car after car
would come by full and leave people waiting at stops. At rush
hour the press was murderous. Hungry and tired, the office
worker and the laborer, in a hurry to get home, would push
their way aboard a car already hopelessly full, each one for
himself, paying no attention to the attempts of the conductor to
keep order. . . . The ferocity in their eyes could be frighten-
ing. . . . The crowds, a black mountain outside a streetcar,
would push and shove and shout, and we could but silently
lament the turmoil and how it brought out the worst in people. . . . They put up with it because they were Japanese, I
heard it said, but if a European or American city were sub-
jected to such things for even a day there would be rioting. . . .
Old Japan had been left behind and new Japan had not yet
come.

It is to be noted that the idea of the city as a cluster of villages is not
credited to Beard but rather is treated as commonplace, and that, like
Beard, Tanizaki remarks upon the quality in deprecatory terms.

We are often told that "those years," the years when Taishō democracy was coming to be, were a time of sybaritism, irresponsibility, and
disenchantment. The characterization itself has about it a disen-

Rain in the Low City. A woodcut by Komura Settai, 1915

chanted look, as if the burden of modernization had become too much. Meanwhile, those who were to bring about the reaction of the thirties were waiting in indignation.

Taishō was the day when such apparently definitive symbols as the Yumeji girl looked as if they themselves, and not merely their bonnets, had been made abroad. The ease with which Taishō democracy surrendered, however, tells us that tradition was strong and near the surface; and a cynicism not far from disenchantment had been affected by the son of Edo. Japan was catching up with the world in respects which had seemed desperately urgent to the people of early Meiji. So the eagerness of the chase had somewhat diminished. There is a Taishō look, but more recent decades seem to inform us that the modern boy and modern girl were not at all inclined to drop out of the race. The Taishō look was another Western element that had been studied well and mastered.

The song everyone was singing in 1923 was both new and old. It was called "The Boatman's Song." The music was by Nakayama

Shimpei, who wrote Matsui Sumako's song in *Resurrection* and is held to have founded modern popular music.

> I am dead grass on the river bank.
> You are dead grass on the bank as well.

So went the refrain. It was thought to be very decadent, but the stylized self-commiseration would have been familiar and congenial to the child of Edo. Among the righteous and the indignant were those who held that it invited destruction, and got what it asked for on September 1, 1923.

NOTES

CHAPTER 1

p. 5 *"he regained consciousness."* Akutagawa Ryūnosuke, in *Daitōkyō Hanjōki (A Chronicle of the Prosperity of Tokyo)*, in two volumes, 1928; *Shitamachi (The Low City)*, 13–14.

12 *A Dutch observer.* Pompe van Meerbevoort, quoted in *Tōkyō Hyakunenshi (A History of the Tokyo Century)*, in six volumes; I, 1973, 1521–22.

15 *wife and daughter.* Tanizaki Junichirō, *Setsuyō Zuihitsu (Osaka Essays)*, 1935, 229–33. Tanizaki uses the French/English "vaudeville."

17 *"Edo townsmen."* Hasegawa Shigure, *Kyūbun Nihombashi (Ancient Tidings of Nihombashi)*, 1935, 232.

CHAPTER 2

25 *by the solar.* The solar or Gregorian calendar was adopted on January 1, 1873. That date corresponded to December 3, 1872, under the lunar calendar, and so the remaining days of the lunar year were dropped. Except when otherwise specified, dates through 1872 have been converted to the Gregorian calendar.

28 *Edo as it was.* *The Poems of Tanizaki Junichirō*, 1977, 348. Composed on August 19, 1962.

32 *drank himself to death.* Hasegawa, *Kyūbun Nihombashi*, 63.

32-33 *"houses are built."* W. E. Griffis, *Guide Book of Yedo*, 11.

34 *into the river.* John Russell Young, *Around the World with General Grant*. Two volumes, 1879. II, 597–98. The Enriokwan, or Enryōkan, was the guest house at the Hama Palace.

p. 35 *Fukuzawa Yukichi. Seiyō Jijō (The Situation in the West)*, second part, 9. In Fukuzawa Yukichi, Collected Works, II, 1898.

41 *florid decorations.* Tanizaki Junichirō, *Yōshō Jidai (My Boyhood)*, in Collected Works, XXIX, 1959, 181–84. "Sanctuary of the Instincts" is Honnōji. A temple by that name, where occurred perhaps the most famous assassination in Japanese history, that of Oda Nobunaga, is situated in Kyoto. Here the name is, of course, used sportively.

42 *an interrupted dream.* Kitahara Hakushū, in *Daitōkyō Hanjōki, Shitamachi*, 166–67. Kinoshita Mokutarō was a well-known poet. Eau-de-vie de Dantzick is in Roman letters in the original.

46 *transfer to Fukagawa.* Nagai Kafū, Collected Works, V, 1948, 80–81.

46 *"Mitsukoshi is today."* Hasegawa, *Kyūbun Nihombashi*, 14.

49 *water from embankments.* The novelist Kikuchi Kan described a more interesting sort of gaffe in the case of the postal service, begun even before the opening of the railroad. The two characters on the post boxes were misconstrued as "urinal." *Meiji Bummei Kidan (Curious Tales of Meiji Civilization)*, 1948, 60.

56 *a school of whitefish.* Osanai Kaoru, *Okawabata (The Bank of the Big River)*, 52–53, 55–56. Masao is of course the hero, closely resembling Osanai. Kimitarō is a geisha. Some of her colleagues go for English lessons to the Summer School in Tsukiji, attended by the young Tanizaki. Nakasu was a restaurant and theater district in Nihombashi. Today it lies mostly beneath expressways.

57 *The River Sumida.* Widely published. See, for instance, *Nihon no Bungaku (Japanese Literature)*, XVIII, 1967, 138.

59 *Mitsui the millionaire.* W. E. Griffis, *The Mikado's Empire*, 1906 (eleventh edition; first published 1876), 365–66, 370.

59 *"latrines of later years."* Ishii Kendō, *Meiji Jibutsu Kigen (Origin of Things Meiji)*, Part 2, 1944, 734.

60 *une laideur Americaine.* Pierre Loti, *Ouevres Complètes*, undated, IV, 473.

60 *"structural hodge-podge."* Philip Terry, *Guide to the Japanese Empire*, 1920, 143.

62 *a famous artist.* Kishida Ryūsei, in *Daitōkyō Hanjōki, Shitamachi*, 360.

64 *someone would say.* Tanizaki, *Yōshō Jidai*, 91. The Kairakuen, in Nihombashi, was the first Chinese restaurant in Tokyo (see page 102). Gen-chan, son of the proprietor, was a close friend of Tanizaki's.

65–66 *connoisseur of fires and firefighting methods.* E. S. Morse, *Japan Day by Day*, 1936, I, 31–32; I, 133; II, 125–26.

67 *willows in full leaf.* Kubota Mantarō, Collected Works, XII, 1948, 250–51.

67 *"capital of the Tycoon."* Sir Rutherford Alcock, *The Capital of the Tycoon*, 1863, I, 115.

p. 71 *dim in mists.* Kubota, Collected Works, XII, 210–11.

76 *lights were to be discerned.* Takahama Kyoshi, in *Daitōkyō Hanjōki, Yamanote (The High City)*, 63–64.

81 *"cry out in astonishment."* Natsume Sōseki, *Gubijinsō (The Poppy)*, 1908, 255.

82 *"wait for pretty boys."* Tanizaki, *Yōshō Jidai*, 73, 75.

84 *"passed away forever."* Griffis, *The Mikado's Empire*, 550.

84 *"Edo was destroyed."* Tayama Katai, Collected Works, XV, 1974, 539.

CHAPTER 3

91 *"old one had not been."* Hasegawa, *Kyūbun Nihombashi*, 117–18.

96 *"trees and foliage."* Basil Hall Chamberlain and W. B. Mason, *Murray's Handbook: Japan*, 1903, 115.

96 *acting to the end.* Cf. *Titus Andronicus*, II, IV: "Enter Demetrius and Chiron, with Lavinia, ravished; her hands cut off, and her tongue cut out."

107 *"erected immediately."* Clara Whitney, *Clara's Diary*, 1979, 257.

107 *"to our honored country."* Ibid., 260–61.

119 *"chatters on and on."* Quoted in *Nishikie Bakumatsu Meiji no Rekishi (A History of Late Edo and Meiji in Woodcuts)*, X, 1978, 82. I have not been able to trace the source in Ryokuu's writings.

121 *behind the grand hall.* Kubota, Collected Works, XII, 55–57.

125 *in vacant lots.* Nagai Kafū, *Hiyorigeta (Good-weather Footgear)*, widely published. See, for instance, *Nihon no Bungaku (Japanese Literature)*, XVIII, 1967, 440–41. The Japanese names of the weeds referred to are *kayatsurigusa, nekojirashi, aka no mamma, ōbako,* and *hakobe.*

133 *of her short stories.* Higuchi Ichiyō, "Takekurabe" ("Growing Up"), widely published. See, for instance, *Nihon no Bungaku (Japanese Literature)*, V, 1968, 98.

137 *oscillations of the boats.* Morse, *Japan Day by Day*, I, 129–31.

138 *hopeless condition spiritually.* Whitney, *Clara's Diary*, 93–94.

140 *sharp and cold.* Nagai Kafū, "The Fox." Widely published. See, for instance, Collected Works, XII, 94. The Japanese title is "Kitsune."

CHAPTER 4

148 *shiver, pleasantly.* Tanizaki, *Yōshō Jidai*, 120–21.

149 *"out of patience."* Whitney, *Clara's Diary*, 277.

149 *illuminate his face.* Morse, *Japan Day by Day*, I, 28–29.

p. 150 *"clean away the decay."* Quoted in *Japanese Music and Dance in the Meiji Era,* compiled and edited by Komiya Toyotaka. Centenary Culture Council Series, III, 1956, 191–92.

155 *"what he had left was Yose."* Osanai Kaoru, quoted in the magazine *Hon,* distributed for advertising purposes by Kōdansha, June, 1980.

158 *busy holiday-makers.* Chamberlain and Hall, *Murray's Handbook: Japan,* 1891, 85 and 87.

160 *upset no one.* Tanizaki, *Yōshō Jidai,* 109–10.

168 *a romantic setting.* Quoted by Kubota, Collected Works, XII, 94.

173 *would not soon forget.* Higuchi Ichiyō, "Growing Up." Widely published. See for instance *Nihon no Bungaku,* V, 98.

CHAPTER 5

194 *air of the degenerate.* Tayama Katai, in *Daitōkyō Hanjōki, Shitamachi,* 300–3, 304–6. *Owai,* "excrement," was the cry of the night-soil draymen as they made their way through the city. "Spectacle Bridge," Meganebashi, was another name for Yorozuyobashi, also known as Manseibashi, in Kanda. The English word "degenerate" is used.

195 *today, assembled.* Hasegawa, *Kyūbun Nihombashi,* 163, 165–66.

195 *affluence in party dress. Ibid.,* 233. *Danna,* something like "master" or "head of the house," is the word rendered "men of affluence."

207 *"Nôtre Dame to Paris."* Griffis, *The Mikado's Empire,* 378.

207 *"at such play." Ibid.,* 388.

209 *"a charred waste."* Akutagawa Ryūnosuke, quoted by Kubota Mantarō in Collected Works, XII, 31–32.

209 *since the earthquake. Ibid.,* 33–34.

211 *attributes of a park. Tokyo Annai (A Guide to Tokyo),* 1907, II, 448. The area of the park converts to about thirteen and a half acres. The Satake were lords of Kubota, the present Akita.

212 *that ancient sadness.* Nagai Kafū, from *Udekurabe (A Test of Skills).* Widely published. See for instance *Nihon no Bungaku (Japanese Literature),* XVIII, 1967, 221.

216 *old Fukagawa was.* Akutagawa, in *Daitōkyō Hanjōki, Shitamachi,* 3, 30, 46. Regions within "the red line" were under the Edo magistracy. In effect it marked the city limits.

217 *"semblance of sanctity."* Chamberlain and Hall, *Murray's Handbook: Japan,* 1903, 88.

218 *"at the head of their lists." Tokyo Annai,* 1907, II, 598, 650.

p. 222 *clams and seaweed. Ibid.,* II, 745–46.

225 *a more revolting form.* Alcock, *The Capital of the Tycoon,* I, 111–13. *Norimono* and *kago* are two words for "sedan chair." The Tocado is more properly the Tōkaidō.

227 *"from other years."* Osanai Kaoru, in *Daitōkyō Hanjōki, Yamanote,* 347.

239 *half of it to ashes.* Arishima Ikuma, *Ibid.,* 94, 96.

242 *"cawing outside the window."* Morse, *Japan Day by Day,* I, 15.

CHAPTER 6

259 *"that suggests Valentino."* Kishida Ryūsei, in *Daitōkyō Hanjōki, Shitamachi,* 362–63.

262 *it rained.* Nagai Kafū, *Hanabi (Fireworks).* Widely published. See for instance, *Kafū Zuihitsu (Kafū's Essays),* III, 1982, 14.

264 *dwell outside it.* Terry, *Guide to the Japanese Empire,* 133.

284 *had not yet come.* Tanizaki, *Setsuyō Zuihitsu,* 215–21.

INDEX

Numbers in italics indicate illustrations.

Abe family, 244
Adults' Day, 138
advertising, 109, 112–13, 279
Akasaka Detached Palace, 22, 235, 241
Akasaka Ward, 134, 236, 240, 246–8
Akihabara district, 213
Akutagawa Ryūnosuke, 4–5, 208, 216
Alcock, Sir Rutherford, 67, 224
alleys, 84; broad, 159, 217
Aoyama Gakuin (missionary school), 203
aqueducts, 283
Arakawa Drainage Channel, 222, 263
Arakawa River, 263
architects, 232, 235
architecture, 67–78, 235, 257; brick
    buildings, 59–61, 78; Edo (Tokugawa
    period), 67–8; government buildings,
    231–3; Western buildings, 68; *see also*
    individual buildings
Arishima family, 239, 247
Arishima Ikuma, 239, 240
aristocracy, 12–13, 185, 186, 248, 249
Arnold, Sir Edwin, 120
art, *see* prints; woodcuts
artists, 249–50
Art Theater (Geijutsuza), 274

Asakusa Kannon Temple, 8, 20, 76, 132,
    158, 206–8
Asakusa opera, 267, 269–71
Asakusa park, 119, 209
Asakusa Twelve Storeys (Ryōunkaku),
    70–3
Asakusa Ward, 6, 8, 20, 21, 55, 88, 142,
    158, 159, 206–10, 254; new, 208, 209;
    during Taishō, 267–71, 268; temples
    and cemeteries in, 207–8
Asuka Hill, 132
Asukayama Park, 119–22, 127–9
automobiles, 49, 266
Azabu Ward, 240, 246–9
Azuma Bridge (Azumabashi), 56, 57

Baldwin (balloonist), 108
balloons, 108
Banchō district, 239–40
bankara (style of dress), 102
Bank of Japan building, 73–4, 78, 188–91
Bank of the Big River, The (Okawabata)
    (Osanai), 54–6
banzai, shouting of, 94
barbershops, 92–3

barracks, military, 248
Barton, William, 71–2
baseball, 166–7, 282
bathhouses, 92
Bauduin, E. A. F., 117
bazaars (*kankōba*), 113–15
beaches, 104–5
Beard, Charles, 34, 276–7
beauty school, 93
beef, eating of, 102
beer, 95
Bird, Isabella, 60, 68, 207
Bird Fair (Tori no Ichi), 133, 173
birds, 130
Black, J. R., 204
blossom-viewing, *see* cherry blossoms;
    peach blossoms; pear blossoms; plum
    blossoms
"Boatman's Song, The," 285–6
boats, pleasure, 19, 53
Bonin (Ogasawara) Islands, 30
boundaries of Tokyo, 29–30
Boys' Day, 135–6
bread, 102
brick buildings, 59–61, 78
Bricktown (Ginza), 45, 59, 60, 199
bridges, 53, 54, 56
British embassy, 232–3, 235
British legation, burning of (1863), 12
broad alleys (*hirokōji*), 159, 217
brothels, 38, 169–72, 175, 177
Buddhism, 102
Bummei Kaika, *see* Civilization and
    Enlightenment
Bungei Kyōkai (Literary Society), 273–4
bureaucracy, Edo, 12
buses, 44, 45
butchers, 102

cafés, 201; *see also* coffee houses
calling cards, 96
canals, 52, 53, 198
cemeteries, 132, 207, 211
chairs, 101
Chamberlain, Basil Hall, 96, 158, 217
chanoyu (tea ceremony), 17–18
Chaplin, Charlie, 274–5
Chaplin caramels, 274, 279
cherry blossoms, 119, 126–9, 132, 173,
    218, 219

Chiba Prefecture, 35
children, 135–6
Children's Day, 136
Chinese cuisine, 102
cholera epidemics, 83
Christianity, 22, 250
chrysanthemums, 129, 131–2, 281
Chūō University, 214
Chūō Ward, 185
Citizens' Day, 30
city council, 30, 31
City Hall, 78
Civilization and Enlightenment (Bummei
    Kaika), 31 37, 61, 81, 91–2, 94, 95;
    meaning of, 35, 36
clams, 127, 130, 220–1
class distinctions, 85, 237
clock tower, Hattori, 200
clothing, *see* dress
coffee houses, 104; *see also* cafés
colleges, 203; *see also* universities
Conder, Josiah, 68, 78, 115, 228, 244
constitution, Meiji, 17
courtesans, 167–9, 171–3
crimes and criminals, 25, 92, 160–3,
    204–5
cultural center, Tokyo as, 87–8

Daiei Building, 74
Daiichi Kangyō Bank, 192
Daimaru store, 46–7
dairy products, 279
dances, Niwaka, 173
dancing, 99, 104
Dangozaka, 131
Danjūrō (Kabuki actor), 149–52, 163
democracy, Taishō, 261, 284–5
department stores, 109, 110–13
detectives, private, 94
diet, changes in, 102–3
Diet building, 232, 233
"double life," the, 90, 109, 139
drainage channel, 222, 263
drama, *see* theater
dress: Meiji, 92, 93, 96–7, 99, 101–2,
    111, 171; Taishō, 257–8, 277–8

earthquake of 1855, 4, 22
earthquake of 1923, 3–9, 14–15
Echigoya (store), 193

Edo (the pre-Restoration city), 4–26;
architecture of, 67–8; aristocracy of,
12–13; as capital and bureaucratic
center, 12; demise of, 9, 182–3;
foreigners in, 19, 22–4; literature of,
250–1; pleasure quarters of, 11, 17,
18, 20, 145; population of, 13, 24;
renamed Tokyo (1868), 26; rice riots
in (1866), 22–4; stores in, 109; streets
and alleys of, 84–5; theaters of,
18–20; transportation in, 19–20; Yose
(variety or vaudeville halls) of, 18–19
Edo castle, 27, 29
Edo culture, 11, 17–21, 32, 86, 144–5,
250–1
education, 87, 203; during Taishō,
279–81; *see also* colleges; schools;
universities
Einstein, Albert, 275, 276
Ekōin Temple, 158–9, 216–17
Electricity Hall, 120
electric lights, 81–2
electric power companies, 82
elevators, 72–3
Elocution Hall (Enzetsukan), 62
embassies and legations, 36, 232–3
Enchō (Yose performer), 156, 157
English period in architecture, 68
Enjū district, 171, 172
enkashi (street minstrels), 163–4
epidemics, 22, 83
era names, 21–2
expositions, 115–16, 257, 285

factories, 86–7, 214, 216
fairs, *see* expositions
farmland, 88, 236
feast days, 132–3
ferries, 218
festivals, 134–8, 282; Yoshiwara, 172–4
fire(s), 6–7, 14, 22, 34, 62–7; of 1872
(Ginza), 58; of 1881 (Kanda), 51,
62–4; of 1911 (Yoshiwara), 63, 174–5;
after 1923 earthquake, 5–6, 23; during
Taishō, 262–3, 266
fire baskets, 64
fire department, 63–4, 262–3
firefighting methods, 65–6, 262
fireflies, 130, 281
First Higher School, 166, 242, 243

First National Bank, *188*, 191, 192
First National Industrial Exposition
(1877), 114, 115
fishing, 88
fish market, central, 82–3
Five Mouths (post-stations), 175–9
flood control, 219–20, 263
floods, 56–8; of 1910, 85, 219, 220; of
Taishō, 263
flowers, 127–32, 281
food, 102–3
footwear, 113; *see also* shoes
foreigners (foreign population), 105–9; in
Edo, 12, 22–4; in Ginza, 203; in
Tsukiji, 36–42; violence against,
103–4, 108
foreign legations and embassies, 36,
232–3
Forty-Seven Loyal Retainers, 48
"Fox, The" (Kafū), 140
Free Theater (Jiyū Gekijō), 272–3
Fūgetsudō (confectioner), 201
Fuji, Mount, 136; miniature, 120
Fujiwara Yoshie, 164
Fukagawa Ward, 39, 214–16, 220–2
Fukuchi Genichirō, 174
Fukuzawa Yukichi, 31, 35–6, 62, 202,
203
funayado (boat lodge or boating inn),
53–4

gakusha-machi (professorial
neighborhood), 244
Gambler's Meadow, *see* Mitsubishi
Meadow
gaslights, 80–1, 149
geese, wild, 130
Geijutsuza (Art Theater), 274
geisha, 94, 169, 171; "town," 179
geisha districts, 179–83; *see also*
individual districts
General Staff Headquarters, 232
German embassy, 232–3
Gilbert, W. S., 27
Gimbura, 61, 199, 206, 264, 265
Ginza district, 9, 10, 44, 53–4, 114, 186,
189, 193, 197–206, 228, 231;
Bricktown in, 59, 60, 199; cafés in,
201; canals of, 198; educational
institutions in, 203; in 1870, 58–9;

Ginza district *(continued)*
 fire of 1872 in, 58; foreign settlement
 in, 203; gaslights in, 81; main street
 of, 198, 266; *narikin (nouveau riche)* of,
 199; newspapers in, 204; rebuilding of
 (after 1872 fire), 59–61; during
 Taishō, 264–6; theaters in, 205;
 willows of, 61–2, 265–6
godowns (warehouses), 23, 64, 190–1
god performances (Kagura), 159–60
god-seat festivals, 133–6
god-seats *(mikoshi)*, 133, 223
Goten Hill, 129
Gotō Shimpei (mayor of Tokyo), 31, 78,
 260, 276
government buildings, 231–3
government of Tokyo, 30–1; Beard's
 views on, 276–7; *see also* city council;
 mayors of Tokyo
Grant, Julia, 105–6, 145–6
Grant, Gen. Ulysses S., 105–7, 137, 145
grasses, 127–9, 131–2, 281
gravel scandal (1920), 31
Great Meiji Flood (1910), 57–8, 219, 220
Griffis, W. E., 26, 32–3, 58–9, 84, 103,
 108, 161, 207

hair styles, 92–3, 278–9
Hamachō geisha quarter, 191
Hama Palace, 69, 198
Hanai O-ume, *see* O-ume
Haneda, 88
Hara Takeshi, 31
Harada Kinu, *see* O-kinu
Hasegawa Shigure, *see* Shigure
hatamoto (lesser military orders), 239
Hashimoto Gahō, 116
Hattori Kintarō, 200
Hearn, Lafcadio, 15
Heian Period, 17
Hepburn, J. C., 96
Hibiya Park, 122–3, 226
High City (Yamanote), 8, 32, 35, 85, 86,
 236–51; earthquake of 1923 and, 5,
 10–11; grand estates of, 241;
 north-south differences in, 240–1;
 pleasure quarters of, 11; streets of,
 237–8
"high-collar," defined, 102

Higuchi Ichiyo, 87, 133, 173
Hikagechō, 229
hikitejaya (teahouses), 169–70, 172, 175
hirokōji (broad alleys), 159
Hōgetsu, 274
holidays, 28; *see also* feast days; festivals;
 seasons and seasonal observances
Hongō Ward, 240–4, 246
Honjo Ward, 214–20, 219, 220
horse-drawn transportation, 44
hospitals, 107
Hoterukan (hotel), 37–8, 186
house numbers, 95–6

Ichimuraza theater, 272
Iemochi (shogun), 24
Imperial Hotel: first, 68, 70, 233, 234,
 262, 275–6; second, 233, 275–6
Imperial Theater, 113, 153, 155, 233,
 235, 268
Imperial University, 241–4
individualism, as new outlook, 250, 251
industrial zones, 214–17, 222; *see also*
 factories
Inoue Kaoru, 98–100
insects, 130, 281
intelligentsia, 279
irises, 130
Iriya district, 130
Ishikawajima Shipyards, 221
Itabashi district, 171, 172, 177
Itō, Prince, 153, 233
Itō Hirobumi, 12, 98–100
Iwasaki estate, 221–2, 244–6
Iwasaki family, 240, 244
Iwo Islands, 30
Izu Islands, 30

Jiyū Gekijō (Free Theater), 272–3
judō and *jujitsu*, 167

Kabuki actors, 145, 149, 151, 273
Kabuki theater, 18, 20, 21, 81, 85, 107,
 145–55; crimes as material for, 160–3;
 in Ginza, 205; lighting for, 147,
 149–50; movement for improvement
 of, 150–1; during Taishō, 267, 271–2

Kabukiza theater, 152–4, 272
Kafū, 11, 16, 54, 60, 66, 104, 128,
    156–7, 169, 182, 201, 213, 226, 238,
    244, 247, 250, 256–7, 271, 283; "The
    Fox," 140; on Fukagawa, 45–6, 216,
    221; on Honjo, 215–16; on Negishi,
    212; on riots of 1918, 262; *The River
    Sumida*, 56–7, 129, 154, 171, 215, 218;
    "A Song in Fukagawa" (*Fukagawa no
    Uta*), 45–6
Kaga estate, 36
Kaga Yashiki, *see* Maeda estate
kagemajaya (shady teahouses), 243
Kagura (god performances), 159–60
Kagurazaka district, 179, 247
Kairakuen restaurant, 102
Kameido district, 128
Kanagaki Robun, *see* Robun
Kanagawa Prefecture, 30
Kanda, 8, 83, 114, 194–5, 224, 236, 243,
    246; Akihabara district of, 213; fire of
    1881 in, 62–4; produce market of, 213;
    universities of, 214; used-book district
    of, 214
Kanda River, 130
Kanda Shrine and festival, 134–5
Kan-eiji temple, 27, 117
Kaneyasu, 14
Kannon Temple, Asakusa, 8, 20, 132,
    158, 206–8
Kanya (impresario), 146–54 *passim*,
    272
karizashiki ("rooms for rent"), 171–2
Kawabata Yasunari, 209–10
Kawarazaki Gonjūrō, 41
Keiki (Yoshinobu) (last shogun), 24, 25
Keiō University, 36, 62, 102, 166, 167
Kikugorō (Kabuki actor), 149, 163
kimono, 97
Kinoshita Mokutarō, 41
Kinoshita O-tsuya, *see* O-tsuya
Kishida Ryūsei, *see* Ryūsei
Kitahara Hakushū, 41–2
Kiyochika (artist), 47, 49–51
Kiyosumi Park, 221–2
Kobayashi Kiyochika, *see* Kiyochika
Koishikawa Ward, 130, 246–7
Kōjimachi Ward, 87, 142, 143, 232–5,
    238–9, 247, 248, 260
Kōjunsha, 201–2

Kokugikan, 165
Koreans, 7
Kotsukappara execution grounds, 16–17,
    161
Kōyōkan restaurant, 227–8
Kubota Mantarō, 66–7, 71, 121, 168, 209
Kudan Hill, 125
Kudan *shōkonsha* (shrine), 125
Kuroda family, 205
Kyōbashi Ward, 8, 10, 53–4, 59, 79, 87,
    185, 186, 197–206, 246; *see also* Ginza
    district
Kyoto, 28, 30, 127, 237; and
    establishment of Tokyo as capital, 26,
    28–9

laver seaweed, 88, 127
law schools, 214
legations and embassies, 36, 232–3
licensed quarters, 167–79; *see also* geisha
    districts; pleasure centers; *and
    individual quarters*
lighting; for Kabuki theater, 147,
    149–50; street, 80–2
Lion café, 201
Li Po, 169
Literary Society (Bungei Kyōkai), 273–4
literature (traditional vs. modern),
    250–1
Lloyd, Harold, 274–5
Londontown, Mitsubishi, 77, 78
Loti, Pierre, 60, 70, 97, 105
lotuses, 130–1
Low City (Shitamachi), 4, 8–11, 34,
    85–6, 189, 236, 237, 249–51, 284; areas
    comprising, 8–9; boundaries of, 206,
    249; earthquake of 1923 and, 4, 5, 9;
    fires in, 64; in Kubota's writings,
    66–7; pleasure quarters of, 11;
    population of, 32; *see also specific wards
    and districts*
lumberyards, 215

machiai, 170
machiaijaya (rendezvous teahouse), 179
Maeda estate, 241–2
Magic Flute, The, 268–9
"mama," use of term, 277

Maria Luz affair (1872), 171
Marine Insurance building, 260
Marunouchi Building, 260
Marunouchi district, 75–9, 231, 260
Masakado (tenth-century general), 134–5
Mason, W. B., 96, 158
Matsui Sumako, *see* Sumako
mayors of Tokyo, 30–1, 260
meat, eating of, 102–3
Meiji Confectionery Company, 274
Meiji constitution, 17
Meiji emperor, 26, 28, 33, 48, 106–7,
    151, 182, 202–3, 235, 255–6; funeral
    of, 254–5; illness and death of, 252–3
Meiji Gakuin (school), 166
Meiji Restoration, 27–9
Meiji Shrine, 31, 254–5
Meiji University, 214
Meijiza theater, 154, 191, 272
Metropole Hotel, 42
Mikado, The (Gilbert and Sullivan), 150
mikoshi (god-seats), 133, 223
military barracks, 248
Minamoto Yoshiie, 107
Ministry of Justice, 232
misdemeanors, 92
Mito Tokugawa estate, 241
Mitsubishi enterprises, 75
Mitsubishi Londontown, 77, 78
Mitsubishi Meadow (Gambler's
    Meadow), 75–80, 232
Mitsui Bank, 73, 187, 191–2
Mitsui Club, 70
Mitsui dry-goods store, 110
Mitsui family, 10
Mitsukoshi Department Store, 5, 73,
    110–13, 264–5
Miura Tamaki, 274
Miyatoza theater, 154, 272
Miyukidōri street, 198
modernism, 250–1
Mori Arinori, 203
Mōri of Nagato, 24
Mori Ogai, *see* Ogai
Morita Kanya, *see* Kanya
Moritaza, *see* Shintomiza theater
Moritoza theater, 267
morning glories, 130
Morse, E. S., 43, 48, 65–6, 68, 91, 137,
    149, 190–1, 242

Morse, W. B., 217
Mount Fuji, 136; miniature, 120
movies, 274–5
movie theaters, 120, 267
Mukōjima district, 218
mulberry trees, 236
music, 163–4, 168; *see also* opera
music halls, 267; *see also* Yose
musumegidayū (theater music), 163, 270

Nagai Kafū, *see* Kafū
Nagoya Tokugawa estate, 241
Nakasu Island, 55
Nakayama Shimpei, 285–6
Nara, 28
narikin (*nouveau riche*), 199
Narushima Ryūhoku, *see* Ryūhoku
National Theater, 156
Natsume Sōseki, 47, 81, 116, 243
Negishi district, 211–12
Nemuro district, 30
neologisms of Taishō period, 277
New Chronicle of Yanagibashi (*Ryūkyo
    Shinshi*), (Ryūhoku), 180–1
New Shimabara licensed quarter, 37–9
newspapers, 204
New Year, 132, 135, 138
Nezu district, 172, 178–9, 242
Nihombashi Bridge, 192, 196
Nihombashi River, 189
Nihombashi Ward, 8–10, 13, 14, 20, 46,
    56, 63, 79, 87, 185–97, 190, 230, 231,
    236, 246; as financial center, 189,
    192–3; fish market in, 82–3, 187;
    pleasure quarters in, 191, 196; pride of
    place of, 196–7; shrines and temples
    of, 191; during Taishō, 264–5
Nihon University, 214
Nikolai Cathedral, 70, 214
Niwaka dances, 173
Nogi Maresuke, Gen., 105, 201, 255
Normanton incident (1886), 100
Nō theater, 125

Occupation, American (after World War
    II), 120
O-den (murderess), 162
Ogai (novelist), 151, 244

Ogasawara (Bonin) Islands, 30
Ogawa Isshin, 78, 231; photographs by, 74–5, 76–7, 94
Okawabata (The Bank of the Big River) (Osanai), 54–6
O-kinu (murderess), 161–2
omnibuses, 44, 45
Omori, shell middens of, 48
Omura Masujirō, 27
opera, 268–71; Asakusa, 267, 269–71
operetta, 269–70
Osaka, 26, 30, 36, 87, 127, 144, 153
Osanai Kaoru, 54, 151, 155–6, 167–8, 182, 227, 272
O-tsuya, murder of (1910), 76
O-ume (murderess), 162–3, 241
Ozaki Yukio, 31, 82

palanquins, 44
"papa," use of term, 277
Parkes, Sir Harry, 104
parks, public, 85, 116–25
parties, during Rokumeikan era, 99–101
peach blossoms, 129
pear blossoms, 129
Peers Club, 70, 100
peragoro (Asakusa opera devotees), 270–1
performers, street, 158–60
Perry, Commodore Matthew Calbraith, 21, 22, 125
Plantain café, 201
pleasure centers (or quarters), 39, 158; of Edo, 11, 17, 18, 20, 145; *see also* licensed quarters; *and individual districts*
plum blossoms, 128
police boxes, 94
political parties, 261
population, 32, 35, 236–7; of Edo, 13, 24; during Taishō, 259
ports, opening of, 22
Portsmouth Treaty (1905), 141–2
post-stations (Five Mouths), 175–9
prints, 49–52, 61, 101
private detectives, 94
produce market (Kanda), 213
professorial neighborhood (*gakusha-machi*), 244
prostitution, 18, 108–9, 170–2, 207;

outlawing of (1958), 175, 177; *see also* brothels; geisha; geisha districts; licensed quarters; pleasure centers

rabbits, 103
railroads, 47–9, 175–7, 222; prints of, 49–52
reading from left to right, 95
rice riots (1866), 22–4
rickshaws, 42–4
Rigoletto, 269–70
riots: of 1918, 261–2; after Portsmouth Treaty (1905), 141–2; rice (1866), 22–4
rivers, 52–8; *see also* floods
River Sumida, The (Kafū), 56–7, 129, 154, 171, 215, 218
Robun (journalist), 162
Rokumeikan, 51, 68–70, 69, 98–100, 233
Rokumeikan era, 97–100, 104
Roppongi, 141, 248
Rossi, G. V., 268–9
Royal movie house, 269
Russia, 105
Russo-Japanese War (1904–1905), 141–3
Ryōgoku, broad alley of, 217
Ryōgoku Bridge, 216–17
Ryokuu (novelist), 119
Ryōunkaku (Twelve Stories), 7–8, 70–3
Ryūhoku (journalist), 180–1
Ryūkyo Shinshi (New Chronicle of Yanagibashi) (Ryūhoku), 180–1
Ryūsei (painter), 159

Sadanji (Kabuki actor), 272–3
Saigō Takamori, 118–19
St. Luke's Hospital, 39
Saionji, Prince, 153
Saitō Ryokuu, *see* Ryokuu
Salvation Army, 108–9
Sanger, Margaret, 275, 276
Sannō festival, 134
Sansom, G. B., 266
Sanyūtei Enchō, *see* Enchō
Sawamura Tanosuke, 96
schools, 87; missionary, 203; Taishō, 280–1
school uniforms, 101
sea bathing, 104–5

seasons and seasonal observances,
126–38, 281–2
Seiyōken Hotel (now restaurant), 42, 118
Senjū (post-station), 175, 177–8
sewage disposal, 83, 84, 282–3
Seward, William H., 105
shadows, Tanizaki on, 80–2
Shiba Detached Palace, 227
Shibaguchi, *see* Shimbashi
Shiba Park, 226–8
Shibaura, 226–7
Shiba Ward, 8, 87, 222–8; temples and
cemeteries of, 225–6
Shibusawa Eiichi, 80–1, 85, 153, 254;
mansion of, 86
Shibuya, 248
Shibuya Station, 48
Shigure (playwright), 17, 32, 46, 90–2,
183, 194–5, 214
Shimamura Hōgetsu, *see* Hōgetsu
Shimazu Saburō, 44
Shimbashi Club, 166
Shimbashi district, 54, 62, 223, 228–9;
geisha quarter in, 181–2, 229
Shimbashi Station, 47, 48, 79, 229–30
Shimizu Kisuke, 37
Shimooka Renjō, 50–1
Shinagawa district, 171, 172, 175–6
Shinjuku district, 29, 83, 171, 172,
175–7, 237
Shinobazu Pond, 117–18, 131
Shintomiza theater, 107, 146–9, 147, 153,
272
Shinto religion, 126
Shirokiya Department Store, 111–12,
264–5
Shiseidō (cosmetics firm), 200–1
Shitamachi, *see* Low City
Shitaya gang, 211
Shitaya Park, 210–11
Shitaya Ward, 130, 206–8, 210–11
Shōchiku company, 153
shoes, 101
shops and shopping, 109–14; *see also*
bazaars; department stores
Shōriki Matsutarō, 261
Shōyo (novelist/dramatist), 273–4
shrine festivals, 134–6
shrines, 125, 132–3, 158, 191; *see also*
god-seats; god-seat festivals

Sino-Japanese War (1894–1895), 140–1
Sixth District (of Asakusa Park), 120–1
snow viewing, 127, 132
Society for Improving the Theater, 150
Spencer (balloonist), 108
sports, *see* baseball; Sumō wrestling
spring, 128–30, 134, 138
street lights, 80–2
street minstrels *(enkashi)*, 163–4
street numbers, 95–6
street pattern, 32–4, 237–8
street performers, 158–60
streets, 84–5; High City, 237–8; house
numbers on, 95–6; traffic on left side
of, 94–5
students, 242–3, 279
student uniforms, 101
Sugawara Michizane, 128
Sullivan, Arthur, 27
Sumako (actress), 168, 273, 274
Sumida embankment, 127, 129, 130, 132,
218, 219, 281–2
Sumida River, 53–6, 55, 217–20;
flood-control devices on, 219–20, 263;
flooding of, 56–8; "opening" of, 106,
136–7, 217
Sumō wrestling, 151, 164–5, 167, 217, 282
Supreme Court, 245
Susaki licensed quarter, 220–1

Taira Masakado, *see* Masakado
Taishō democracy, 261, 284–5
Taishō emperor, 255–6
Taishō Hakurankai (Taishō Exposition)
(1914), 257
Taishō look, 256–9, 285
Taishō Period, 256–86
Tajiri Inajirō, 260
Takahama Kyoshi, 76
Takahashi O-den, *see* O-den
Takehisa Yumeji, *see* Yumeji
Tama district, 30
Tameike Pond, 130–1
Tameike reservoir, 53
Tanizaki Junichirō, 10, 14–15, 28, 66,
88, 91, 104, 126–7, 130, 148, 159–60,
189, 194, 210, 283–4; at English
school, 39–41; and fire baskets, 64; on
shadows and dark places, 80–2

Tatsuno, 48
taxis, 44
Tayama Katai, 84, 193–5
tea bushes, 236
tea ceremony (*chanoyu*), 17–18
teahouses, 38; brothels and, 169–70, 172, 175, 243; rendezvous (*machiaijaya*), 179; shady (*kagemajaya*), 243; theater, 147, 148, 153
teeth, blackening of, 91
telephone service, 111, 278
temples, 132–3, 158–9, 191, 207–8, 211, 246
Tempō sumptuary edicts, 21
Tennōji Temple, 211
Terry, Philip, 60, 257, 264
theaters, 253; of Edo, 18–20; Kabuki, *see* Kabuki theater; movie, 120, 267; Nō, 125; Western, 272–4; *see also* Yose
theater teahouses, 147, 148, 153
Tōkaidō highway, 185, 198
Tokiwa bridge, 9, 192
Tokuda Shōsei, 238, 243
Tokugawa castle, 63
Tokugawa cemetery (tombs), 224, 228
Tokugawa regime, 8, 11–13; end of, 22–7, 28
Tokutomi Roka, 237
Tokyo: boundaries of, 29–30, 259–60; as capital district, 30; as a collection of villages, 34, 277, 284; establishment of, as capital, 26–8; government of, 30–1, 276–7; pronunciations of name, 26; *see also* Edo; High City; Low City
Tokyo Central Station, 47, 62, 78–80, 80, 114
Tokyo Hotel, 233
Tokyo Prefecture, 29–30
Tokyo School of English, *see* First Higher School
Tokyo Shibaura (manufacturing firm), 226, 227
Tomioka Hachiman, 221
tourist buses, 281
traffic on left side of street, 94–5
transportation, 42–9, 85, 283; in Edo, 19–20; *see also specific modes of transportation*
trolleys, 44–7, 226
Tsubouchi Shōyo, *see* Shōyo

Tsukiji quarter, 36–42, 40
Twelve Storeys (Ryōunkaku), 6, 7–8, 70–3, 72

Ueno, 27, 79, 116, 210
Ueno Park, 27, 116–20, 128–30, 210
Uguisudani (Warbler Valley), 130
uniforms, student, 101
United States embassy, 232, 233
United States legation, 36, 233; attack on (1905), 142
universities, 214, 242
Ushigome Ward, 240, 247

vacant lots, Kafū on, 124–5
variety or vaudeville halls (Yose), 18–19, 21

Wakayama Tokugawa estate, 241
wards of Tokyo, 230–1, 246
Waseda, 132
Waseda University, 166, 167
waste disposal, 83, 84, 282–3
watch of the twenty-sixth night, 133–4
Waters, Thomas, 59, 68
water supply, 84, 283
water vendors, 84
waterways, 19–20, 52–8; *see also* canals
weddings, 94
weeds, Kafū on, 124–5
wells, 7, 283
Westerners, *see* foreigners
Western influences, 90–143
Whitney, Clara, 101, 107, 137–8, 149, 225
willows, 61–2, 265–6
Wirgman, Charles, 50
wisteria, 128
women: clothing of, 96–7; in the performing arts, 163, 169; Sumō and, 164; during Taishō, 257–8, 273, 277–8; tooth-blackening by, 91
Women's Higher Normal School, 242
woodcuts, 53
World War I, 260, 261, 269
Wright, Frank Lloyd, 275, 276
writers, 249–50

Yamanote, *see* High City

Yanagibashi district, 54, 229, 230; geisha quarter in, 179–81

Yanaka district, 211

Yasuda Zenjirō, 31

Yasukuni Jinja (shrine), 125, 126

Yokohama, 26, 39, 44, 47, 48, 96

Yomiuri (newspaper), 261

Yose (variety or vaudeville halls), 18–19, 21, 155–8

Yoshiwara district, 8, 18, 20, 22, 29, 63, 167–76, 170, 174, 212; festivals in, 172–4; fires in, 63, 174–5; rebuilding of (after 1911 fire), 175

Yotsuya Ward, 29, 35, 236, 240, 241, 247

Young, John Russell, 34, 277

Yumeji (artist), 258, 259

Yumeji girl, 258–9

Yushima quarter, 243

Yushima Shrine, 128

A NOTE ABOUT THE AUTHOR

Edward Seidensticker divides his time between Tokyo, where he lives half of each year, and New York City, where he is Professor of Japanese at Columbia University. As one of the country's most distinguished translators, Mr. Seidensticker has been responsible for introducing the works of a number of important modern Japanese novelists to the English-speaking world, among them Mishima Yukio, Tanizaki Junichirō, and Kawabata Yasunari. His translation of Kawabata's *The Sound of the Mountain* brought him a National Book Award in 1970, and his widely praised translation of *The Tale of Genji* was published in 1976.

A NOTE ABOUT THE TYPE

The main body of the book was set, via computer-driven cathode-ray tube, in Fairfield, a type face designed by the distinguished American artist and engraver Rudolph Ruzicka. This type displays the sober and sane qualities of a master craftsman whose talent was long dedicated to clarity. Rudolph Ruzicka was born in Bohemia in 1883 and came to America in 1894. He designed and illustrated many books and created a considerable list of individual prints in a variety of techniques.

Composed by York Graphic Services, Inc.,
York, Pennsylvania

Printed and bound by Murray Printing Company,
Westford, Massachusetts

Typography by Joe Marc Freedman